AUTHENTIC TRANSCRIPTIONS
WITH NOTES AND TABLATURE

HIM - DARK LIGHT

HIM

Music transcriptions by Pete Billmann

ISBN-13: 978-1-4234-1258-3
ISBN-10: 1-4234-1258-8

7777 W. Bluemound Rd. P.O. Box 13819 Milwaukee, WI 53213

In Australia Contact:
Hal Leonard Australia Pty. Ltd.
4 Lentara Court
Cheltenham, Victoria, 3192 Australia
Email: ausadmin@halleonard.com

Visit Hal Leonard Online at
www.halleonard.com

HIM

4 VAMPIRE HEART
14 RIP OUT THE WINGS OF A BUTTERFLY
20 UNDER THE ROSE
30 KILLING LONELINESS
39 DARK LIGHT
48 BEHIND THE CRIMSON DOOR
59 THE FACE OF GOD
67 DRUNK ON SHADOWS
74 PLAY DEAD
81 IN THE NIGHTSIDE OF EDEN

92 GUITAR NOTATION LEGEND

Vampire Heart

Words and Music by Ville Valo

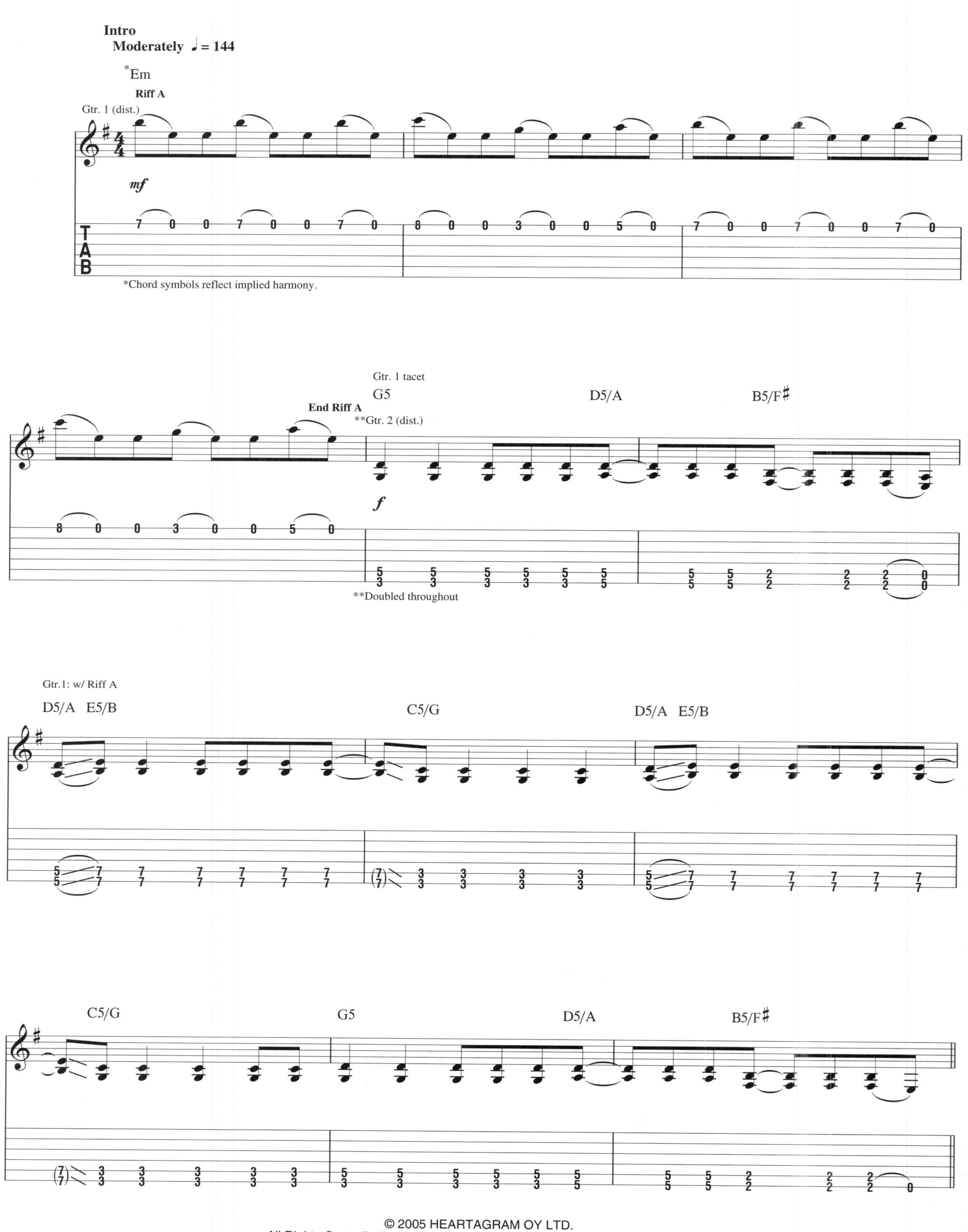

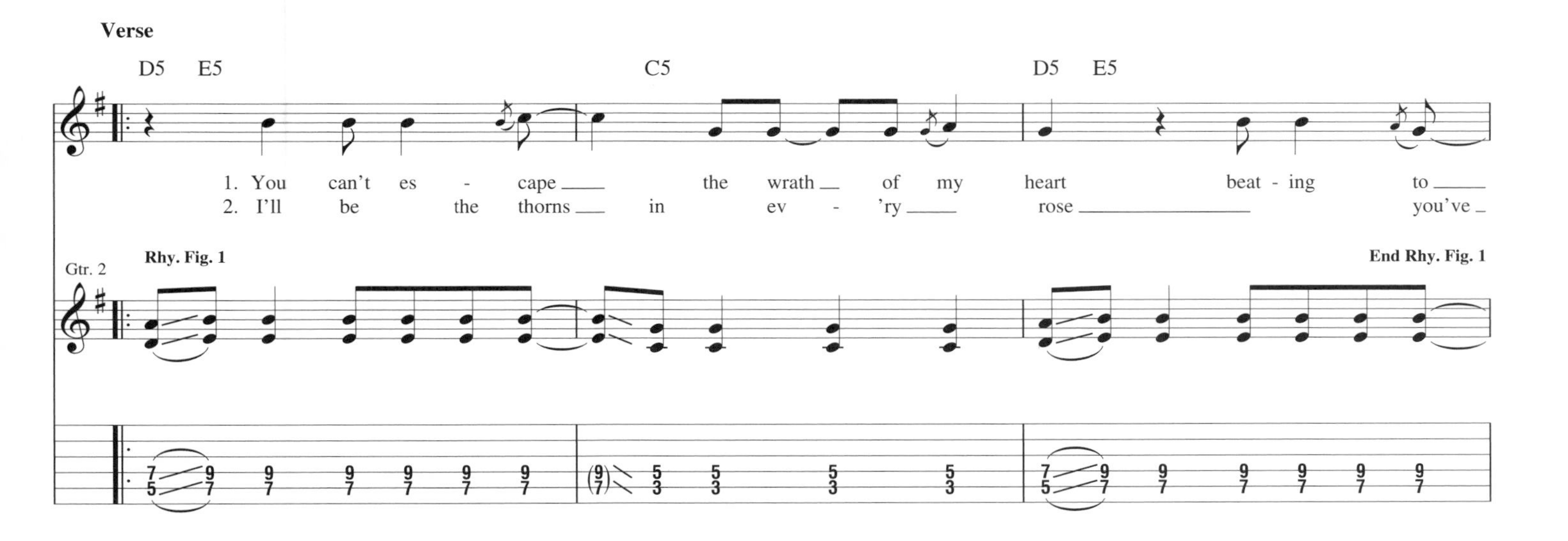
Verse
D5 E5
C5
D5 E5
1. You can't es - cape the wrath of my heart beat - ing to
2. I'll be the thorns in ev - 'ry rose you've
Gtr. 2
Rhy. Fig. 1
End Rhy. Fig. 1

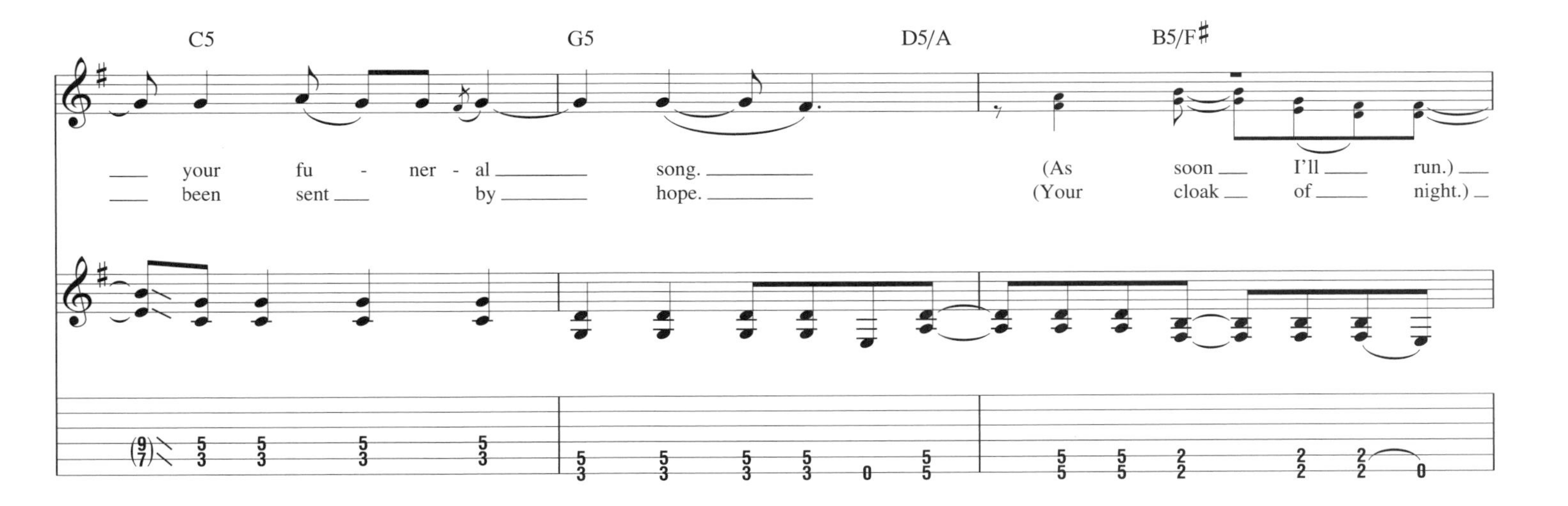
C5
G5
D5/A
B5/F♯
your fu - ner - al song. (As soon I'll run.)
been sent by hope. (Your cloak of night.)

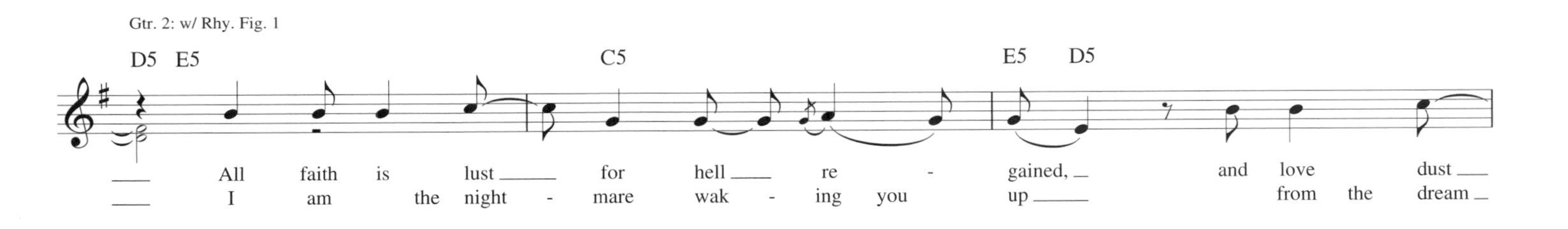
Gtr. 2: w/ Rhy. Fig. 1
D5 E5
C5
E5 D5
All faith is lust for hell re - gained, and love dust
I am the night - mare wak - ing you up from the dream

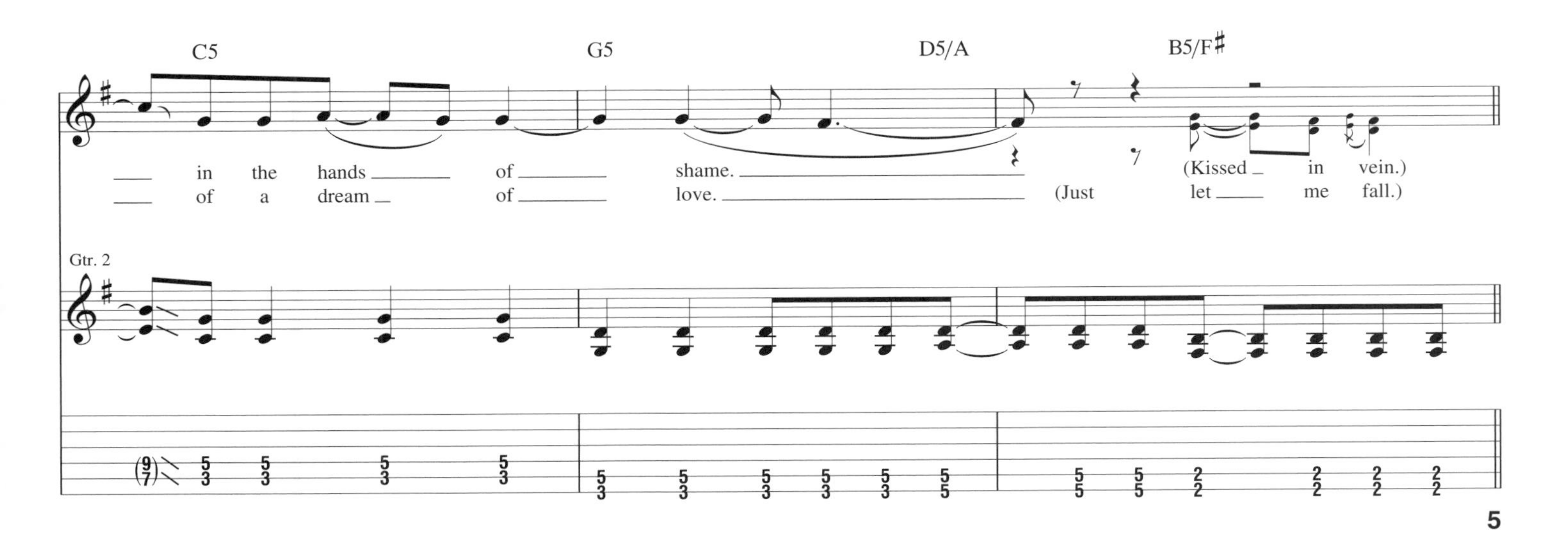
C5
G5
D5/A
B5/F♯
in the hands of shame. (Kissed in vein.)
of a dream of love. (Just let me fall.)
Gtr. 2

Pre-Chorus
*G/C
Dadd4/C
G
Dadd4
Let me bleed you this song of my heart de - formed,
Let me weep you this po - em as heav-en's gates close,
Riff B2
Gtr. 4 (clean)
End Riff B2
mf
let ring throughout
Riff B1
Gtr. 3 (clean)
End Riff B1
mf
let ring throughout
Riff B
Gtr. 2
End Riff B
P.M.
*Chord symbols reflect combined harmony, next 14 meas.
Gtr. 2: w/ Riff B
Gtrs. 3 & 4: w/ Riffs B1 & B2 (2 times)
G/C
Dadd4/C
G
Dadd4
lead you a - long this path in the dark
paint you my soul, scarred and a - lone,
G/C
Dadd4/C
Em7
Dadd4/F♯
where I be - long 'til I feel your
wait-ing for your kiss to take me back
Gtr. 2
P.M.

Chorus
Half-time feel
Gtrs. 3 & 4 tacet
G
B5
E5
warmth.
home.
Hold me like you
Riff C
Gtr. 4
Gtr. 1
Gtr. 3
Gtr. 2
*P.M.
*Gradually lift P.M.
C5/G
G5
C5/G
G5
held on - to life, when all fears came a - live and en - tombed
End Riff C
Rhy. Fig. 2
End Rhy. Fig. 2

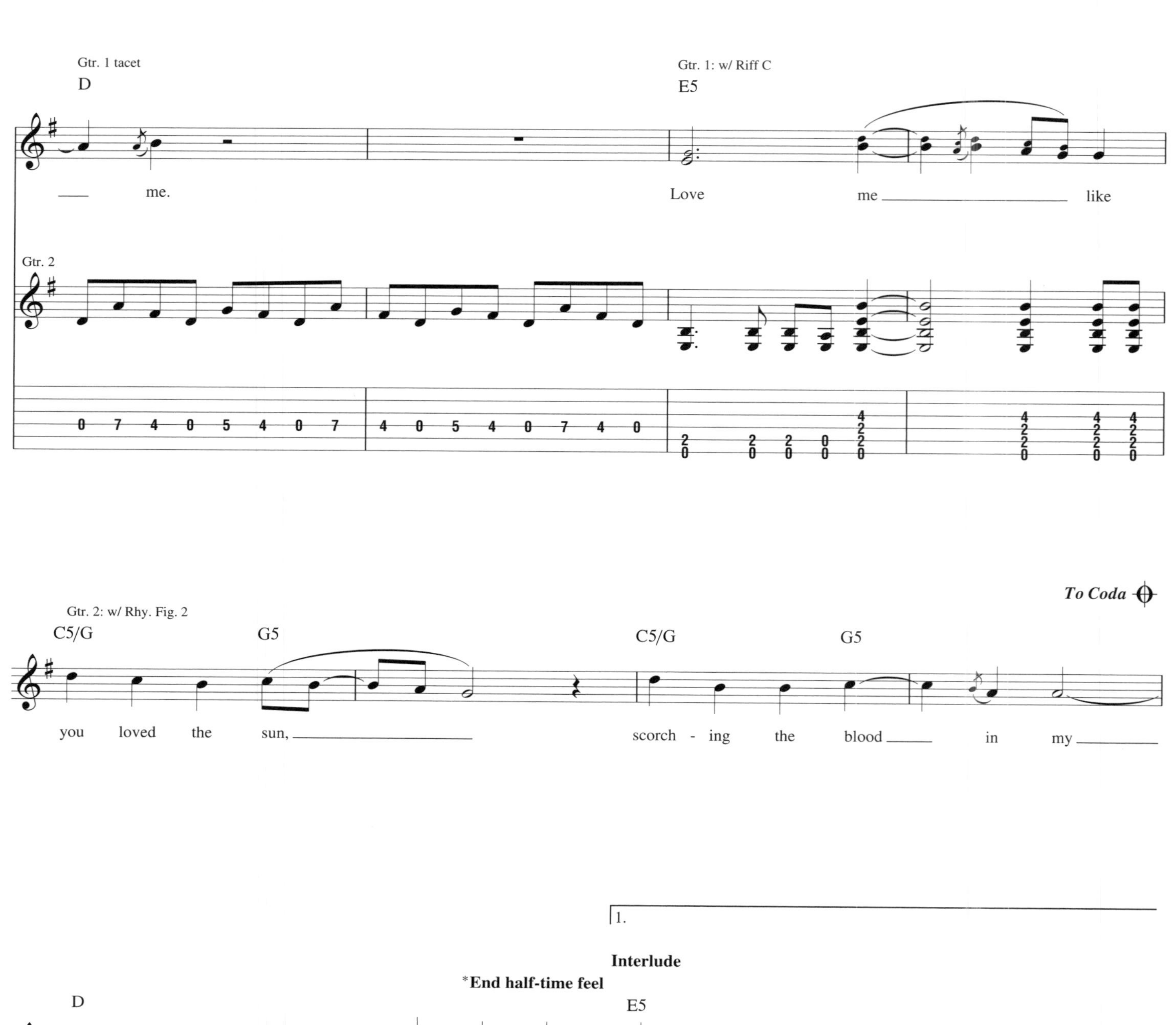
Gtr. 1 tacet
D
me.
Gtr. 1: w/ Riff C
E5
Love
me
like
Gtr. 2
Gtr. 2: w/ Rhy. Fig. 2
C5/G
G5
you
loved
the
sun,
C5/G
G5
scorch - ing
the
blood
in
my
To Coda

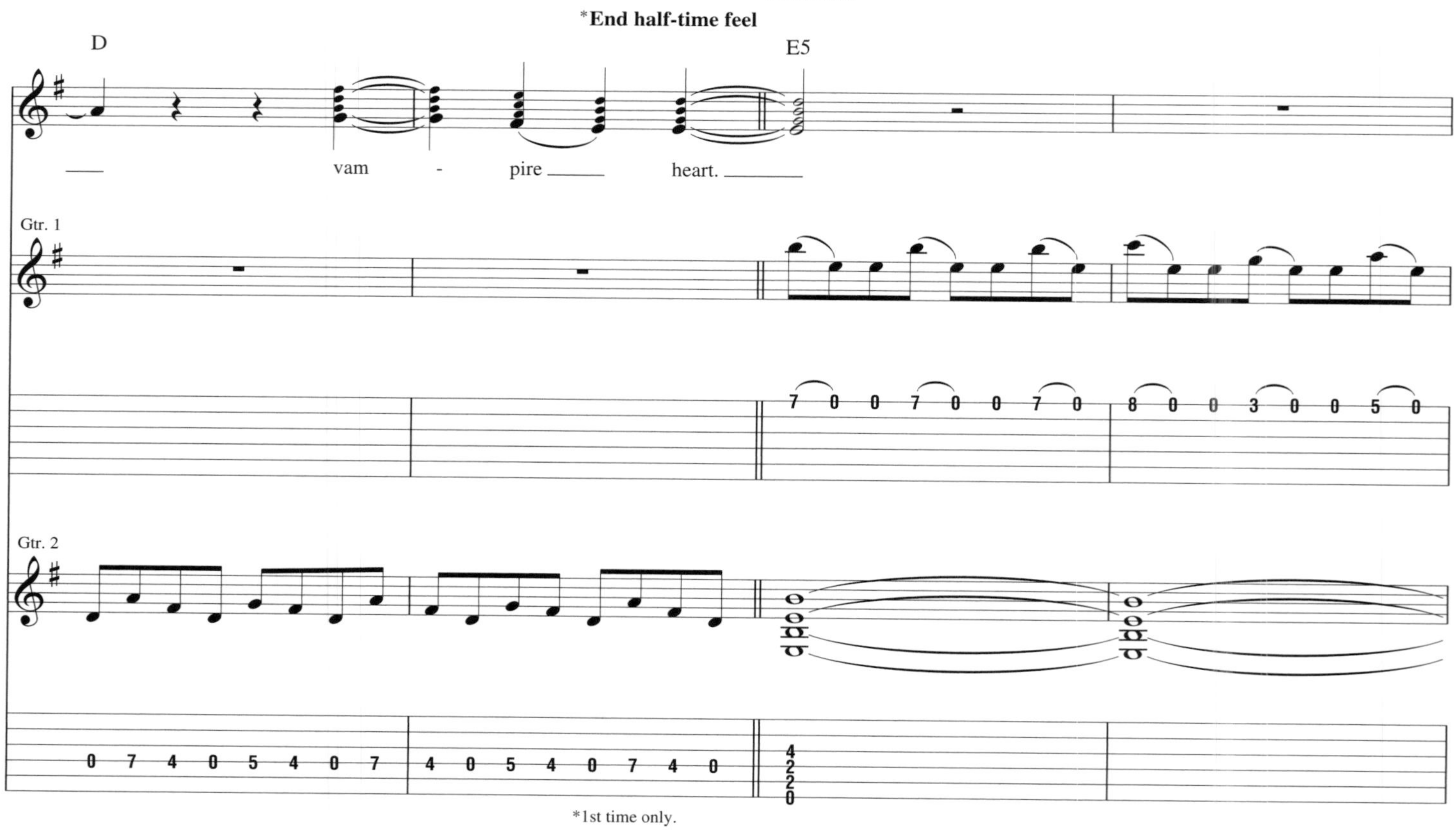
1.
Interlude
*End half-time feel
D
vam - pire
heart.
E5
Gtr. 1
Gtr. 2
*1st time only.

Gtr. 1 tacet
G5
D5/A
B5/F♯
steady gliss.
2.
Interlude
E5
Riff D
Gtr. 2
End Riff D
P.M.
P.H.

End half-time feel
Gtr. 2: w/ Riff D
*Gtr. 5
mf
let ring throughout
*Kybds. arr. for gtr.

1.
Gtr. 5 tacet
D5 B5 C5 B5 D5 B5 C5 B5 A5 D5 B5 C5 B5 D5 B5 C5 B5 A5
8va
Gtr. 6 (dist.)
f
P.H.
Pitch: E
Gtr. 7 (dist.)
Gtr. 2
2.
D.S. al Coda
Gtrs. 6 & 7 tacet
B5 C5 B5 A5 N.C.

Coda
Chorus
D
D5/A
F#5
vam - pire
Whispered: heart.
(Hold me
Gtr. 1
Riff E
Gtr. 2
Rhy. Fig. 3
D/A
A
D/A
A
Hold me like you held on - to life,
like you held on - to life, when all fears came a - live
let ring
let ring

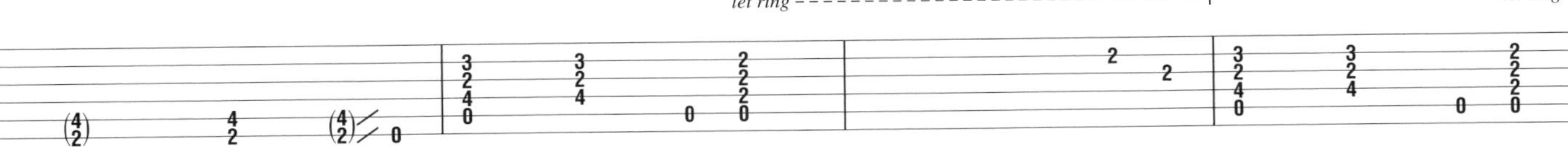

Gtr. 1 tacet

E

my vam - pire heart.

and en - tombed me.

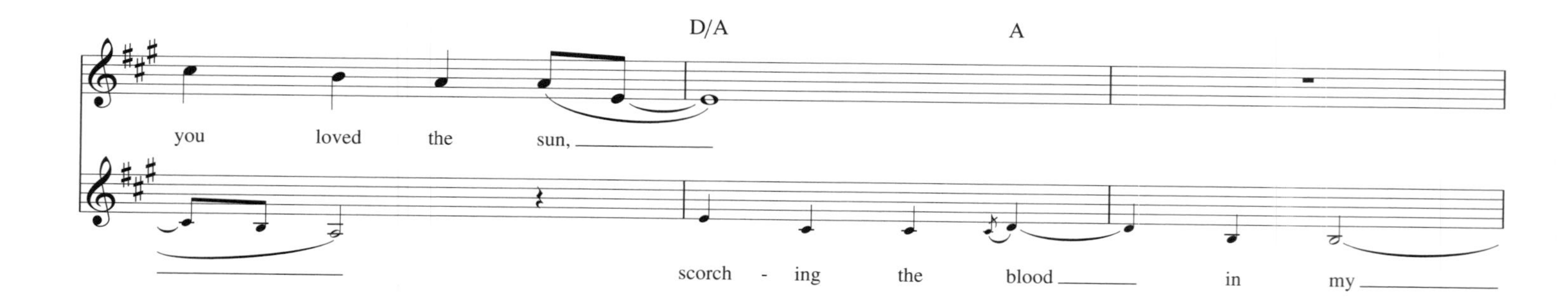

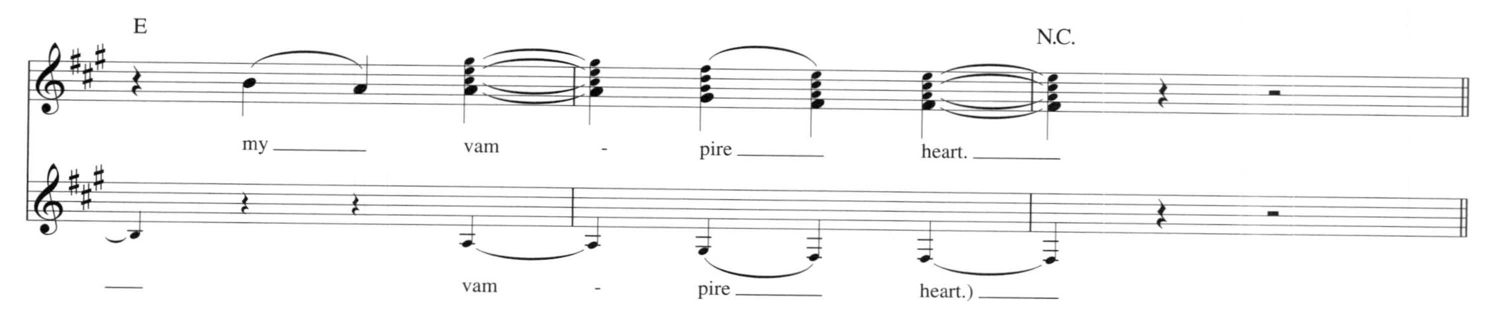

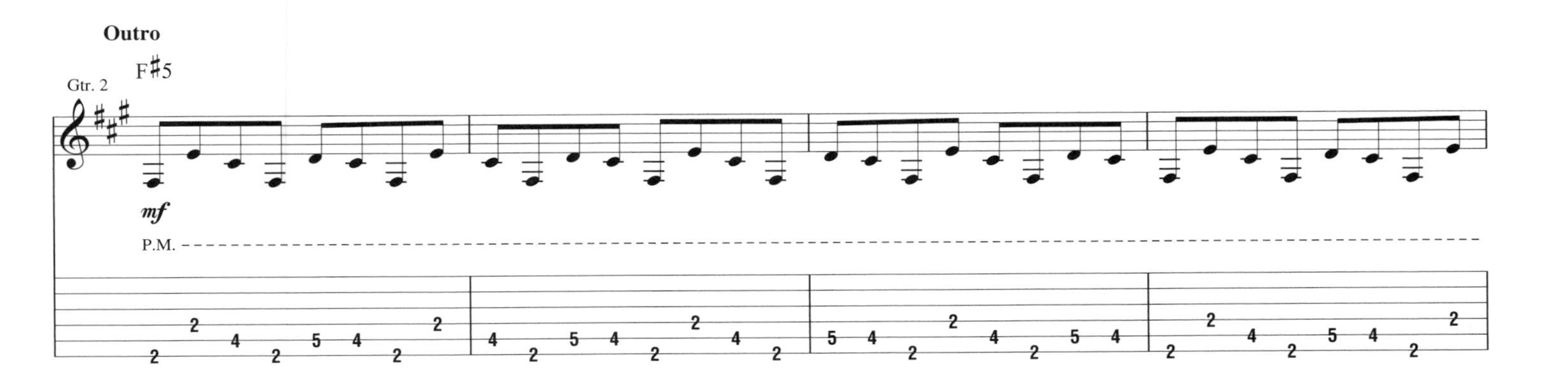
Outro
F♯5
Gtr. 2
mf
P.M.

P.M.

P.M.

P.M.

P.M.

Rip Out the Wings of a Butterfly

Words and Music by Ville Valo

Drop D tuning, down 1/2 step:
(low to high) D♭-A♭-D♭-G♭-B♭-E♭

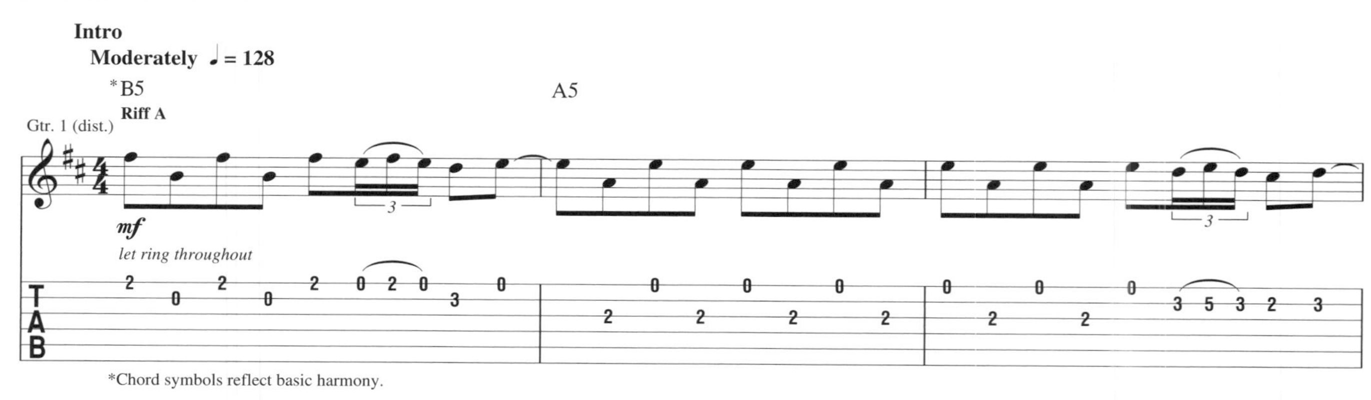

*Chord symbols reflect basic harmony.

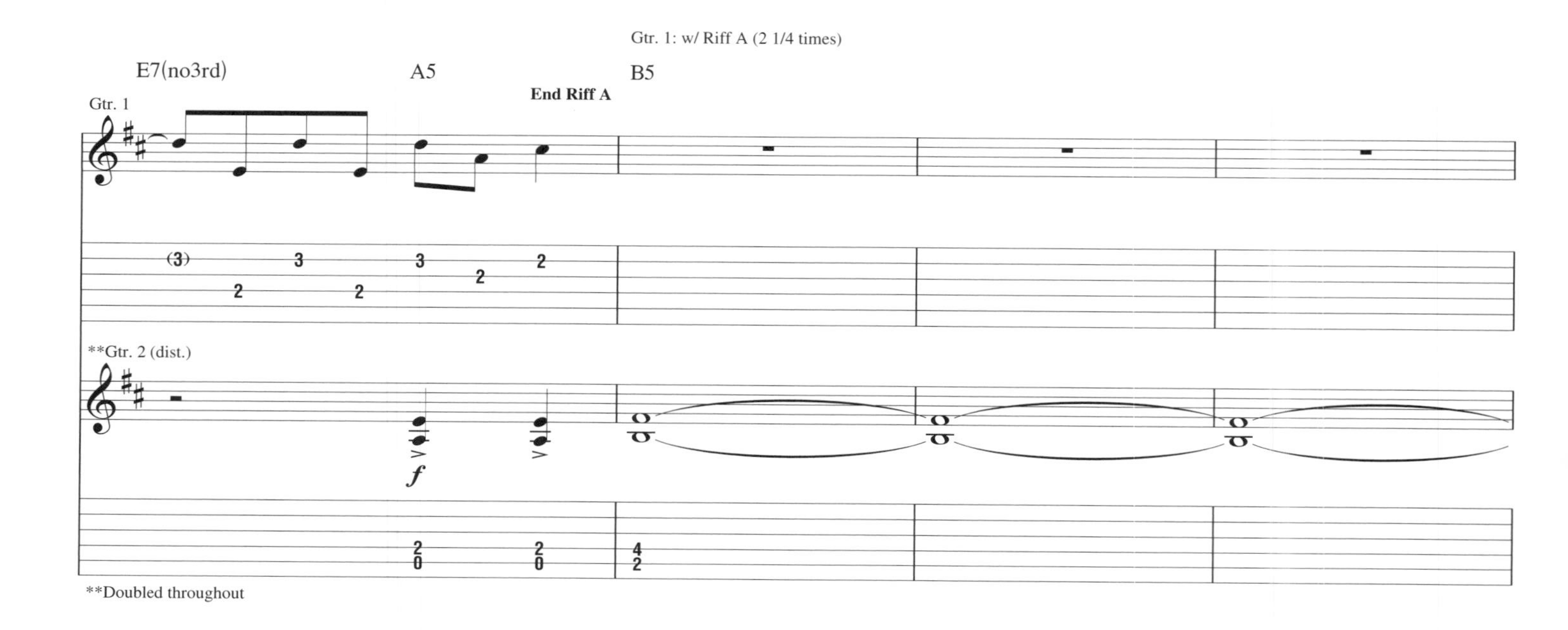

**Doubled throughout

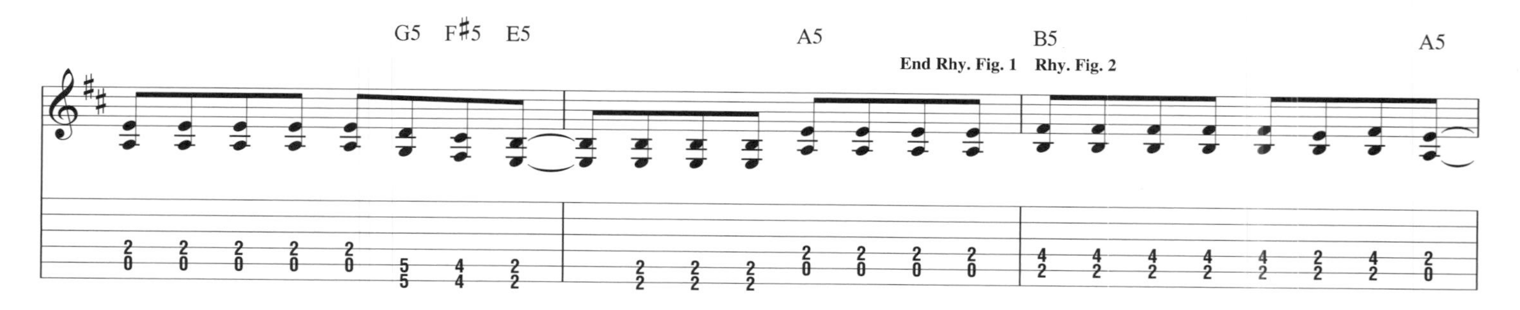

Gtr. 1
G5 F♯5 E5
Gtr. 2
End Rhy. Fig. 2

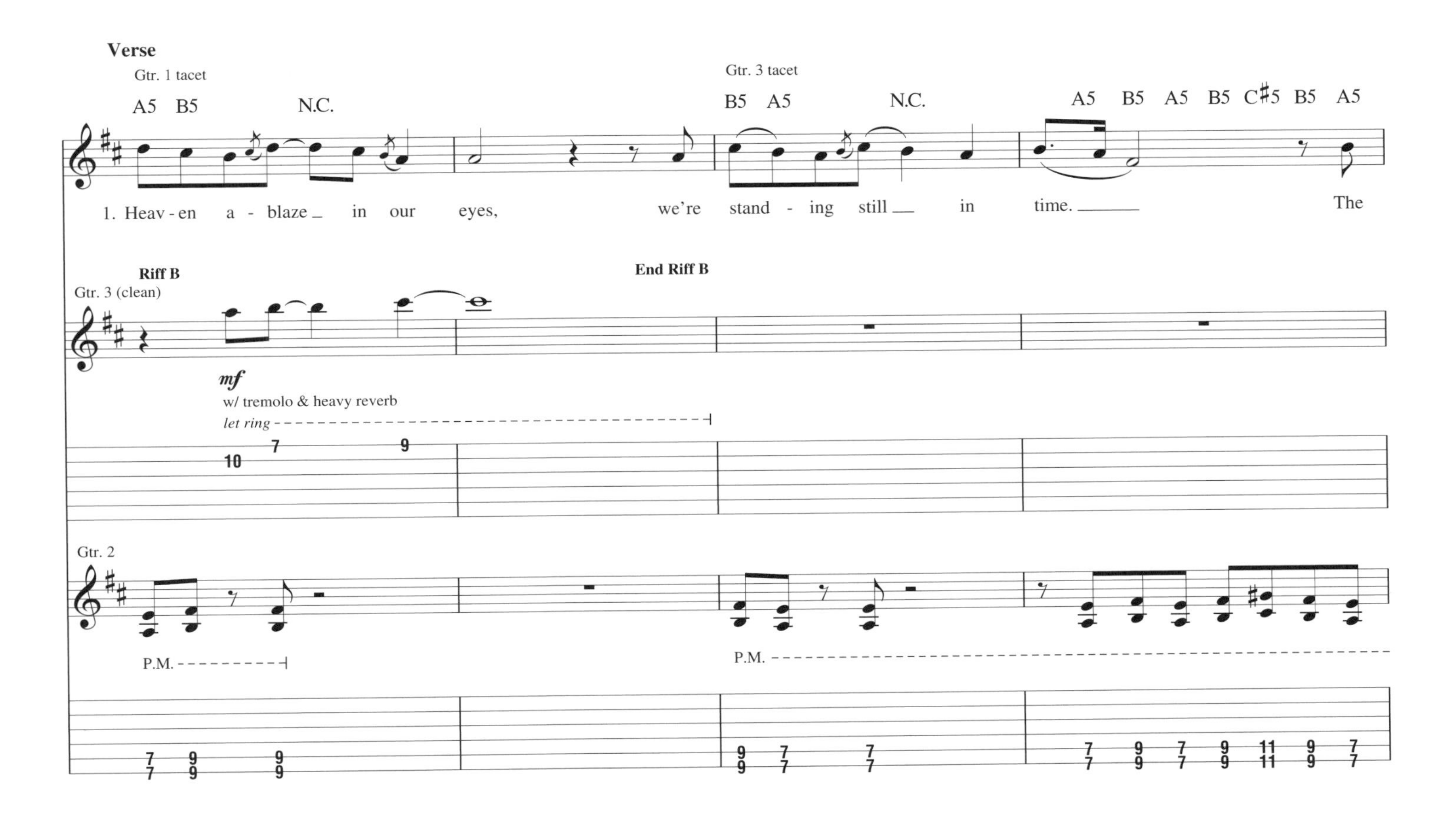
Verse
Gtr. 1 tacet
A5 B5 N.C.
Gtr. 3 tacet
B5 A5 N.C.
A5 B5 A5 B5 C♯5 B5 A5
1. Heav - en a - blaze in our eyes, we're stand - ing still in time. The
Riff B
Gtr. 3 (clean)
End Riff B
mf
w/ tremolo & heavy reverb
let ring
Gtr. 2
P.M.
P.M.

B5 N.C.
A5
B5 A5 N.C.
blood on our hands is the wine we of - fer as sac - ri -
Gtr. 2
P.M.
w/ reverse effect
P.M.

A5 B5 A5 B5 C♯5 B5 A5 E5 A5
fice.
Come on and
P.M.
Chorus
Gtr. 2: w/ Rhy. Fig. 1 (2 times)
3rd time, Gtr. 1: w/ Riff A (2 times)
B5 A5 G5 F♯5 E5 A5
show them your love.
Rip out the wings of a but - ter - fly for your
To Coda 1
To Coda 2
B5 A5 G5 F♯5 E5 A5
soul, my love.
Rip out the wings of a but - ter - fly for your
Interlude
Gtr. 2: w/ Rhy. Fig. 2
B5 A5 G5 F♯5 E5
soul.
Gtr. 1
2. This
Verse
Gtr. 1 tacet
Gtr. 3: w/ Riff B
A5 B5 N.C. A5 B5 A5 N.C.
end - less mer - cy mile,
we're crawl - ing side by
Gtr. 2
P.M.

A5 B5 A5 B5 C♯5 B5 A5 B5 N.C. A5
side. With hell freez - ing o - ver in our eyes, gods
Gtr. 3
let ring
Gtr. 2
P.M.
w/ reverse effect
P.M.

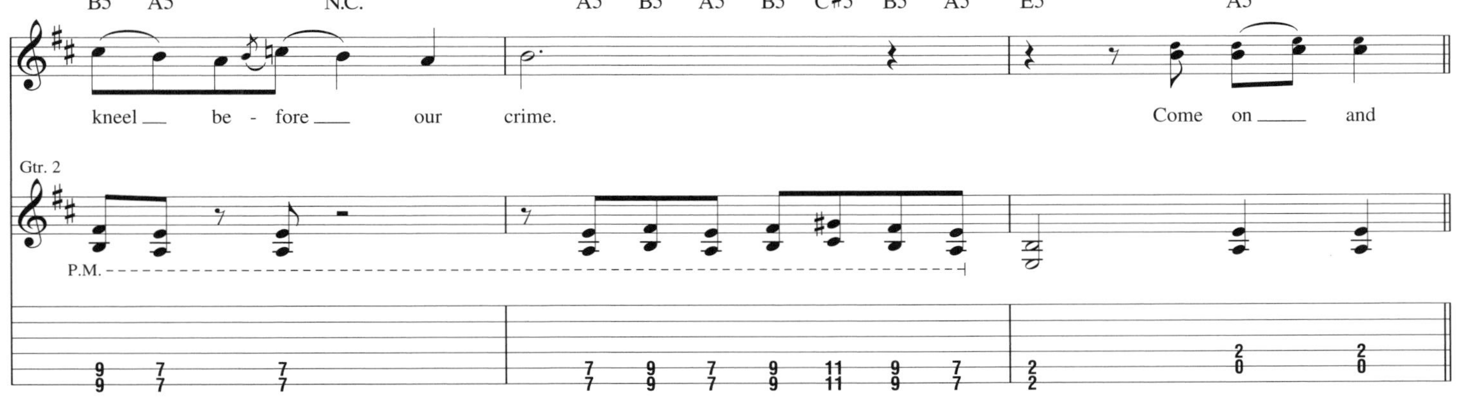
D.S. al Coda 1
Gtr. 3 tacet
B5 A5 N.C. A5 B5 A5 B5 C♯5 B5 A5 E5 A5
kneel be - fore our crime. Come on and
Gtr. 2
P.M.

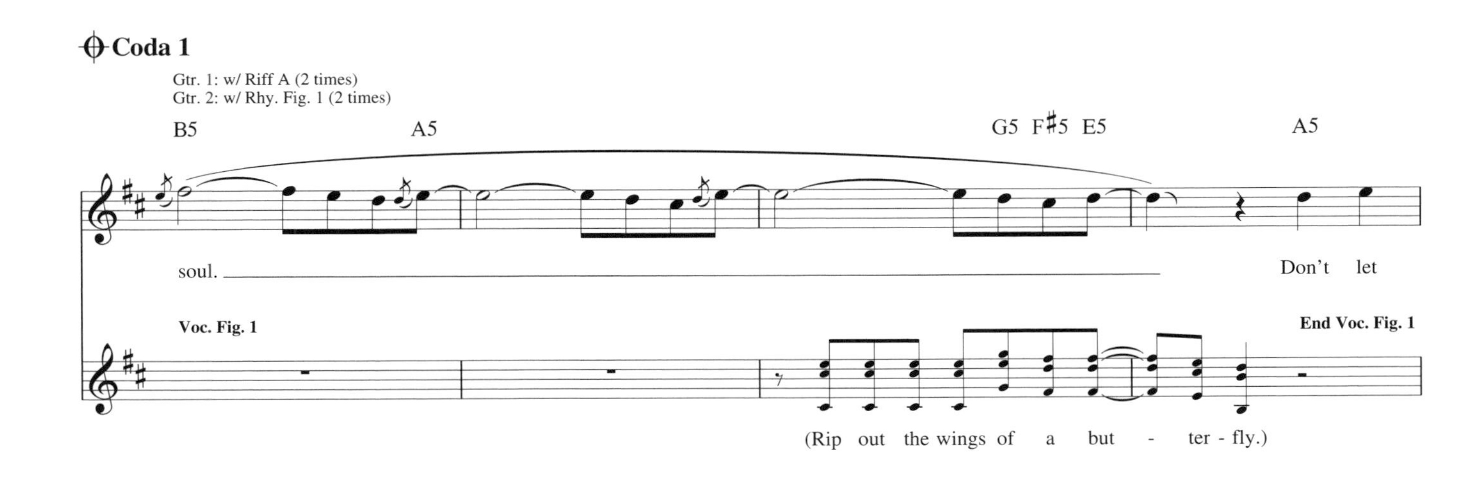
Coda 1
Gtr. 1: w/ Riff A (2 times)
Gtr. 2: w/ Rhy. Fig. 1 (2 times)
B5 A5 G5 F♯5 E5 A5
soul. Don't let
Voc. Fig. 1
End Voc. Fig. 1
(Rip out the wings of a but - ter - fly.)

Bkgd. Vocs.: w/ Voc. Fig. 1
B5 A5 G5 F♯5 E5 A5
go. For your

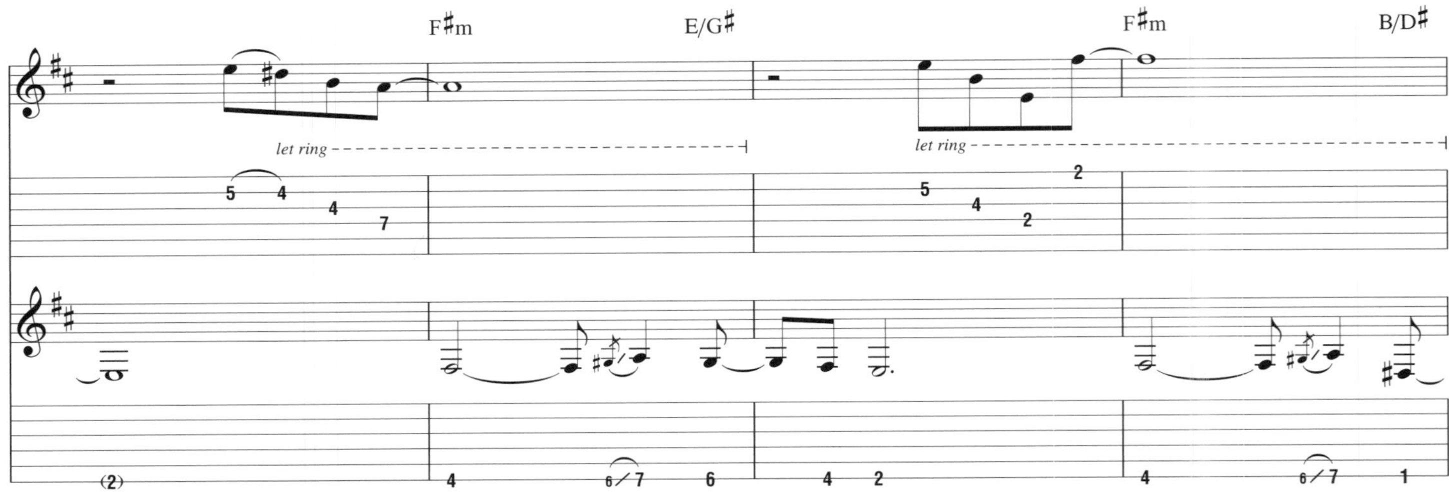

End half-time feel

Gtr. 3 tacet

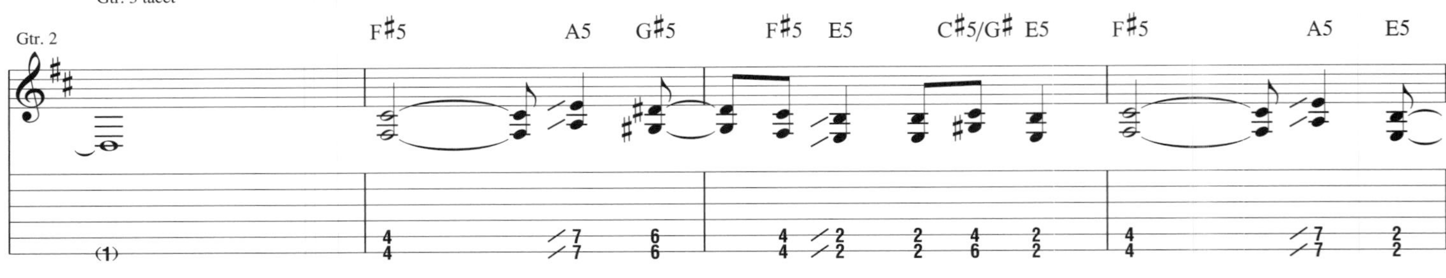

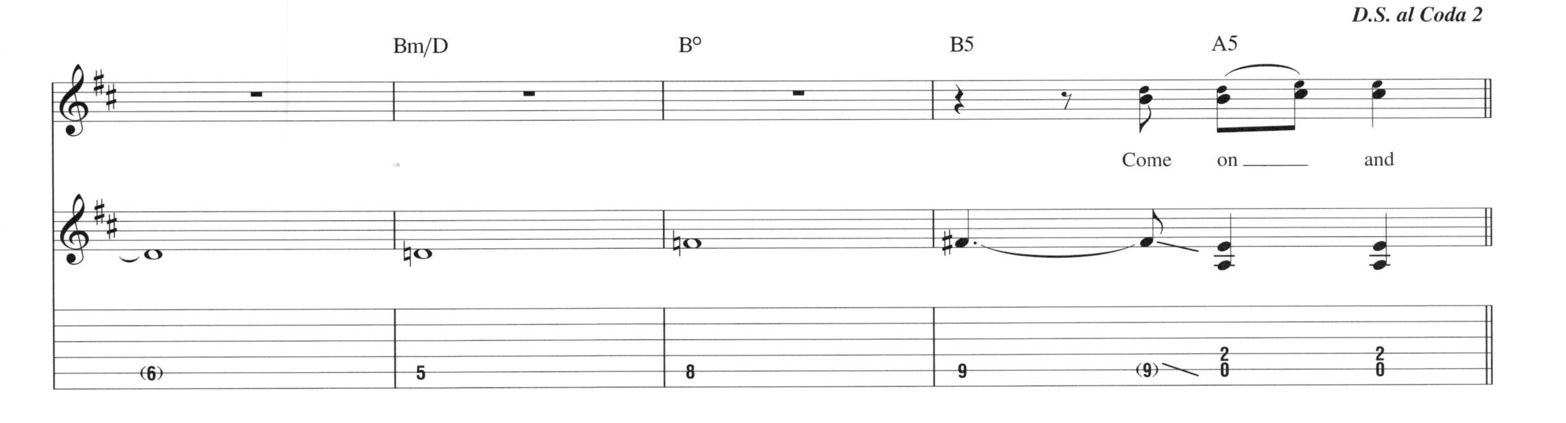
D.S. al Coda 2
Bm/D
B°
B5
A5
Come on and

Coda 2

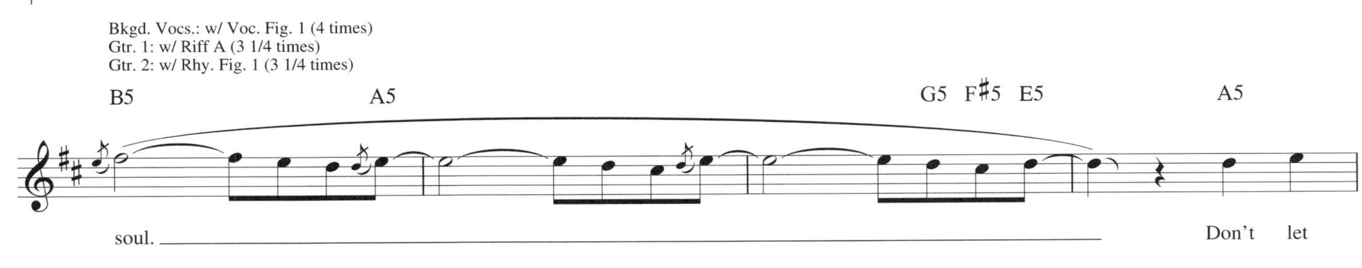
Bkgd. Vocs.: w/ Voc. Fig. 1 (4 times)
Gtr. 1: w/ Riff A (3 1/4 times)
Gtr. 2: w/ Rhy. Fig. 1 (3 1/4 times)
B5
A5
G5 F♯5 E5
A5
soul.
Don't let

B5
A5
G5 F♯5 E5
A5
go.
For your

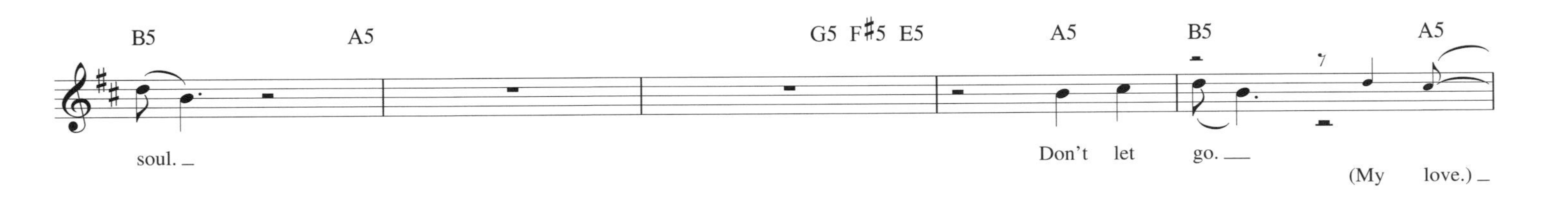
B5
A5
G5 F♯5 E5
A5
B5
A5
soul.
Don't let
go.
(My love.)

G5 F♯5 E5
A5
N.C.
Rip out the wings of a but - ter - fly for your soul.
Gtr. 1
Gtr. 2

Under the Rose

Words and Music by Ville Valo

Gtrs. 1 & 2: w/ Riffs B & B1 (2 times)
E5
D5 E5
A5 E5 A5 B5
Riff C
End Riff C
Gtr. 4 (acous.)
mp
Rhy. Fig. 1
End Rhy. Fig. 1
Gtr. 3

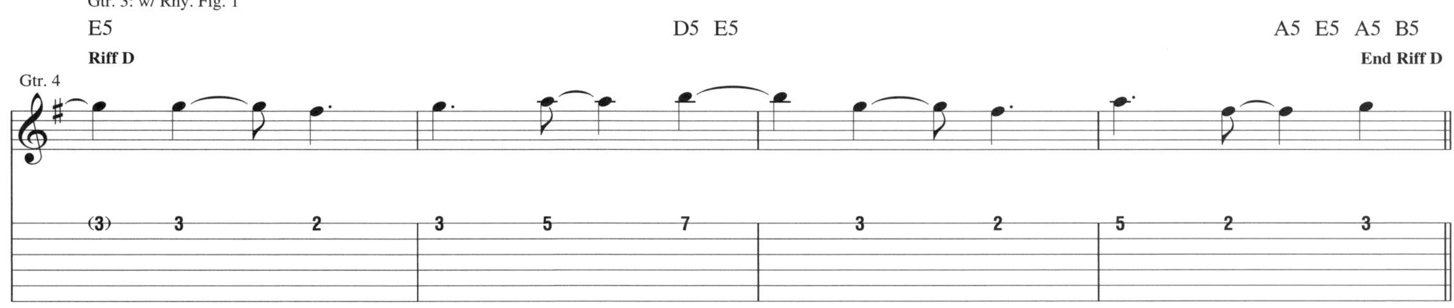
Gtr. 3: w/ Rhy. Fig. 1
E5
D5 E5
A5 E5 A5 B5
Riff D
End Riff D
Gtr. 4

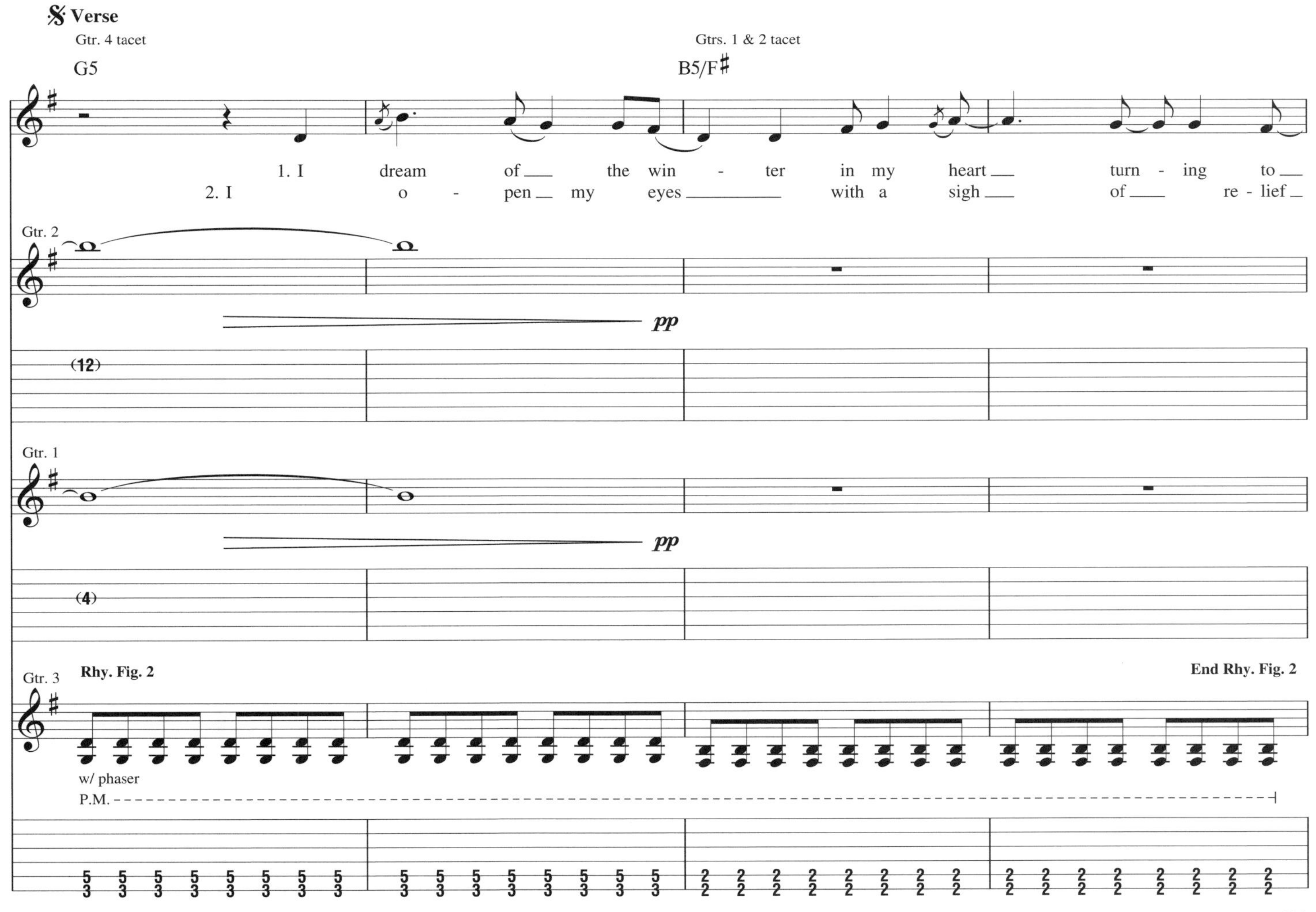
Verse
Gtr. 4 tacet
Gtrs. 1 & 2 tacet
G5
B5/F♯
1. I dream of the win - ter in my heart turn - ing to
2. I o - pen my eyes with a sigh of re - lief
Gtr. 2
pp
Gtr. 1
pp
Gtr. 3
Rhy. Fig. 2
End Rhy. Fig. 2
w/ phaser
P.M.

Gtrs. 1 & 2: w/ Riffs A & A1
*Gtr. 3: w/ Rhy. Fig. 1
Gtr. 4: w/ Riff C
E5
D5 E5
A5 E5 A5 B5
spring
*Phaser off
Gtr. 3: w/ Rhy. Fig. 2
2nd time, Gtr. 2: w/ Riff B1
1st time, Gtrs. 1 & 2 tacet
Gtr. 4 tacet
2nd time, Gtr. 1: w/ Fill 2
G5
B5/F♯
while the ice gives way un - der my
as the warmth of sum - mer's sun - light danc - es a - round
Fill 1
End Fill 1
Gtr. 2
Gtr. 4
divisi
Fill 1A
End Fill 1A
Gtr. 1
Gtrs. 1 & 2: w/ Riffs A & A1
Gtr. 3: w/ Rhy. Fig. 1
Gtr. 4: w/ Riff C
E5
D5 E5
A5 E5 A5 B5
feet.
me.
And that's you
Fill 2
Gtr. 1

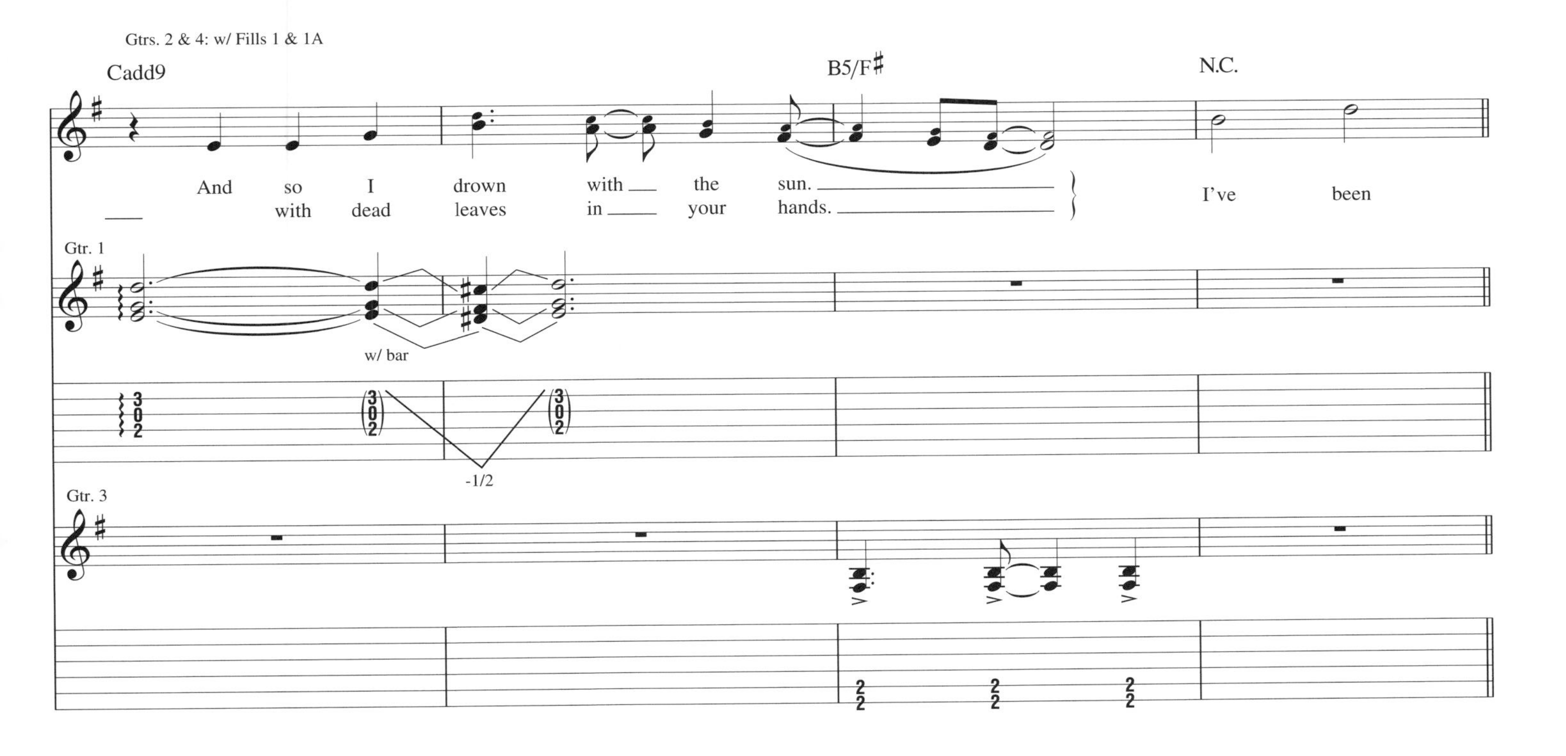

Gtrs. 2 & 4: w/ Fills 1 & 1A
Cadd9
B5/F♯
N.C.
And so I drown with the sun.
with dead leaves in your hands.
I've been
Gtr. 1
w/ bar
-1/2
Gtr. 3

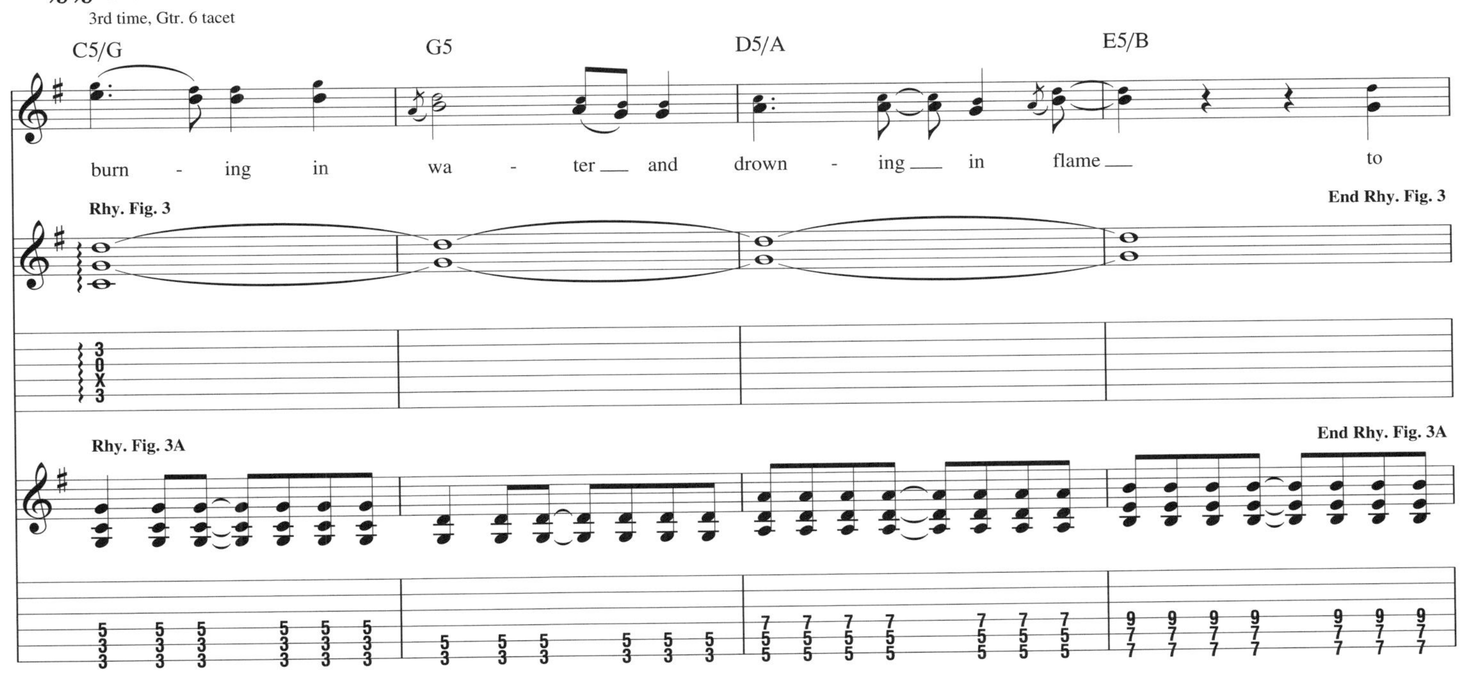

𝄋𝄋 Chorus
3rd time, Gtr. 6 tacet
C5/G
G5
D5/A
E5/B
burn - ing in wa - ter and drown - ing in flame to
Rhy. Fig. 3
End Rhy. Fig. 3
Rhy. Fig. 3A
End Rhy. Fig. 3A

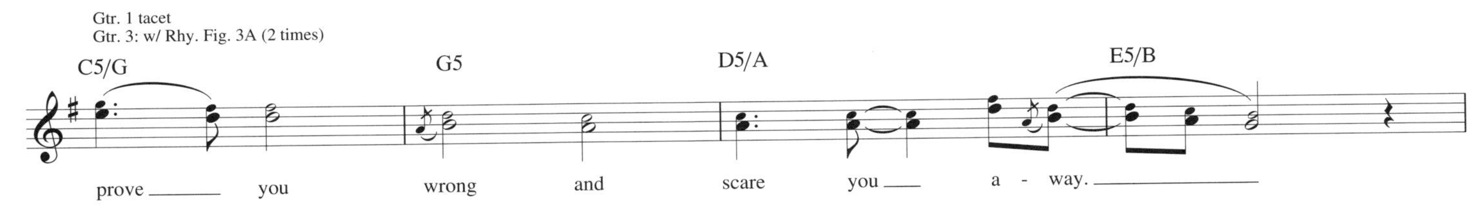

Gtr. 1 tacet
Gtr. 3: w/ Rhy. Fig. 3A (2 times)
C5/G
G5
D5/A
E5/B
prove you wrong and scare you a - way.

To Coda 1
To Coda 2
Gtr. 1: w/ Rhy. Fig. 3
C5/G
G5
D5/A
E5/B
I ad - mit my de - feat and want back home in your

Csus2
D/A
Em
A5 E5 A5 B5
heart
un - der
the rose.
Gtr. 1
w/ bar
-1 1/2
Gtr. 3
Interlude
Gtrs. 1 & 2: w/ Riffs A & A1
Gtr. 3: w/ Rhy. Fig. 1 (2 times)
Gtr. 4: w/ Riff C
E5
D5 E5
A5 E5 A5 B5
Gtrs. 1 & 2: w/ Riffs B & B1
Gtr. 4: w/ Riff D
D.S. al Coda 1
E5
D5 E5
A5 E5 A5 B5
Coda 1
Csus2
D/A
Em
heart
un - der
the rose.
Gtr. 1
w/ bar
-1/2
Gtr. 3

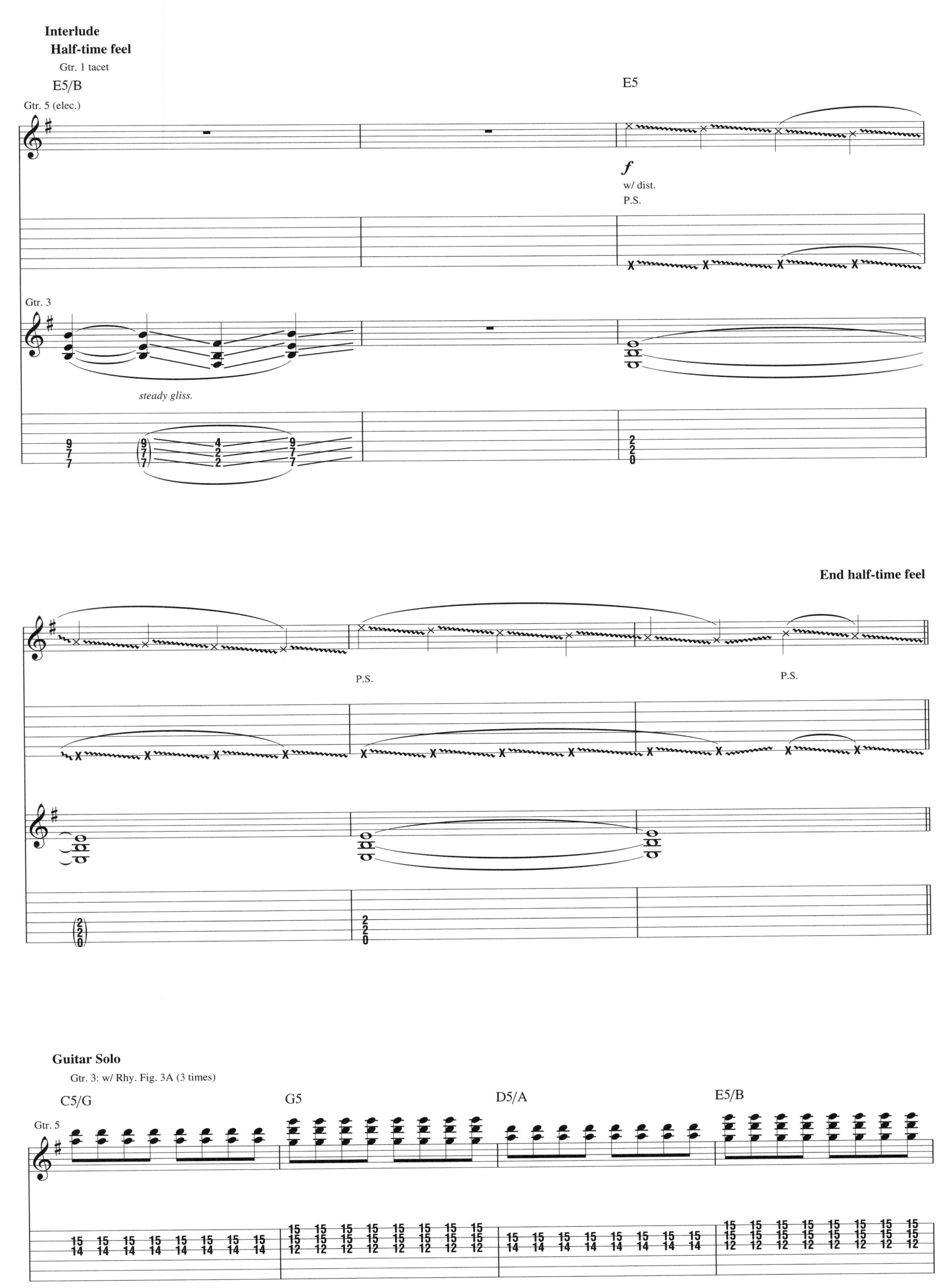
Interlude
Half-time feel
Gtr. 1 tacet
E5/B
E5
Gtr. 5 (elec.)
f
w/ dist.
P.S.
Gtr. 3
steady gliss.
End half-time feel
P.S.
P.S.
Guitar Solo
Gtr. 3: w/ Rhy. Fig. 3A (3 times)
C5/G
G5
D5/A
E5/B
Gtr. 5

C5/G
G5
D5/A
E5/B
(Un - der the
rose.)
Gtr. 5 tacet
Gtr. 6 (elec.)
mf
w/ dist.
let ring
Gtr. 5
D.S.S. al Coda 2
I've been
Gtr. 6
Gtr. 3

Coda 2

Gtr. 1: w/ Rhy. Fig. 3
Gtr. 3: w/ Rhy. Fig. 3A (3 times)
Csus2
D/A
C5/G
G5
heart un - der the rose. Burn - ing in wa - ter and
Gtr. 1
Gtr. 3

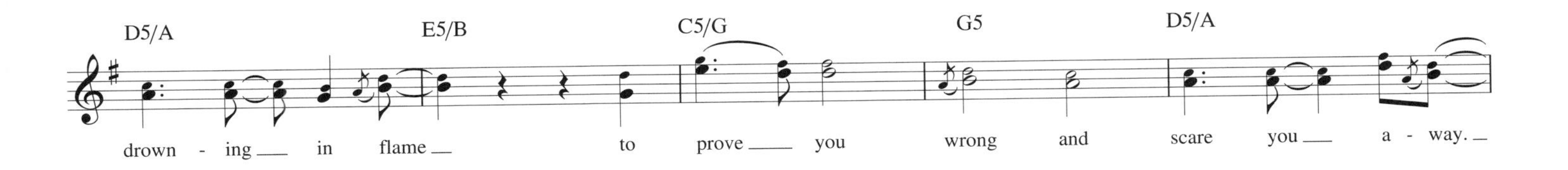

D5/A
E5/B
C5/G
G5
D5/A
drown - ing in flame to prove you wrong and scare you a - way.

Gtr. 1: w/ Rhy. Fig. 3
E5/B
C5/G
G5
D5/A
E5/B
I ad - mit my de - feat and want back home in your

Csus2
Rhy. Fig. 4
D/A
Em
End Rhy. Fig. 4
Gtr. 1
heart un - der the rose. In your
Gtr. 2
Gtr. 3

Gtr. 1: w/ Rhy. Fig. 4 (2 times)

Csus2 D/A Em

heart under the rose. Oh, in your

Gtr. 2 — Riff E — End Riff E

(15) 12 14 12 13 15

Gtr. 3 — Rhy.Fig. 5 — End Rhy.Fig. 5

5 3 3 | 7 5 5 | 0 3 0 0 2 0 0 | 3 0 0 5 0 0 5 7

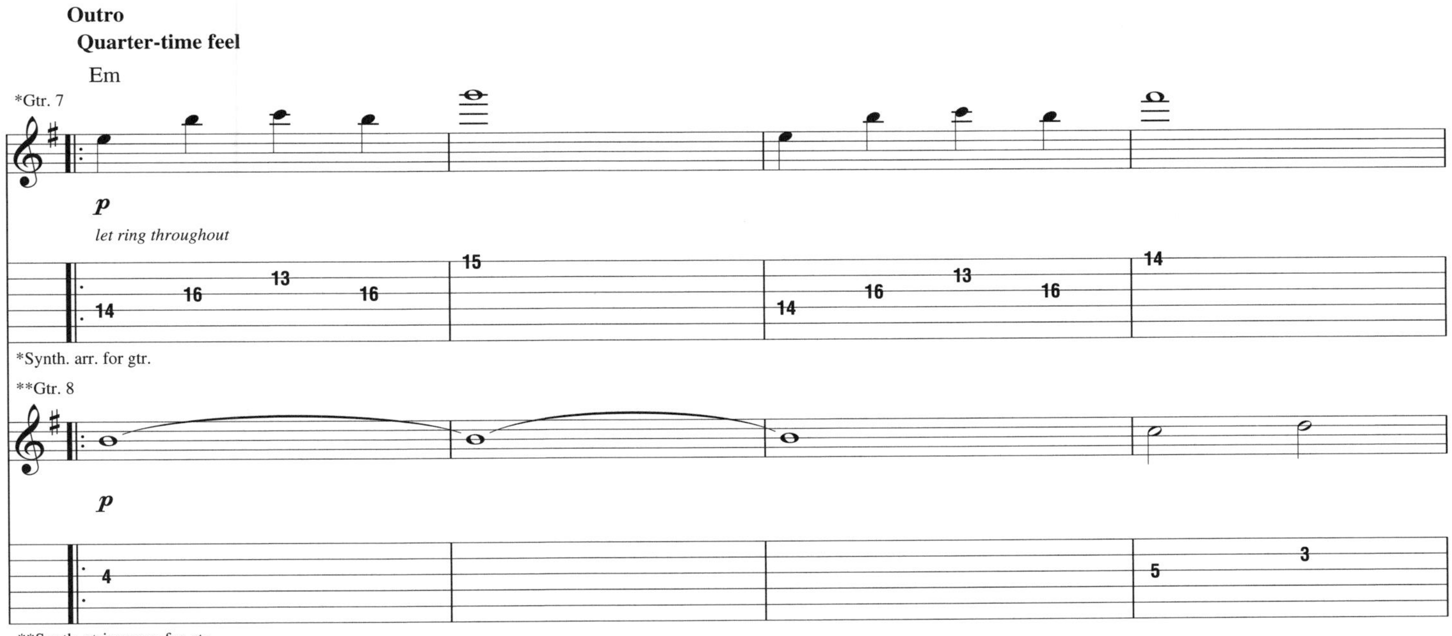
Outro
Quarter-time feel
Em
*Gtr. 7
p
let ring throughout
14 16 13 16
15
14 16 13 16
14
*Synth. arr. for gtr.
**Gtr. 8
p
4
5 3
**Synth. strings arr. for gtr.

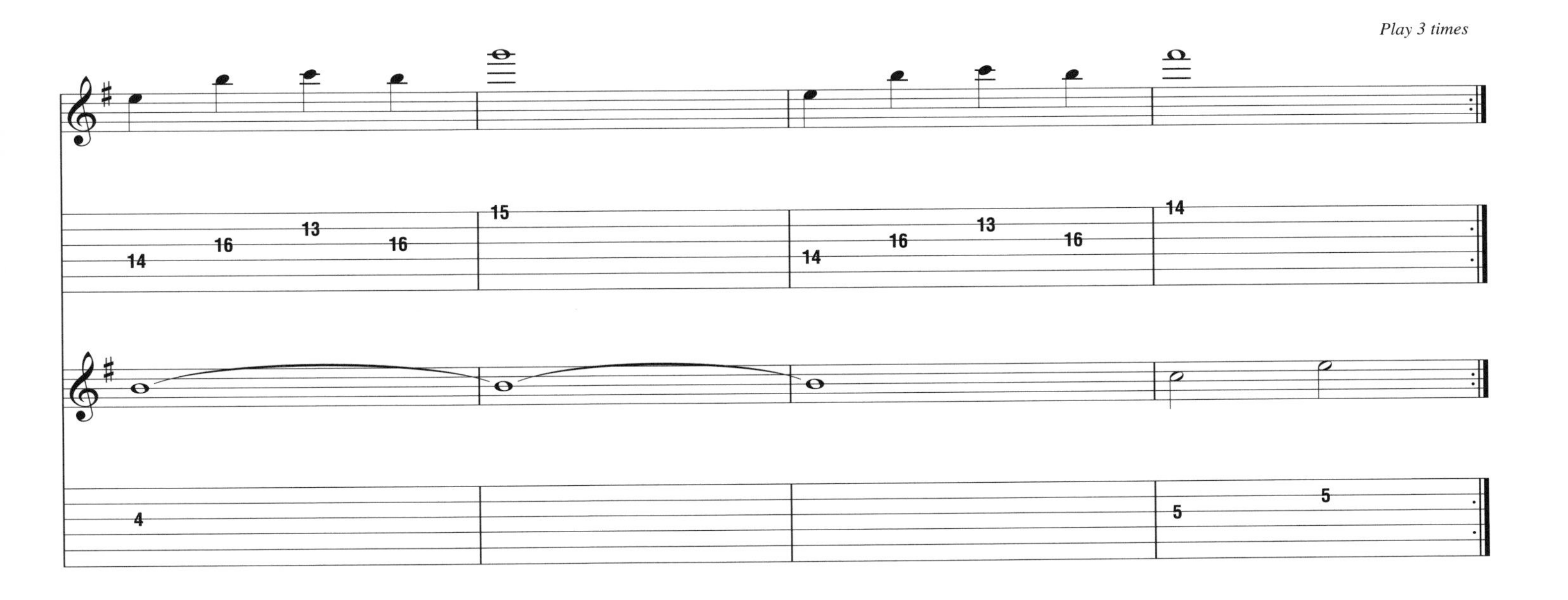
Play 3 times
14 16 13 16
15
14 16 13 16
14
4
5 5

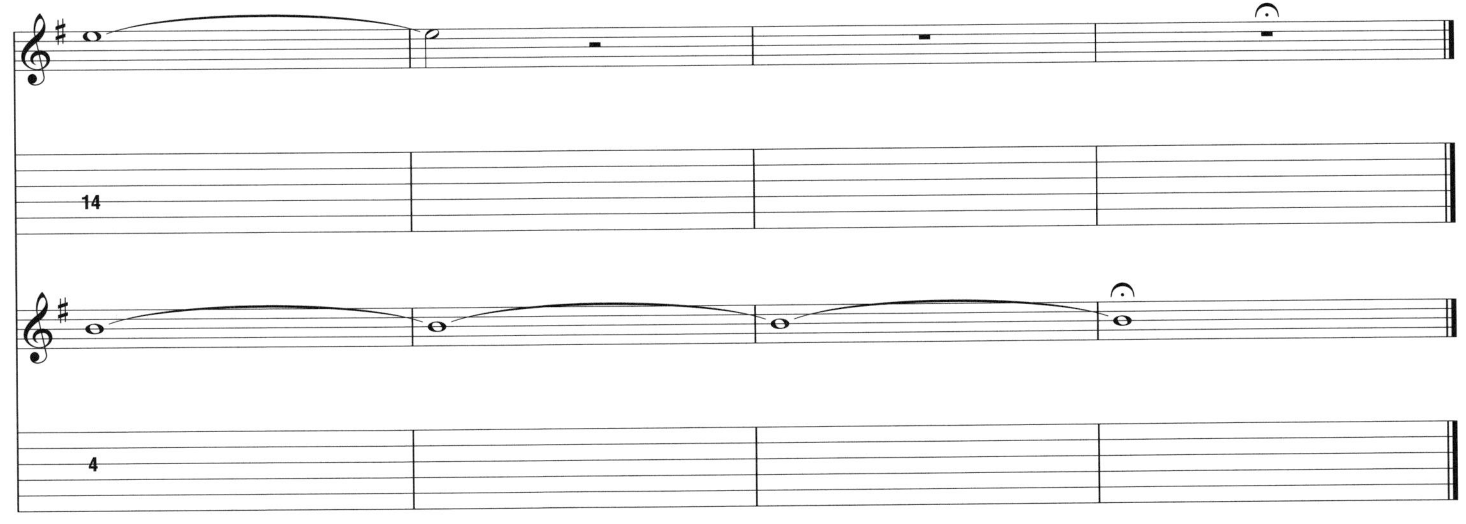
14
4

Killing Loneliness

Words and Music by Ville Valo

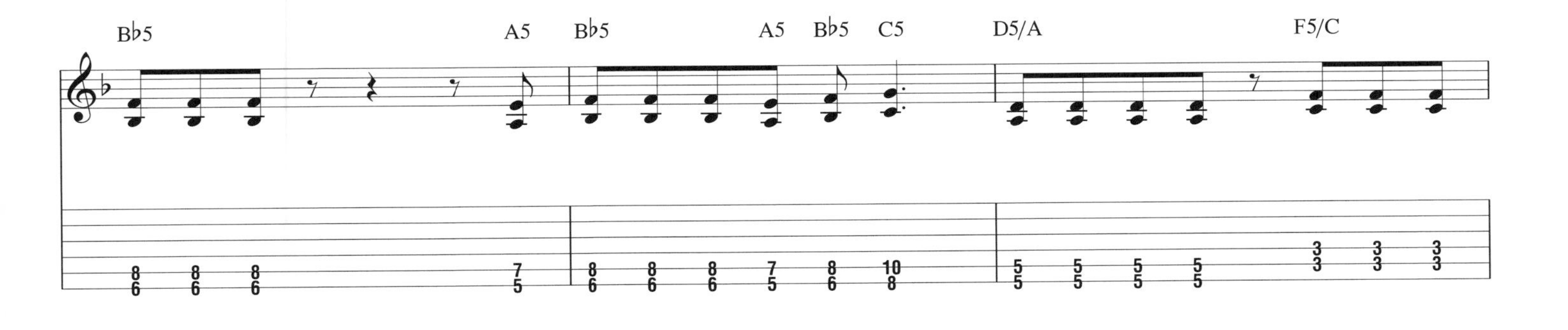
B♭5
A5
B♭5
A5
B♭5
C5
D5/A
F5/C

C5
A5
B♭5
A5
B♭5
A5
B♭5
A5
End Rhy. Fig. 1

Verse
Gtrs. 4 & 5 tacet
*Dm
Am
1. Mem - o - ries sharp as dag - gers
2. Nailed to a cross to - geth - er
Gtr. 3
P.M.
*Chord symbols reflect overall harmony.

Gm
pierce in - to the flesh of to - day.
as sol - i - tude begs us to stay.
P.M.

B♭
Dm
Su - i - cide of love
Oh, we dis - ap - pear
w/ dist.
mf
Gtr. 6 (elec.)
Gtr. 5
divisi
P.M.
Gtr. 4
P.M.
Gtr. 3
P.M.

Gtrs. 3 & 6 tacet
Am
took a - way all that mat - ters and
in the lie for - ev - er and de -
Gtr. 5
P.M.
Gtr. 4
P.M.

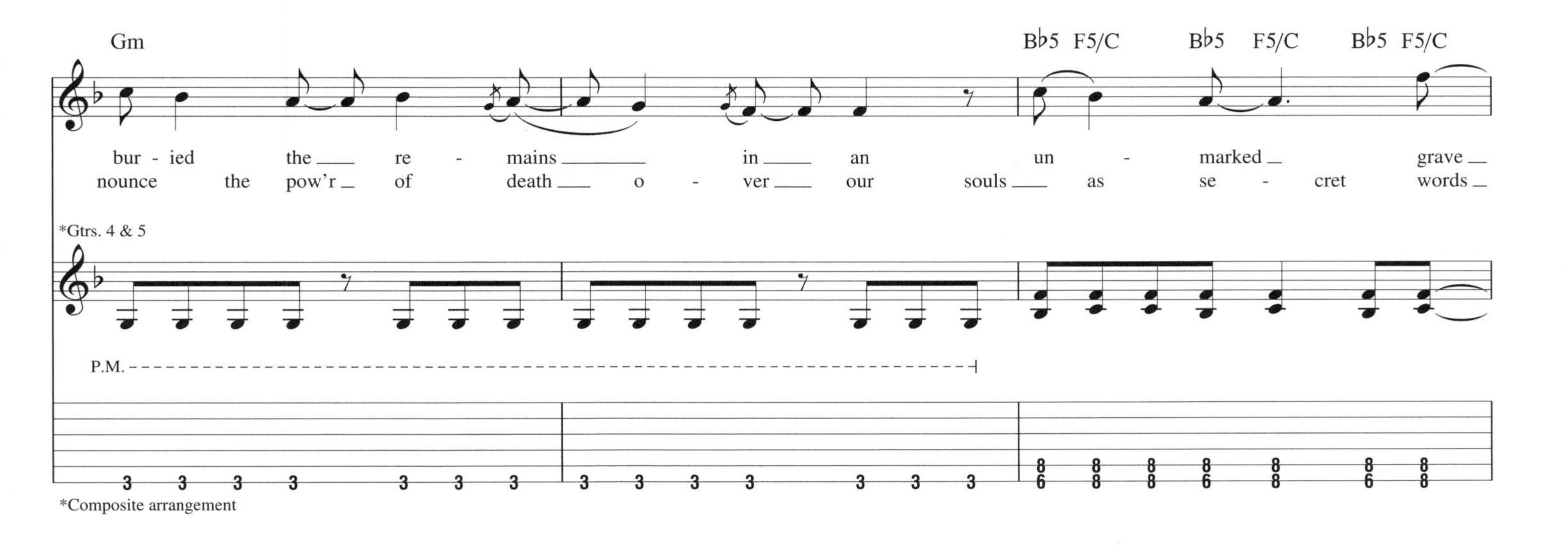
Gm
B♭5 F5/C B♭5 F5/C B♭5 F5/C
bur - ied the re - mains in an un - marked grave
nounce the pow'r of death o - ver our souls as se - cret words
*Grts. 4 & 5
P.M.
3 3 3 3 3 3 3 3 3 3 3 3 3 3
8 6 8 8 8 8 8 8 8 6 8 8 8 6 8 8
*Composite arrangement

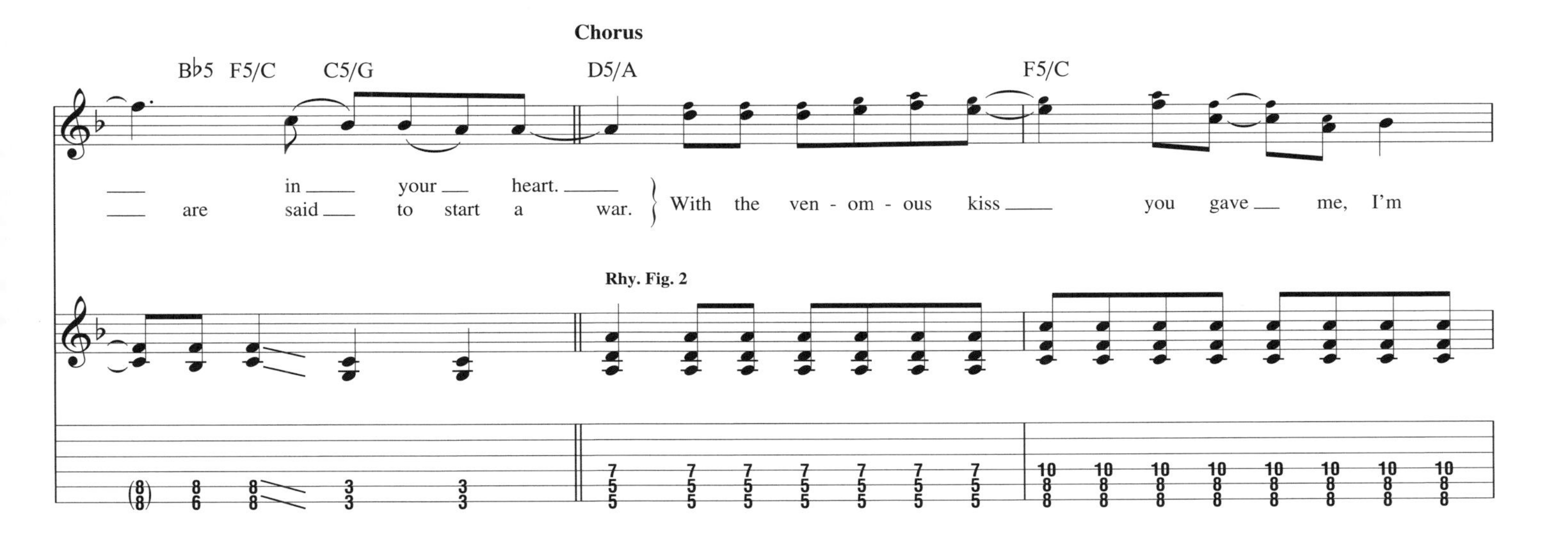
Chorus
B♭5 F5/C C5/G
D5/A
F5/C
in your heart.
are said to start a war.
With the ven - om - ous kiss you gave me, I'm
Rhy. Fig. 2

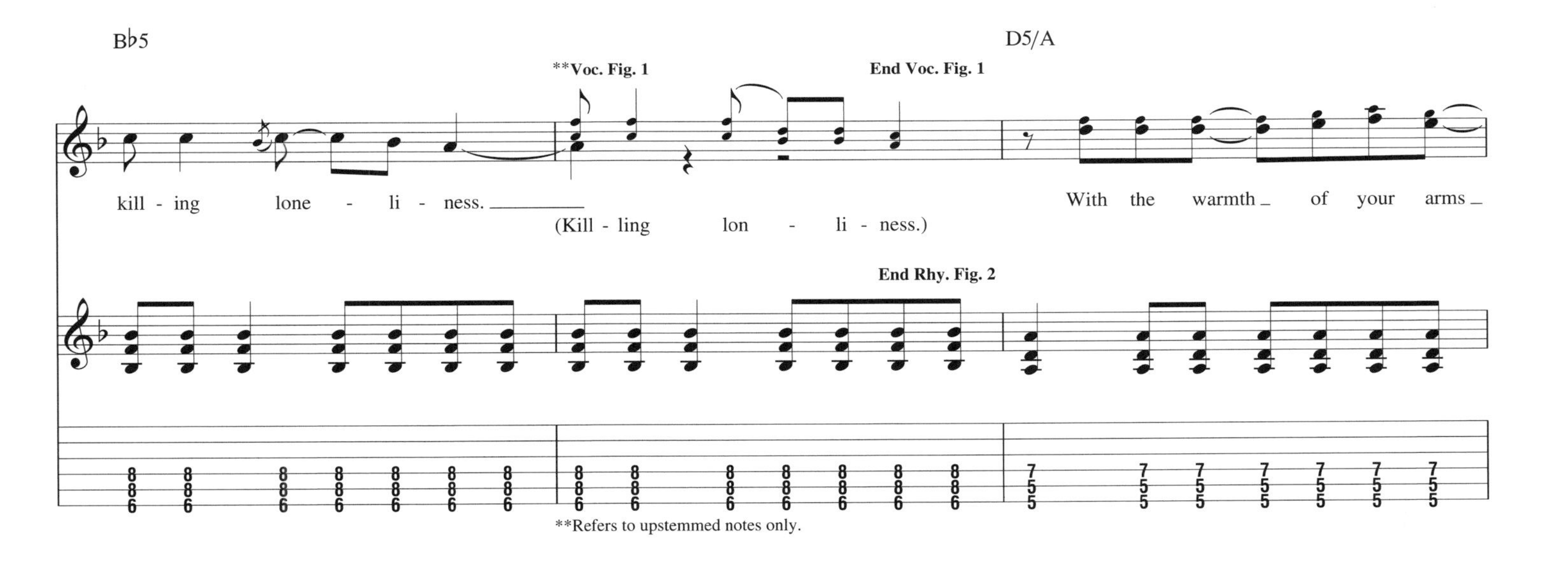
B♭5
D5/A
**Voc. Fig. 1
End Voc. Fig. 1
kill - ing lone - li - ness.
(Kill - ling lon - li - ness.)
With the warmth of your arms
End Rhy. Fig. 2
**Refers to upstemmed notes only.

Gtrs. 4 & 5: w/ Rhy. Fig. 2 (last 3 meas.)
F5/C
B♭5
you saved me.
Oh, I'm kill - ing lone - li - ness with

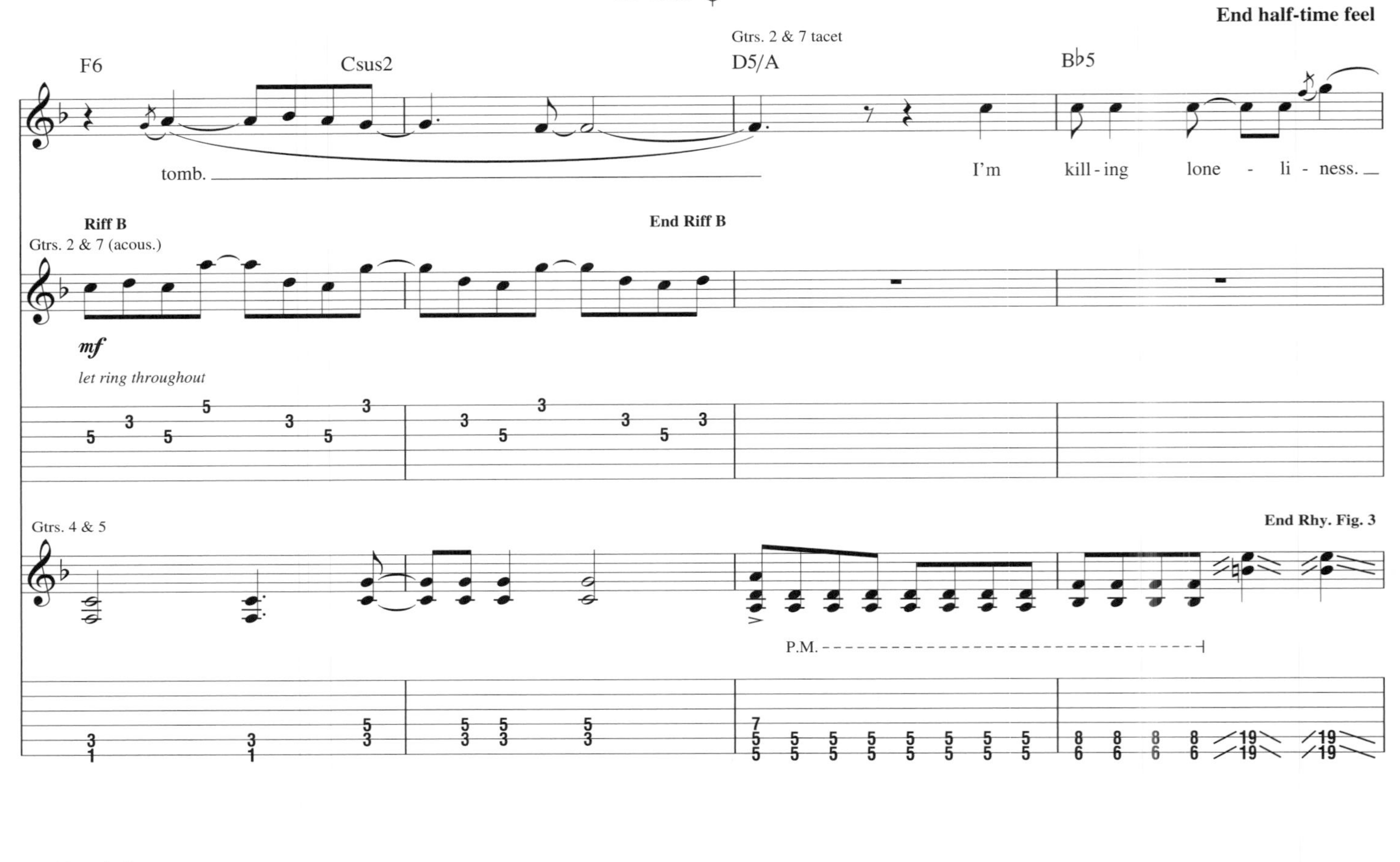

Interlude

Gtrs. 1 & 2: w/ Riffs A & A1 (2 times)
Gtrs. 4 & 5: w/ Rhy. Fig. 1

D5/A F5/C C5 A5 B♭5 A5 B♭5 A5 B♭5 C5

D.S. al Coda

D5/A F5/C C5 A5 B♭5 A5 B♭5 A5 B♭5 A5

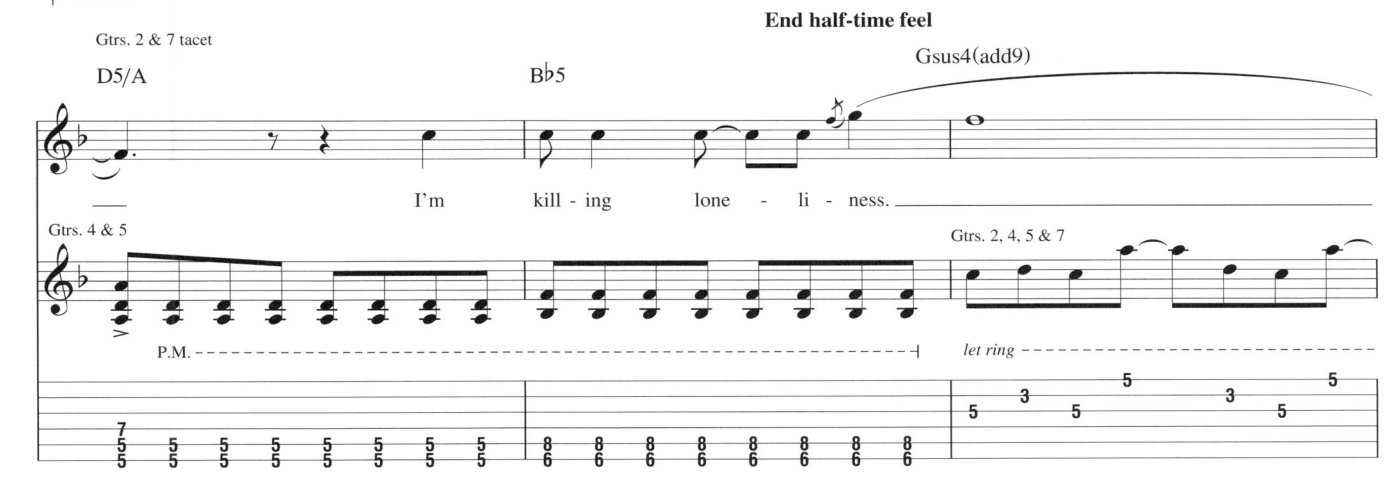

Coda
End half-time feel
Gtrs. 2 & 7 tacet
D5/A
B♭5
Gsus4(add9)
I'm kill - ing lone - li - ness.
Gtrs. 4 & 5
Gtrs. 2, 4, 5 & 7
P.M.
let ring

B♭6/9
I'm kill - ing lone - li - ness.
let ring

Interlude
D5/A F5/C D5/A Dm
Dsus4
Dm
D5/A F5/C D5/A Dm
Dsus4
Dm
Gtr. 1
Riff C
End Riff C
*w/ delay
*Set for quarter-note regeneration w/ one repeat.
Riff C1
End Riff C1
Gtrs. 2 & 7
Gtrs. 4 &5

Half-time feel
Gtr. 1: w/ Riff C (1st 2 meas.)
Gtrs. 2 & 7: w/ Riff C1 (1st 2 meas.)
Gtr. 1: w/ Riff C (2 times)
Gtrs. 2 & 7: w/ Riff C1 (2 times)
Gtrs. 4 & 5
End half-time feel
Chorus
Gtrs. 4 & 5: w/ Rhy. Fig. 2 (2 times)
Gtr. 3
I'm
kill - in' lone - li - ness.
With the ven - om - ous kiss you gave me, I'm

Bkgd. Vocs.: w/ Voc. Fig. 1
B♭5
D5/A
kill - ing lone - li - ness.
With the warmth of your arms

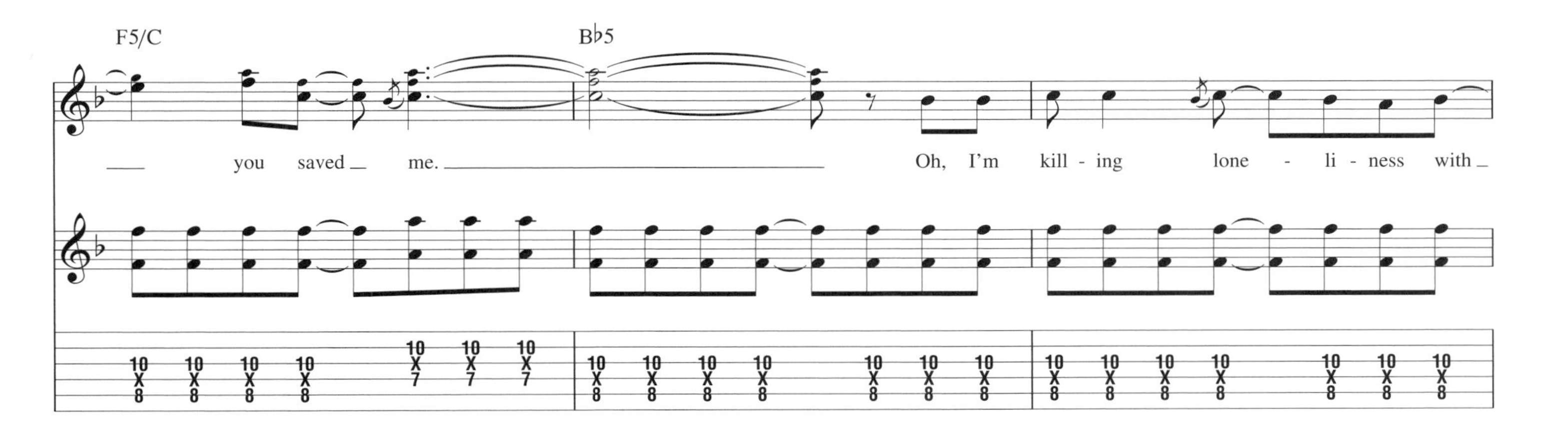
F5/C
B♭5
you saved me.
Oh, I'm kill - ing lone - li - ness with

Half-time feel
Gtr. 3 tacet
Gtrs. 4 & 5: w/ Rhy. Fig. 3
F5/C
C5
D5/A N.C.
B♭5 N.C.
B♭5
you.
We're kill - ing lone - li - ness that turned my heart in - to a

Gtrs. 2 & 7: w/ Riff B
End half-time feel
F6
Csus2
D5/A
B♭5
tomb.
I'm kill - ing lone - li - ness.
Outro
*Gtrs. 1 & 2: w/ Riffs A & A1 (6 times)
Gtrs. 4 & 5: w/ Rhy. Fig. 1 (2 times)
Bkgd. Vocs.: w/ Voc. Fig. 1
D5/A
F5/C
C5
A5
B♭5
A5
B♭5
A5
B♭5
C5
I'm kill - ing lone - li - ness with
Gtr. 6
Riff D
End Riff D
*Gtr. 1: delay off

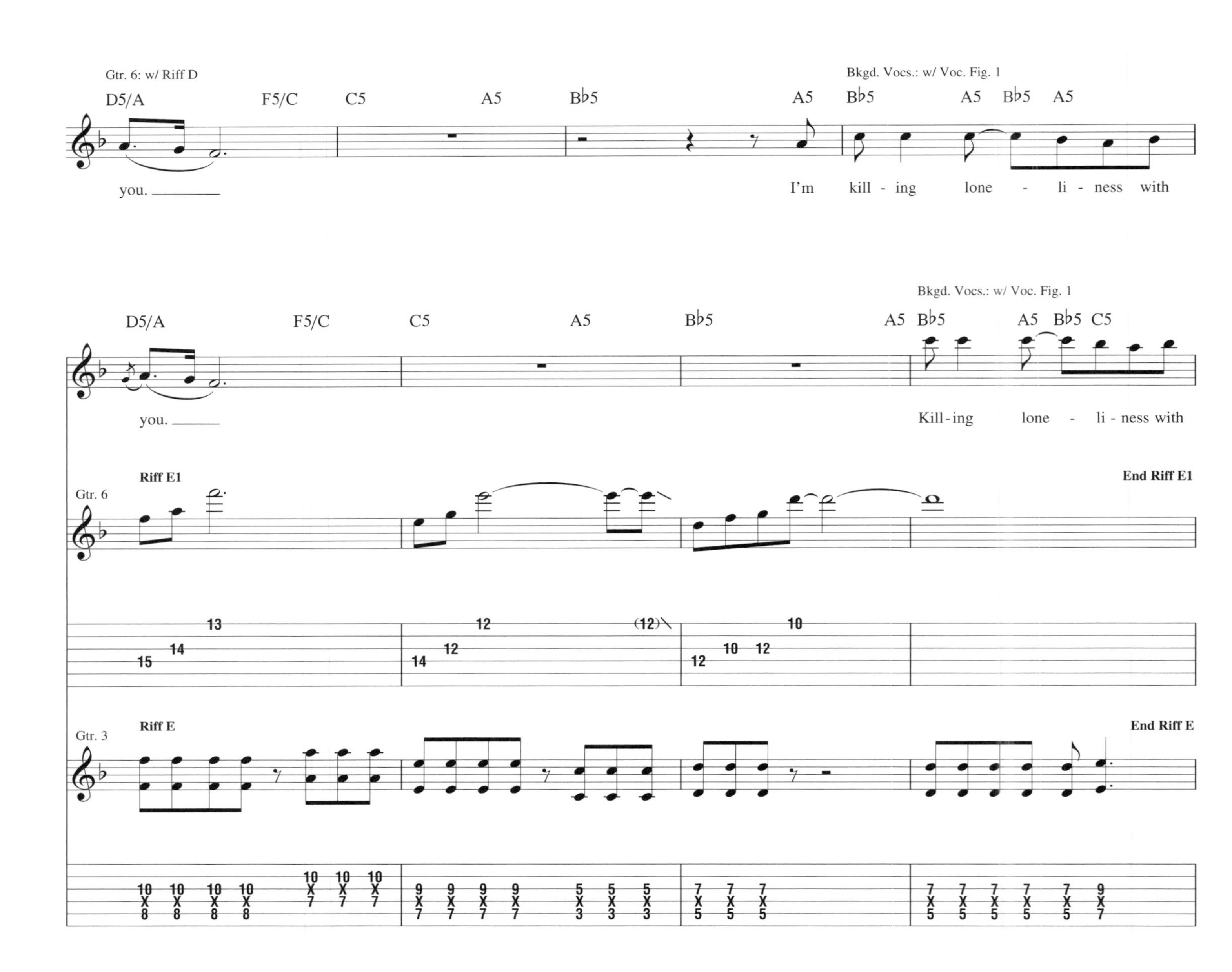
Gtr. 6: w/ Riff D
D5/A F5/C C5 A5 B♭5 A5
Bkgd. Vocs.: w/ Voc. Fig. 1
B♭5 A5 B♭5 A5
you. I'm kill - ing lone - li - ness with
D5/A F5/C C5 A5 B♭5 A5
Bkgd. Vocs.: w/ Voc. Fig. 1
B♭5 A5 B♭5 C5
you. Kill-ing lone - li - ness with
Riff E1
Gtr. 6
End Riff E1
Riff E
Gtr. 3
End Riff E

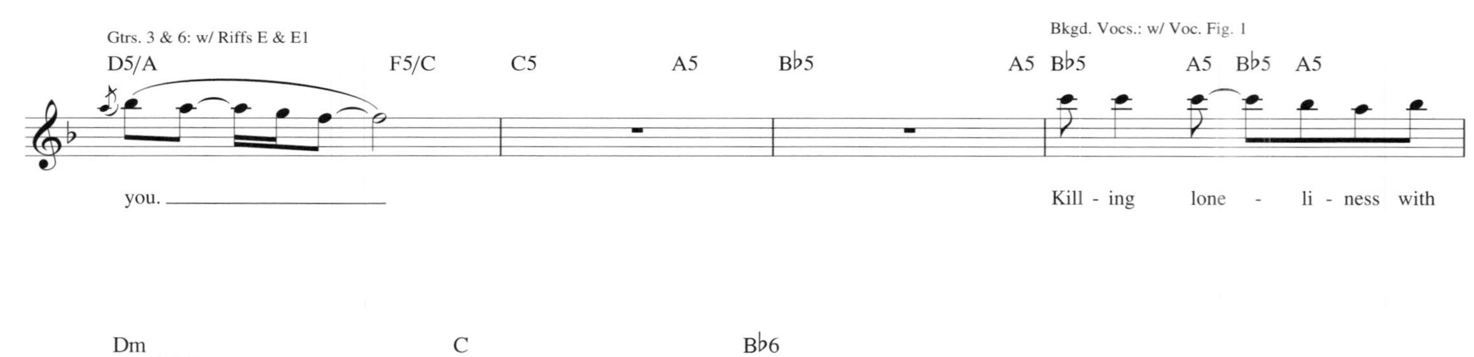
Gtrs. 3 & 6: w/ Riffs E & E1
D5/A F5/C C5 A5 B♭5 A5
Bkgd. Vocs.: w/ Voc. Fig. 1
B♭5 A5 B♭5 A5
you. Kill - ing lone - li - ness with

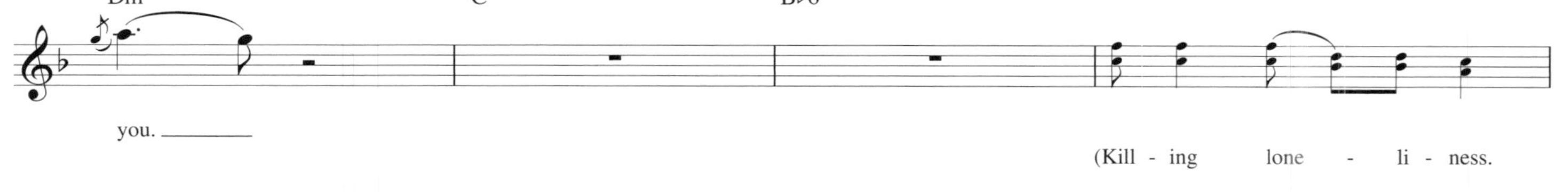
Dm C B♭6
you. (Kill - ing lone - li - ness.

Dm C B♭6 Dm
Kill - ing lone - li - ness.)

Dark Light

Words and Music by Ville Valo

Gtrs. 7, 8 & 9: Capo II

Intro
Moderately slow ♩ = 78

F♯11(no3rd)

End Riff A

End Rhy. Fig. 1

Gtr. 4: w/ Rhy. Fig. 1
Aadd9
Gtr. 1
Gtrs. 2 & 3

F♯11(no3rd)

Verse

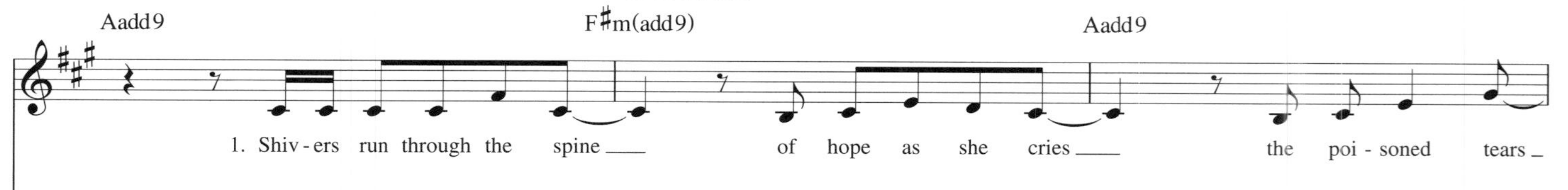
Gtr. 1 tacet
Gtrs. 2 & 3 tacet
Aadd9
F♯m(add9)
Aadd9
1. Shiv-ers run through the spine
of hope as she cries
the poi-soned tears

Gtrs. 2 & 3
Gtr. 5 (elec.)
mp
w/ clean tone
let ring throughout

Gtr. 5 tacet
F#m(add9)
D5/A
E5/B
A
D5/A
A
of a life denied in the raven-black night.
Gtr. 4
f
P.M.

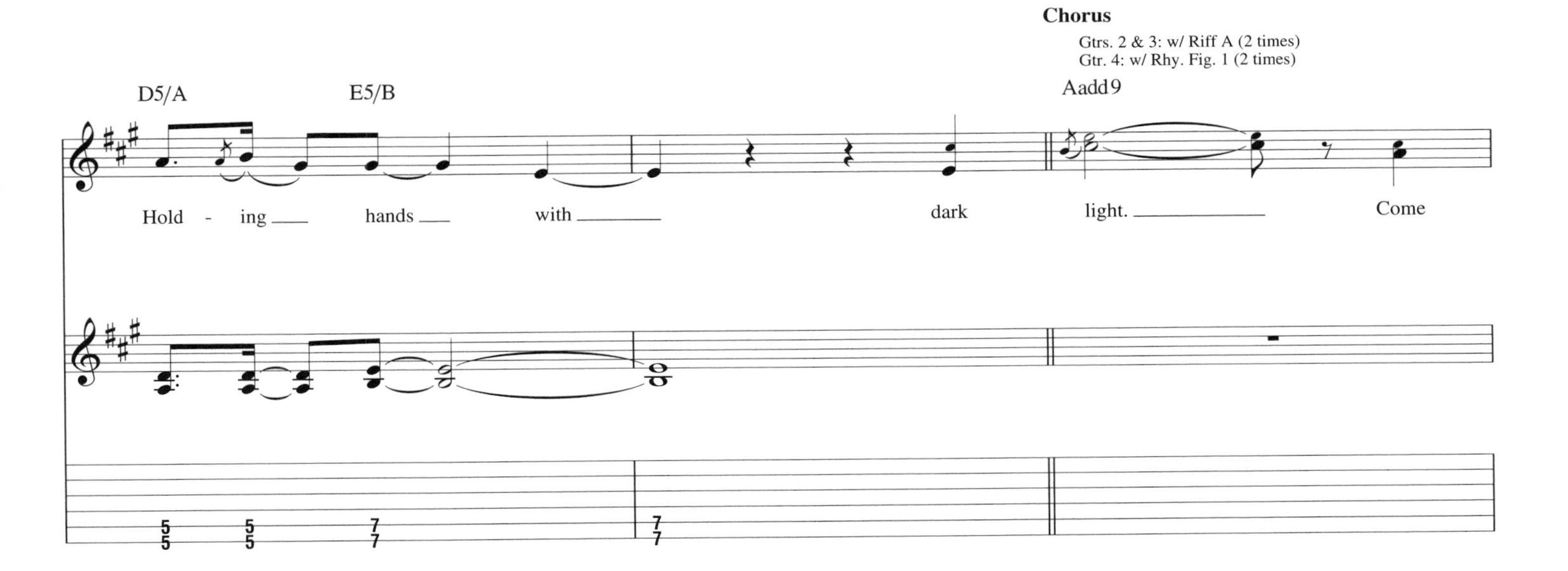
Chorus
Gtrs. 2 & 3: w/ Riff A (2 times)
Gtr. 4: w/ Rhy. Fig. 1 (2 times)
D5/A
E5/B
Aadd9
Holding hands with dark light. Come

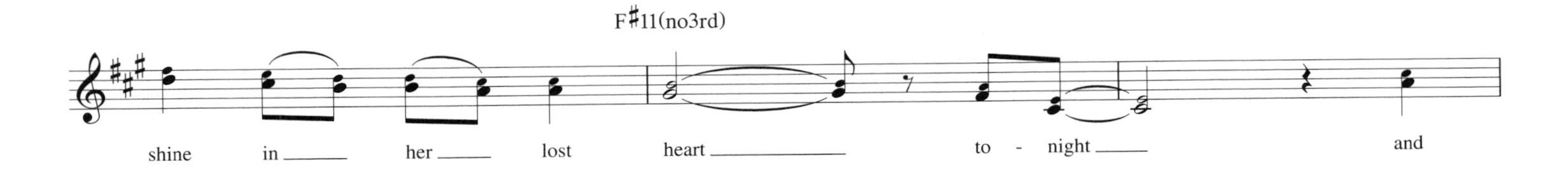
F#11(no3rd)
shine in her lost heart tonight and

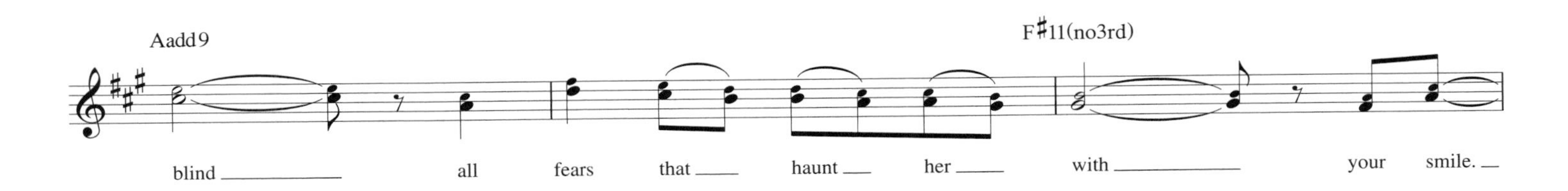
Aadd9
F#11(no3rd)
blind all fears that haunt her with your smile.

Verse
Aadd9
F♯m(add9)
Dark light. 2. In ob - liv - i - on's gar - den her bod - y's on fire,
Gtr. 5

Aadd9
F♯m(add9)
Gtr. 5 tacet
D5/A
E5/B
writh - ing to - wards the an - gel de - filed to
Gtr. 4

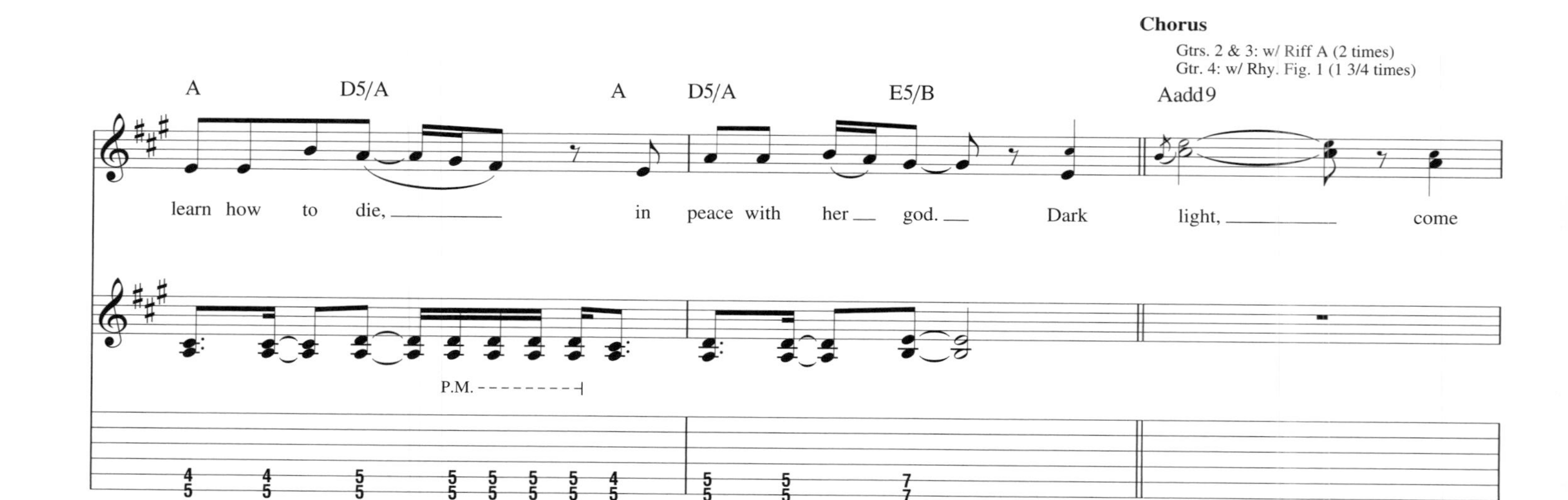
Chorus
Gtrs. 2 & 3: w/ Riff A (2 times)
Gtr. 4: w/ Rhy. Fig. 1 (1 3/4 times)
A
D5/A
A
D5/A
E5/B
Aadd9
learn how to die, in peace with her god. Dark light, come
P.M.

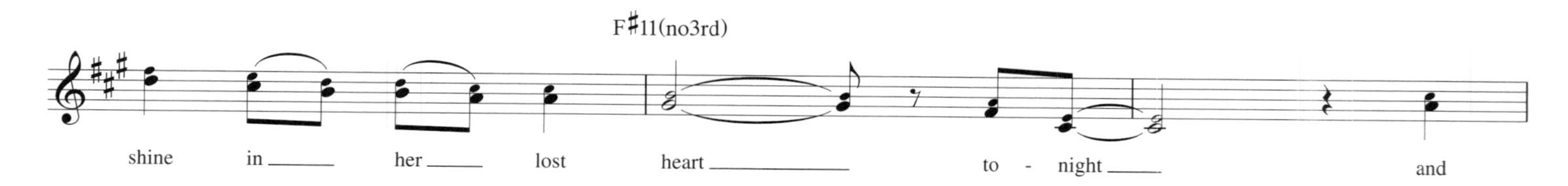
F♯11(no3rd)
shine in her lost heart to - night and

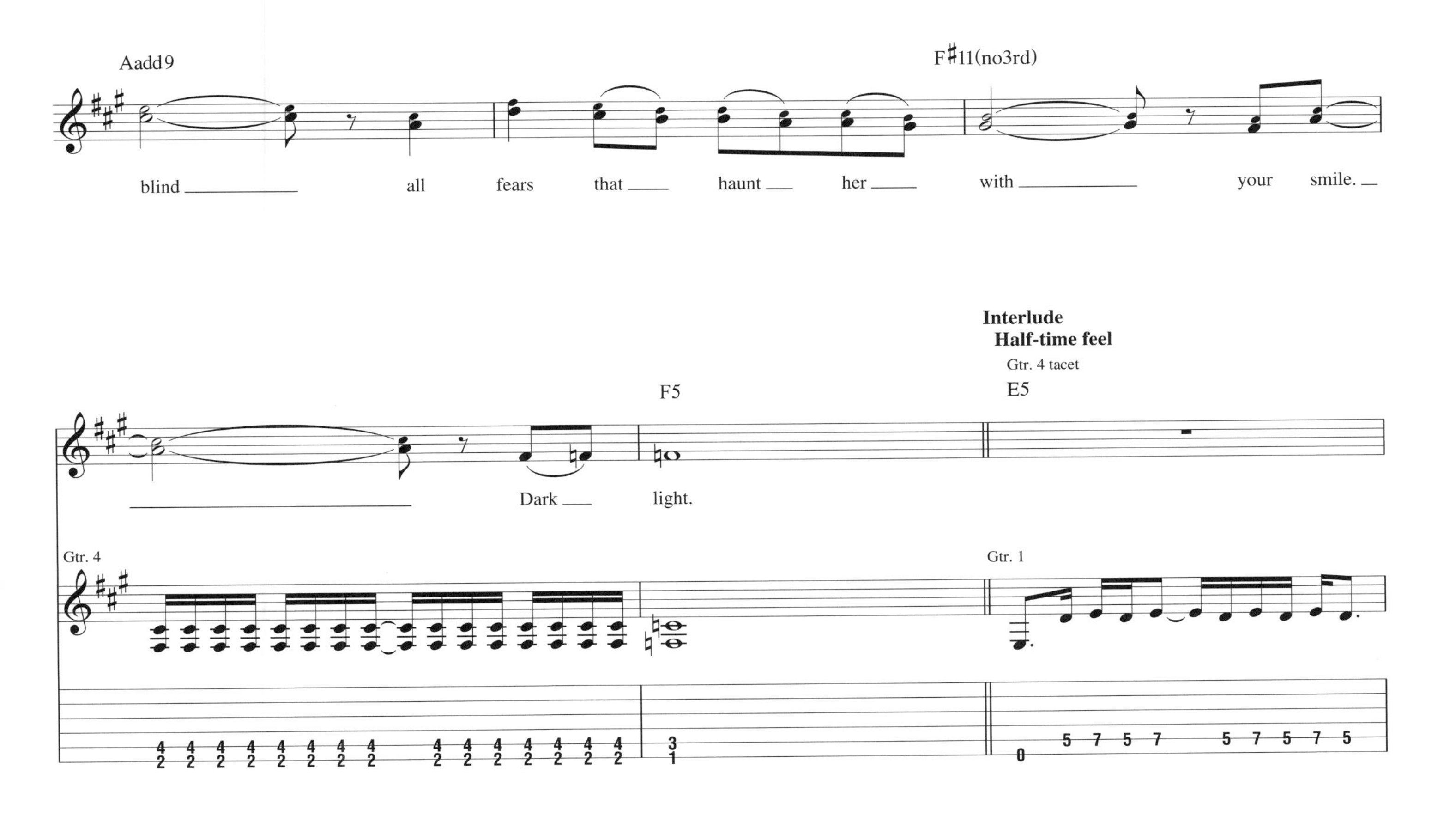

Aadd9
F♯11(no3rd)
blind all fears that haunt her with your smile.
Interlude
Half-time feel
Gtr. 4 tacet
F5
E5
Dark light.
Gtr. 4
Gtr. 1

End half-time feel
G5
A5
F5
E5
Gtr. 1
Gtr. 6 (elec.)
mf
w/ dist.

Chorus

*Symbols in parentheses represent chord names respective to capoed guitar. Symbols above reflect actual sounding chords. Capoed fret is "0" in tab.

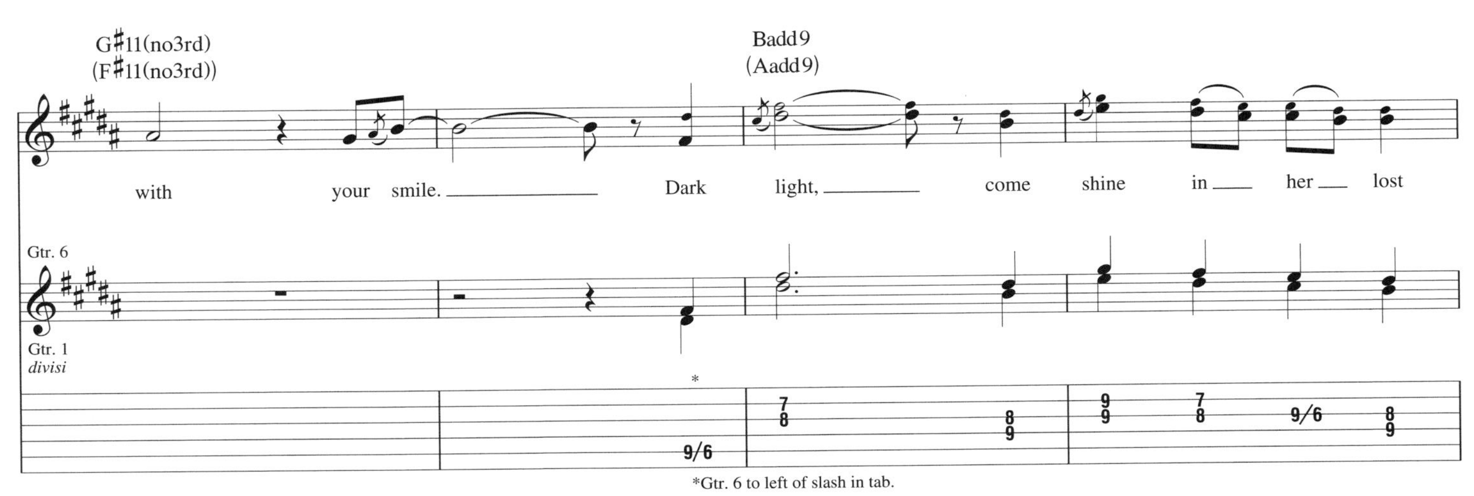

*Gtr. 6 to left of slash in tab.

G♯11(no3rd)
(F♯11(no3rd))
Badd9
(Aadd9)
heart to - night and blind all fears that haunt her
Gtr. 6
Gtr. 1
G♯11(no3rd)
(F♯11(no3rd))
G5
with your smile. Dark light.
Gtr. 6
Gtr. 1
Gtr. 4

Outro

Gtrs. 1, 4 & 6 tacet
G♯m7add11
(F♯m7add11)
Gtr. 8
p

Gmaj7add11
(Fmaj7add11)

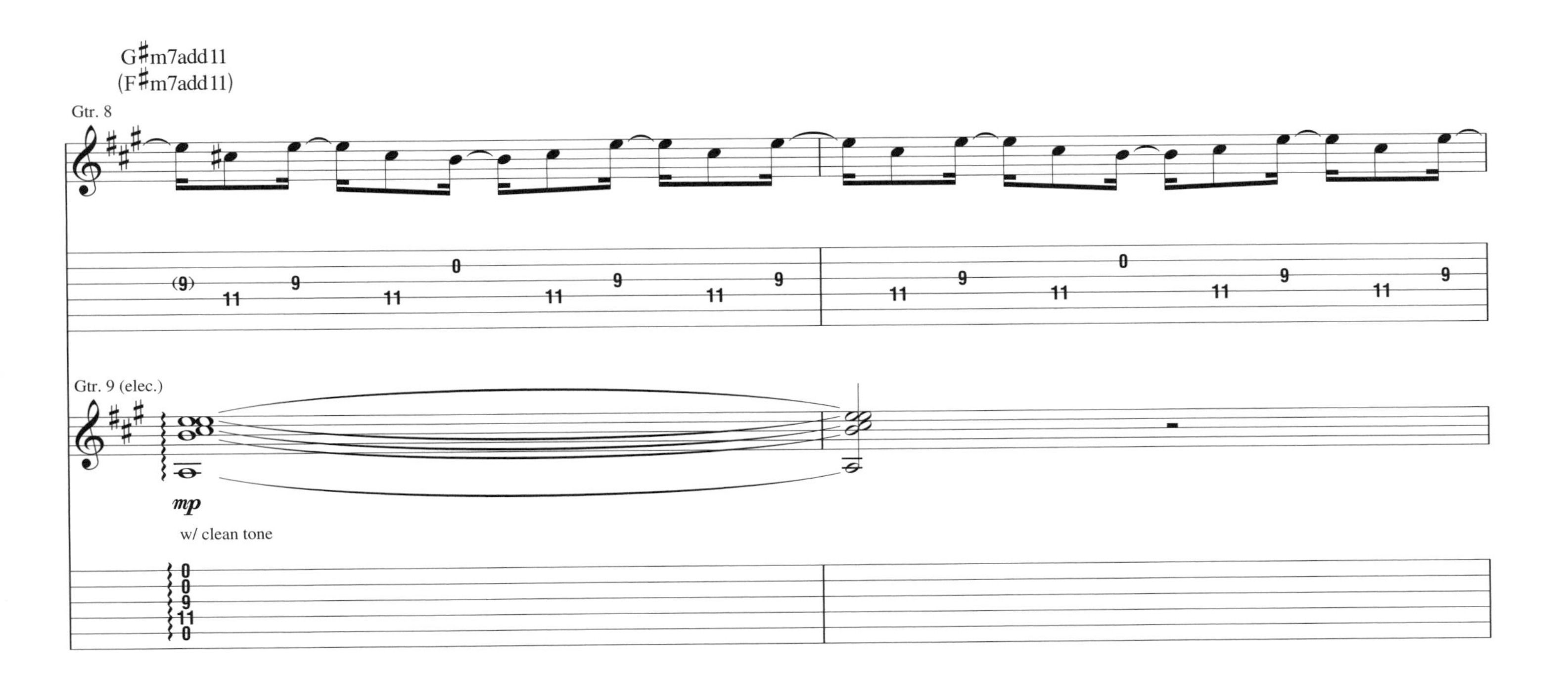
G♯m7add11
(F♯m7add11)
Gtr. 8
Gtr. 9 (elec.)
mp
w/ clean tone

Gtr. 9 tacet
Gmaj7add11
(Fmaj7add11)
Gtr. 8

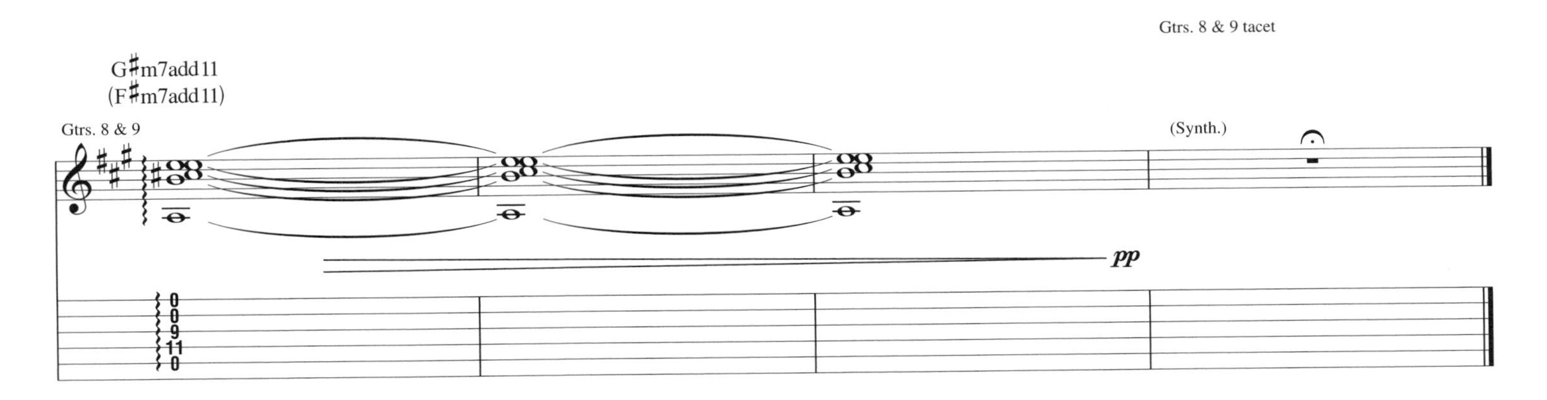
Gtrs. 8 & 9 tacet
G♯m7add11
(F♯m7add11)
Gtrs. 8 & 9
(Synth.)
pp

Behind the Crimson Door

Words and Music by Ville Valo

Intro
Moderately ♩ = 141

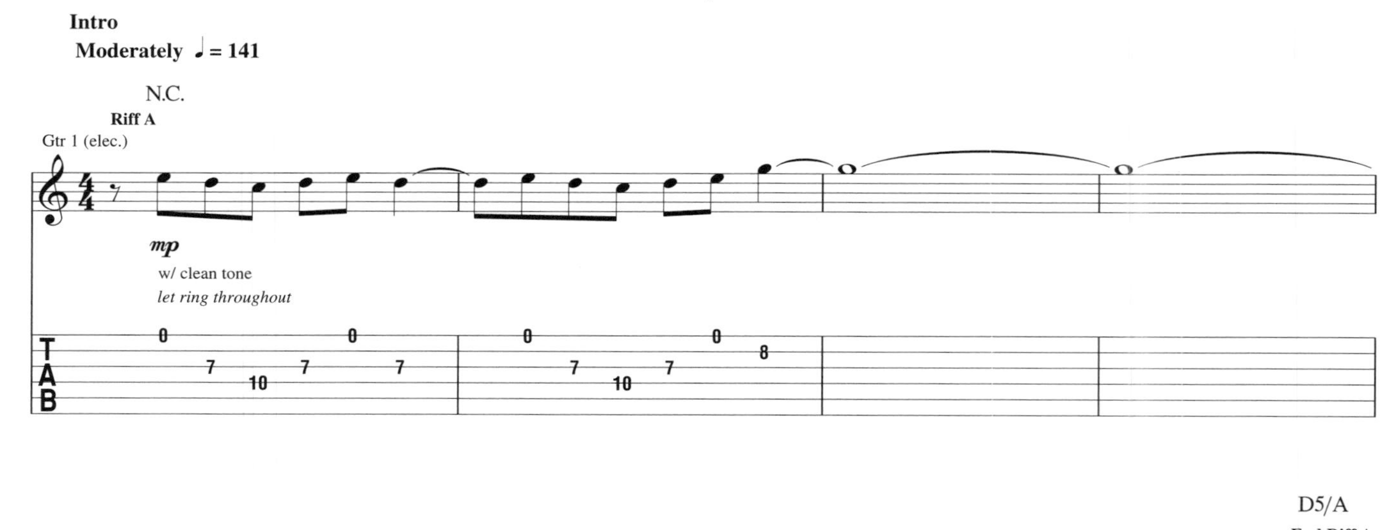

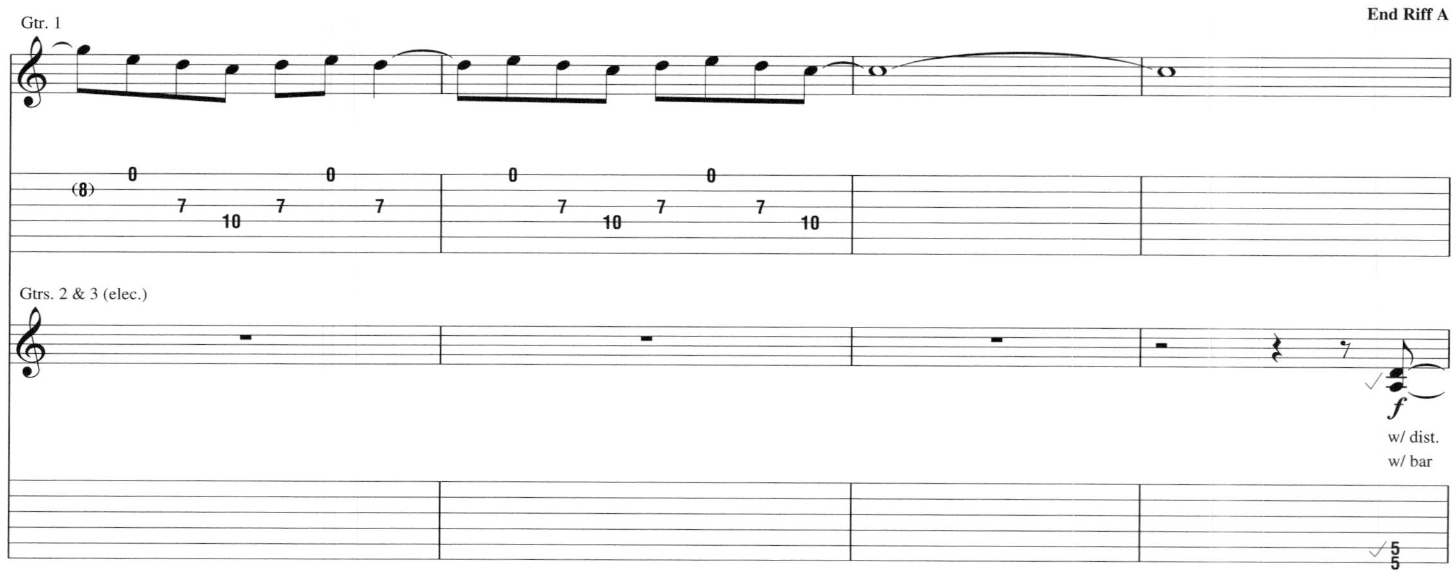

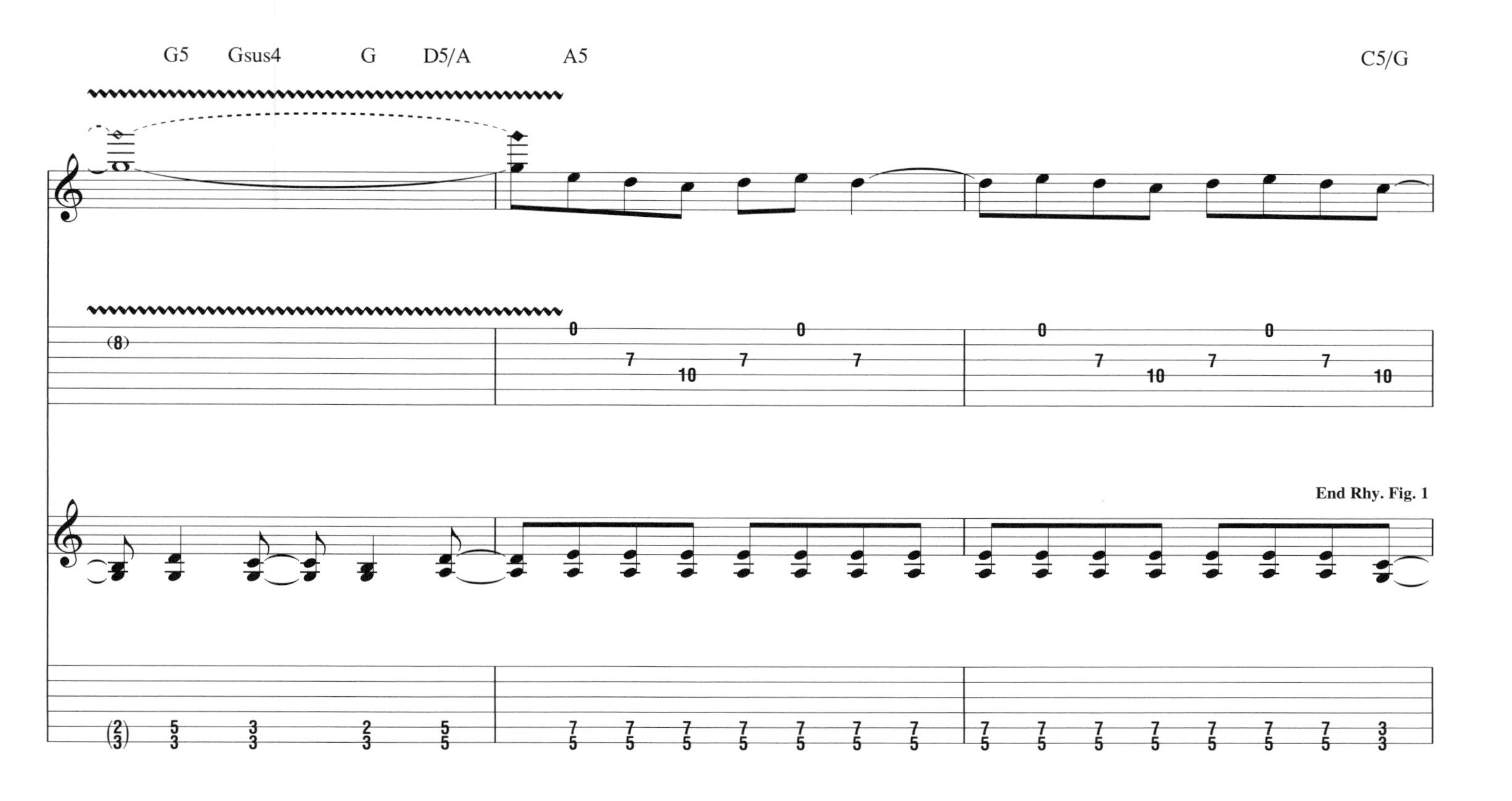

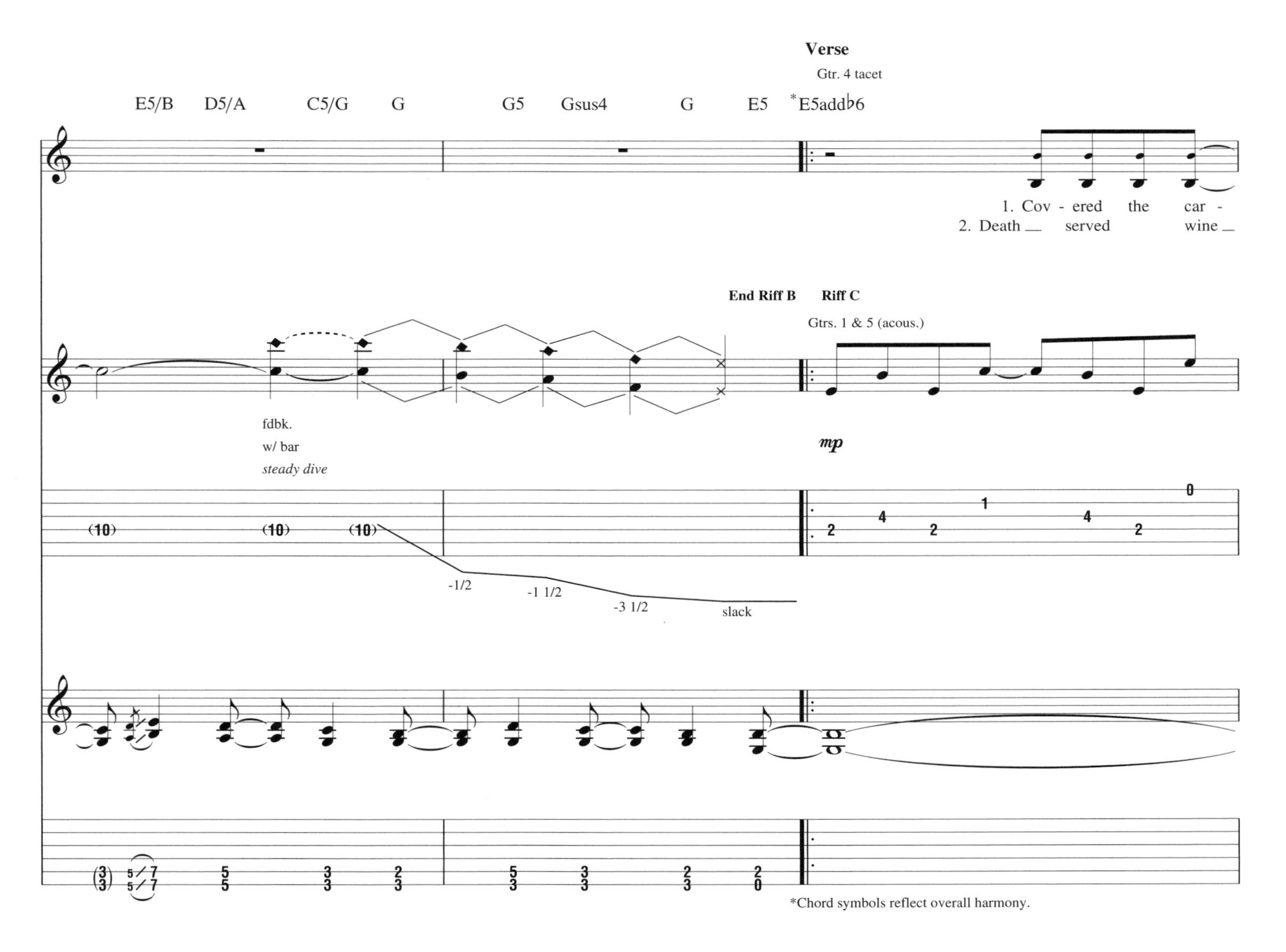

*Chord symbols reflect overall harmony.

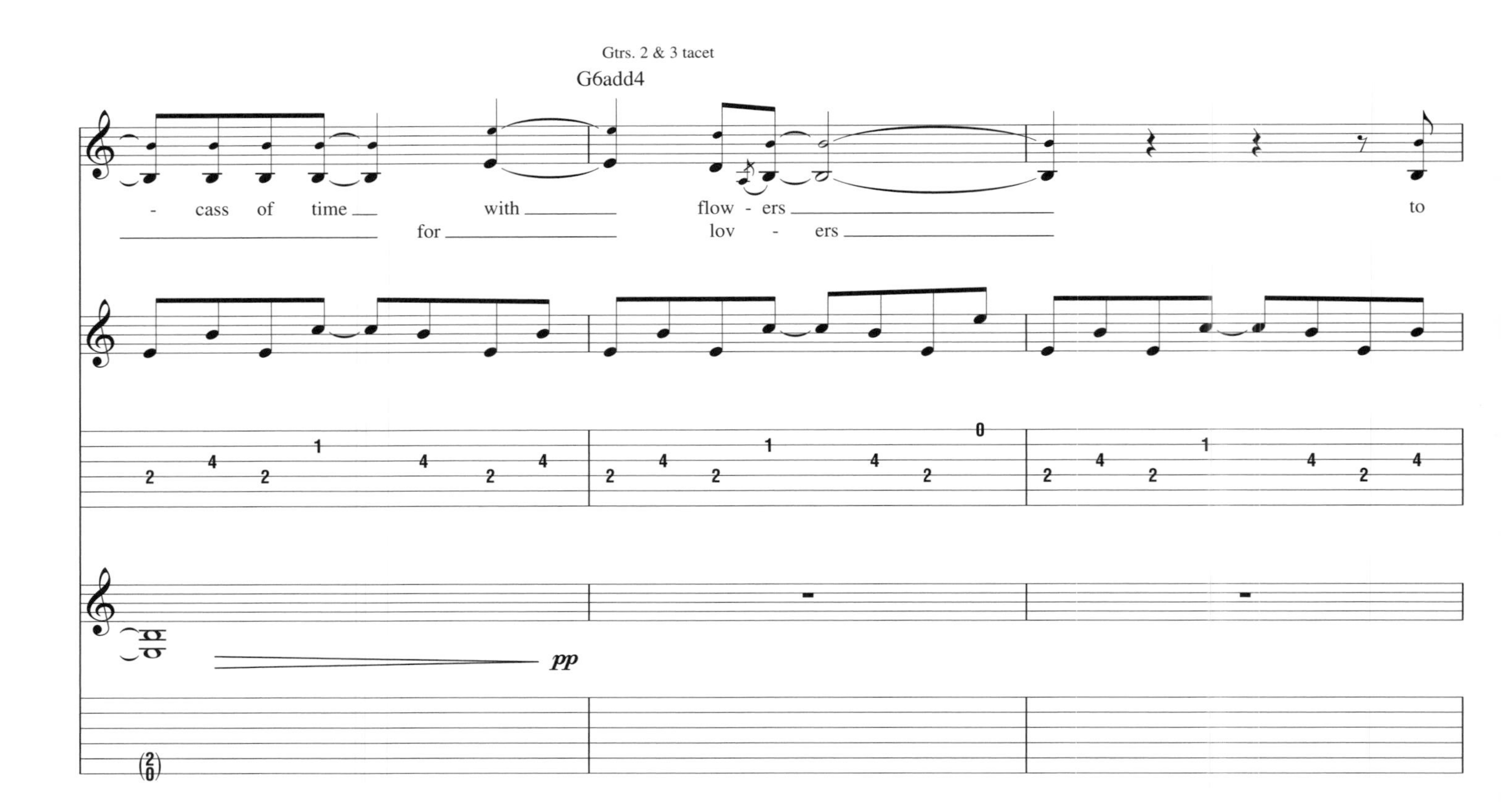
Gtrs. 2 & 3 tacet
G6add4
- cass of time with flow - ers to
for lov - ers
pp

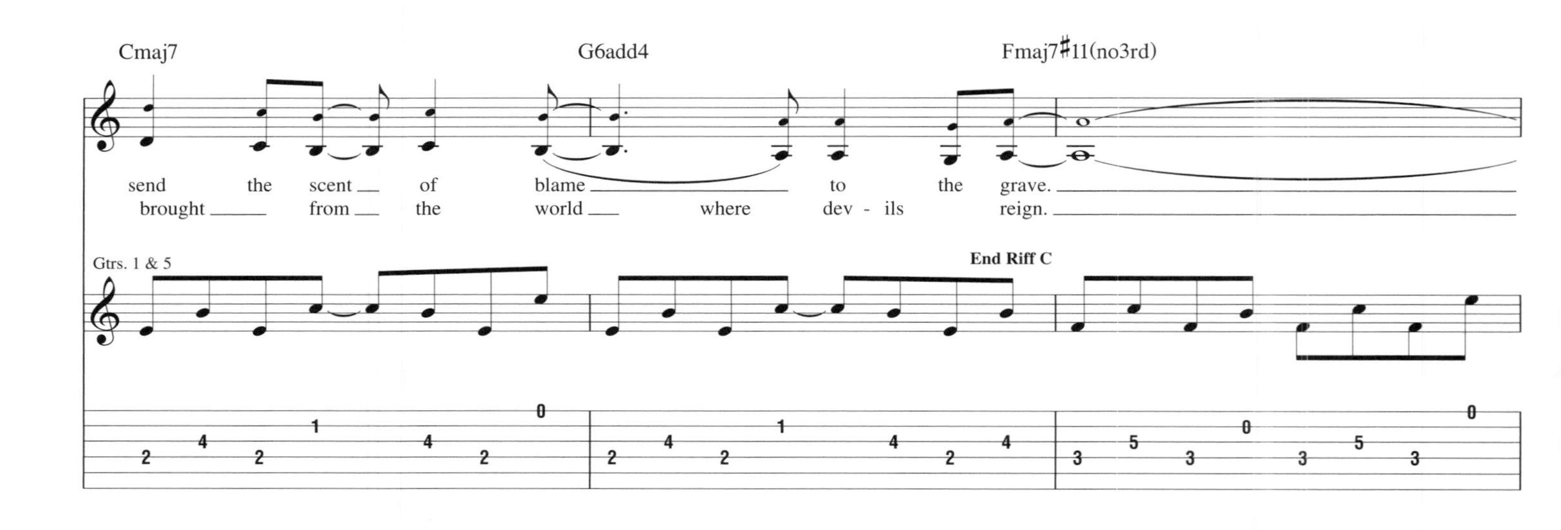
Cmaj7
G6add4
Fmaj7♯11(no3rd)
send the scent of blame to the grave.
brought from the world where dev - ils reign.
Gtrs. 1 & 5
End Riff C

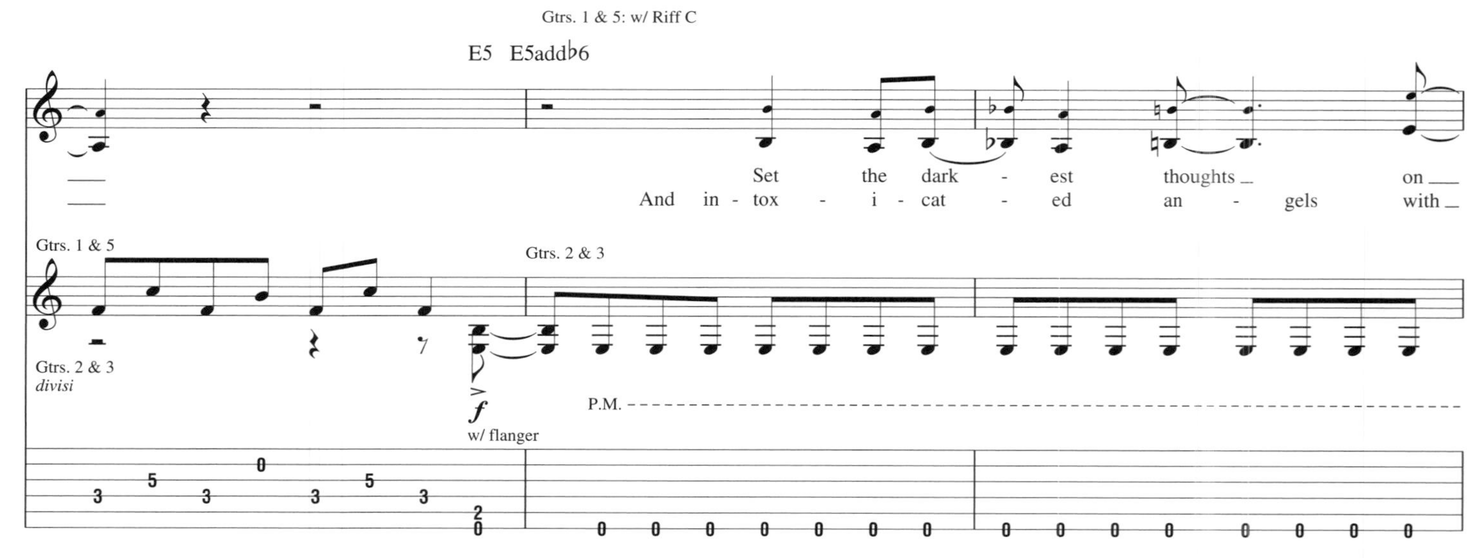
Gtrs. 1 & 5: w/ Riff C
E5 E5add♭6
Set the dark - est thoughts on
And in - tox - i - cat - ed an - gels with
Gtrs. 1 & 5
Gtrs. 2 & 3
Gtrs. 2 & 3
divisi
f
w/ flanger
P.M.

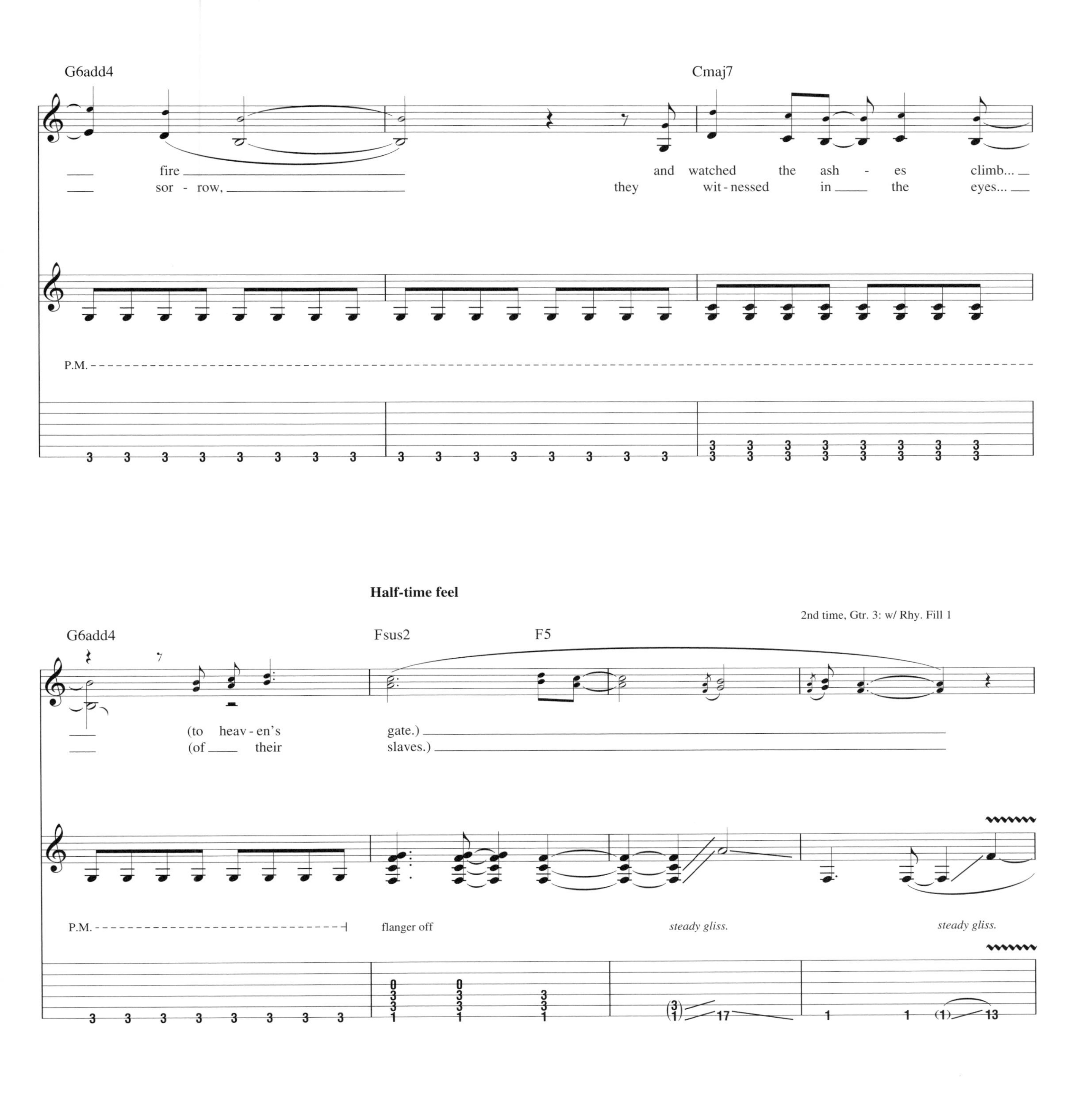
G6add4
Cmaj7
fire
and watched the ash - es climb...
sor - row,
they wit - nessed in the eyes...
P.M.
Half-time feel
2nd time, Gtr. 3: w/ Rhy. Fill 1
G6add4
Fsus2
F5
(to heav - en's
gate.)
(of their
slaves.)
P.M.
flanger off
steady gliss.
steady gliss.

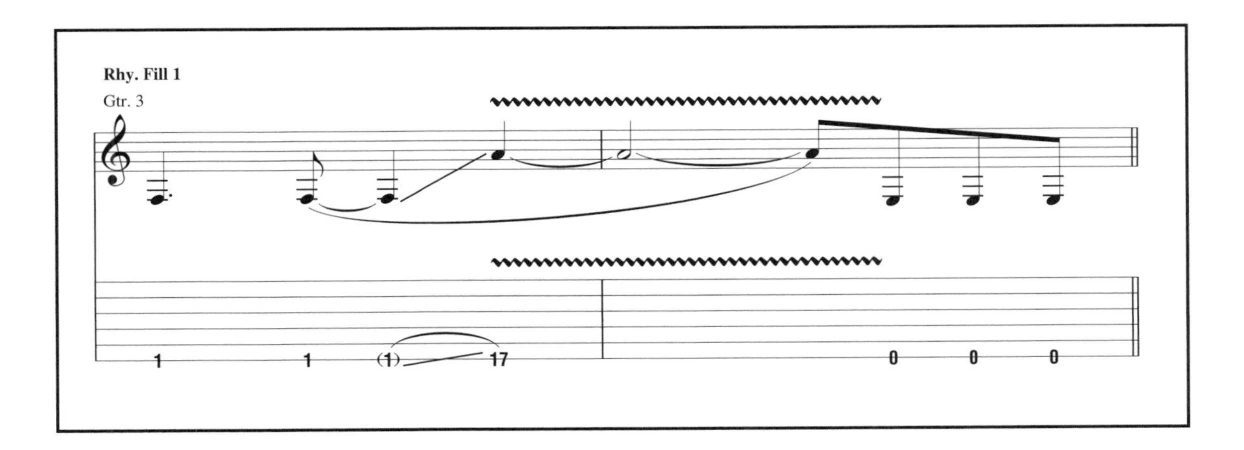
Rhy. Fill 1
Gtr. 3

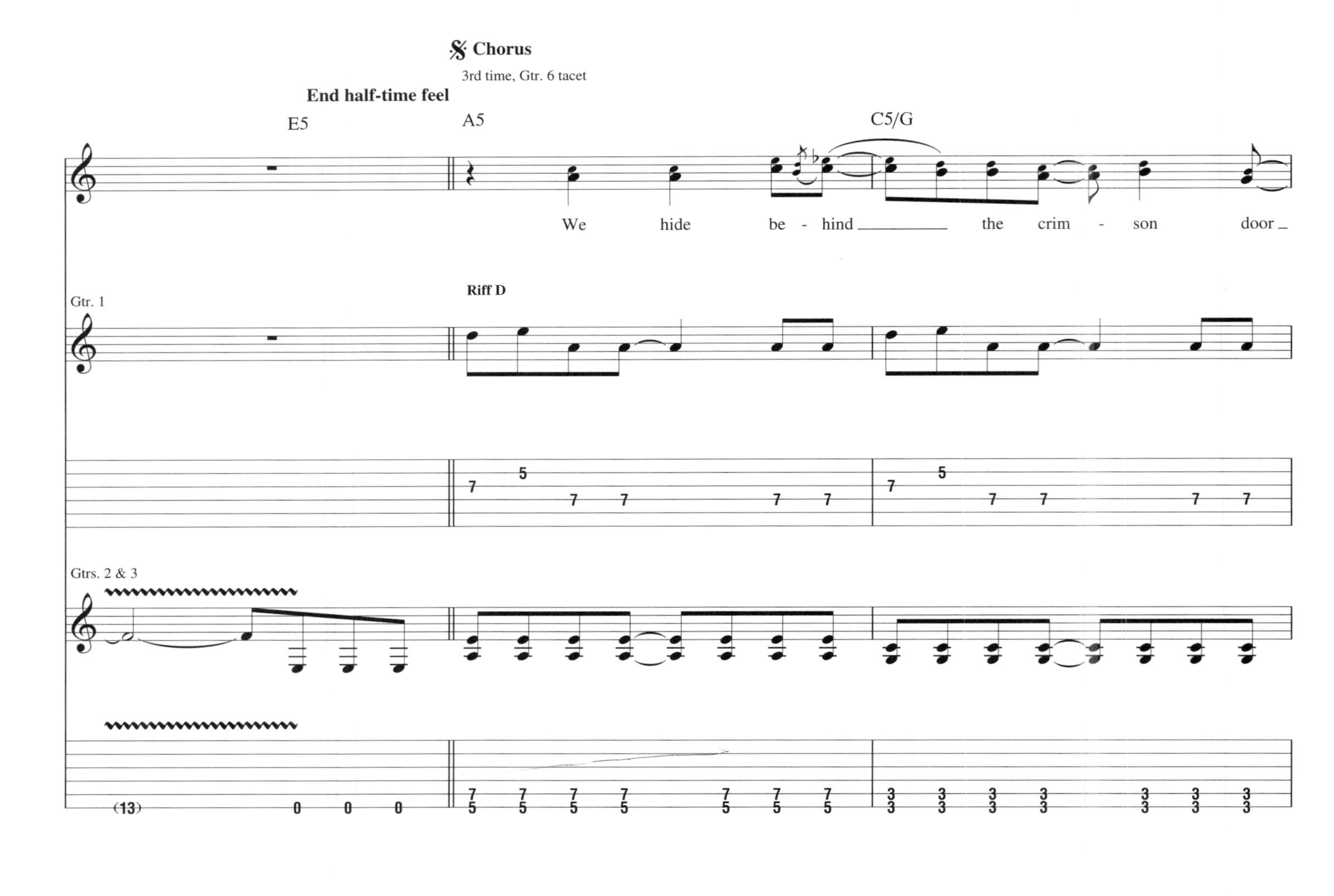

Chorus
3rd time, Gtr. 6 tacet
End half-time feel
E5
A5
C5/G
We hide be - hind the crim - son door
Gtr. 1
Riff D
Gtrs. 2 & 3

G5
D5/A
A5
while the sum - mer's killed by the fall. A - live be - hind

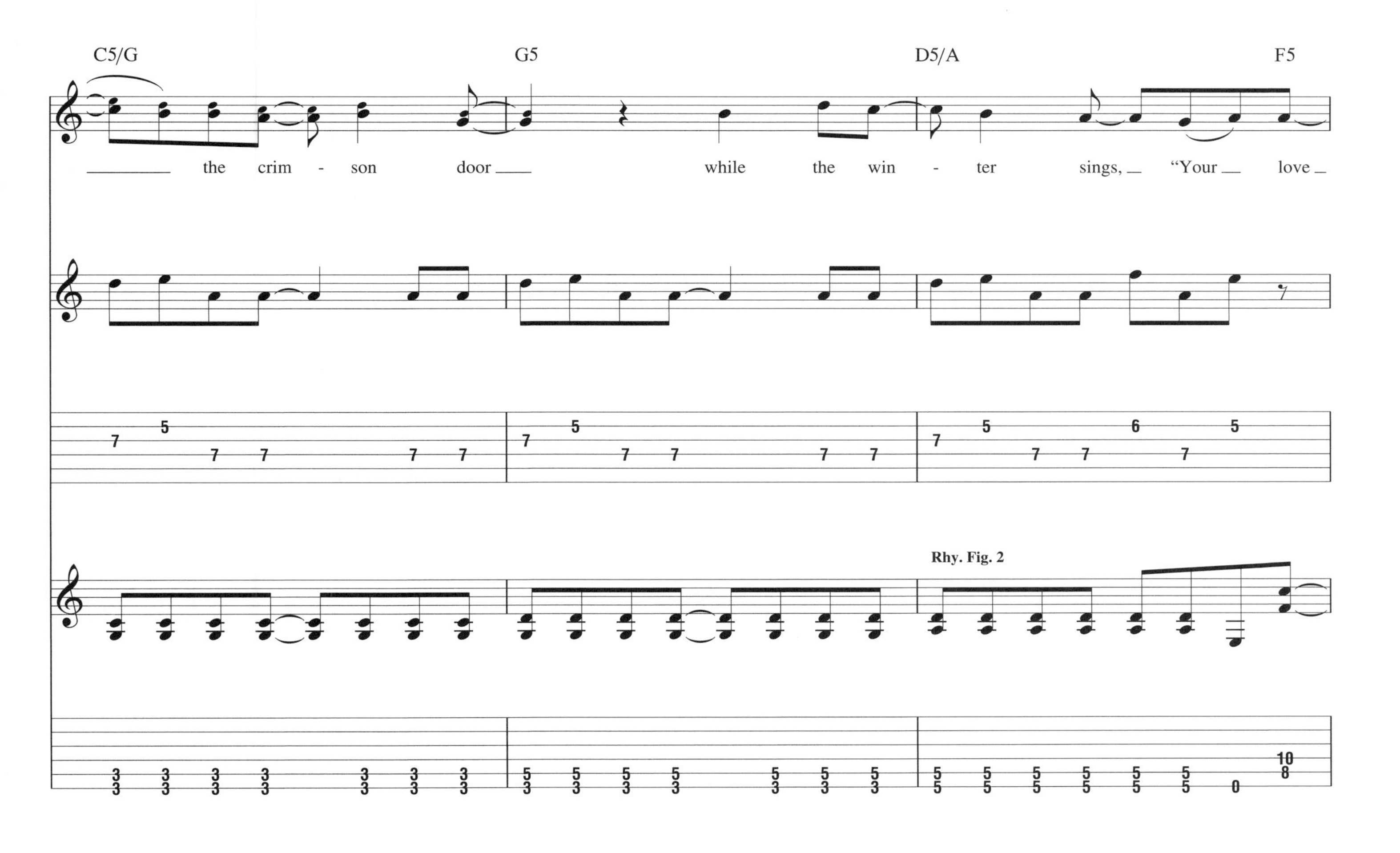
C5/G
G5
D5/A
F5
the crim - son door while the win - ter sings, "Your love
Rhy. Fig. 2

G5
D5/A
A5
C5/G
will be the death of me.
(Death

1.
To Coda
Interlude
Gtr. 1 tacet
Gtr. 1: w/ Riff A
Gtrs. 2 & 3: w/ Rhy. Fig. 1
Gtr. 4: w/ Riff B
A5
F5
G5
D5/A
A5
Your love will be the death of me."
of me.)
End Riff D
End Rhy. Fig. 2
C5/G
E5/B
D5/A
C5/G
G
G5
Gsus4
G
D5/A
A5
C5/G
E5/B
D5/A
C5/G
G
G5
Gsus4
G
E5
2.
G5
be the death
Gtrs. 2 & 3

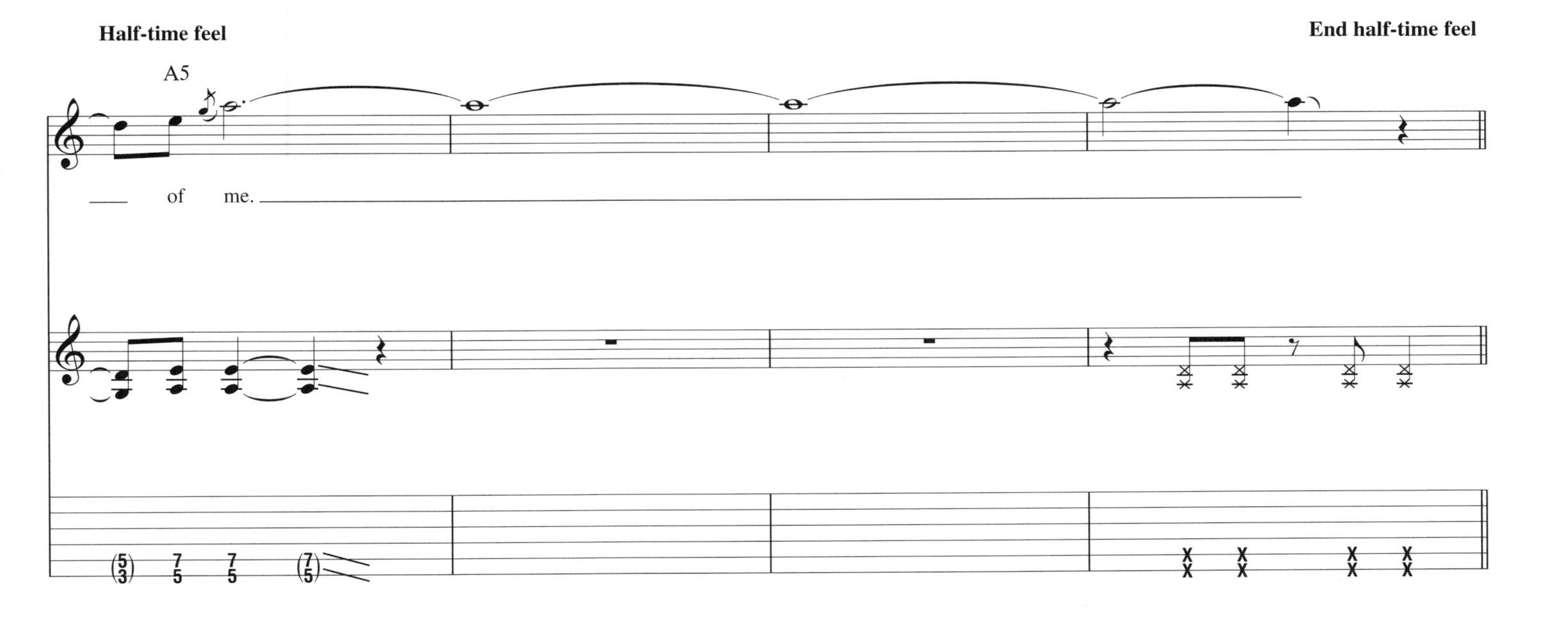
Half-time feel
End half-time feel
A5
of me.

Interlude

A5

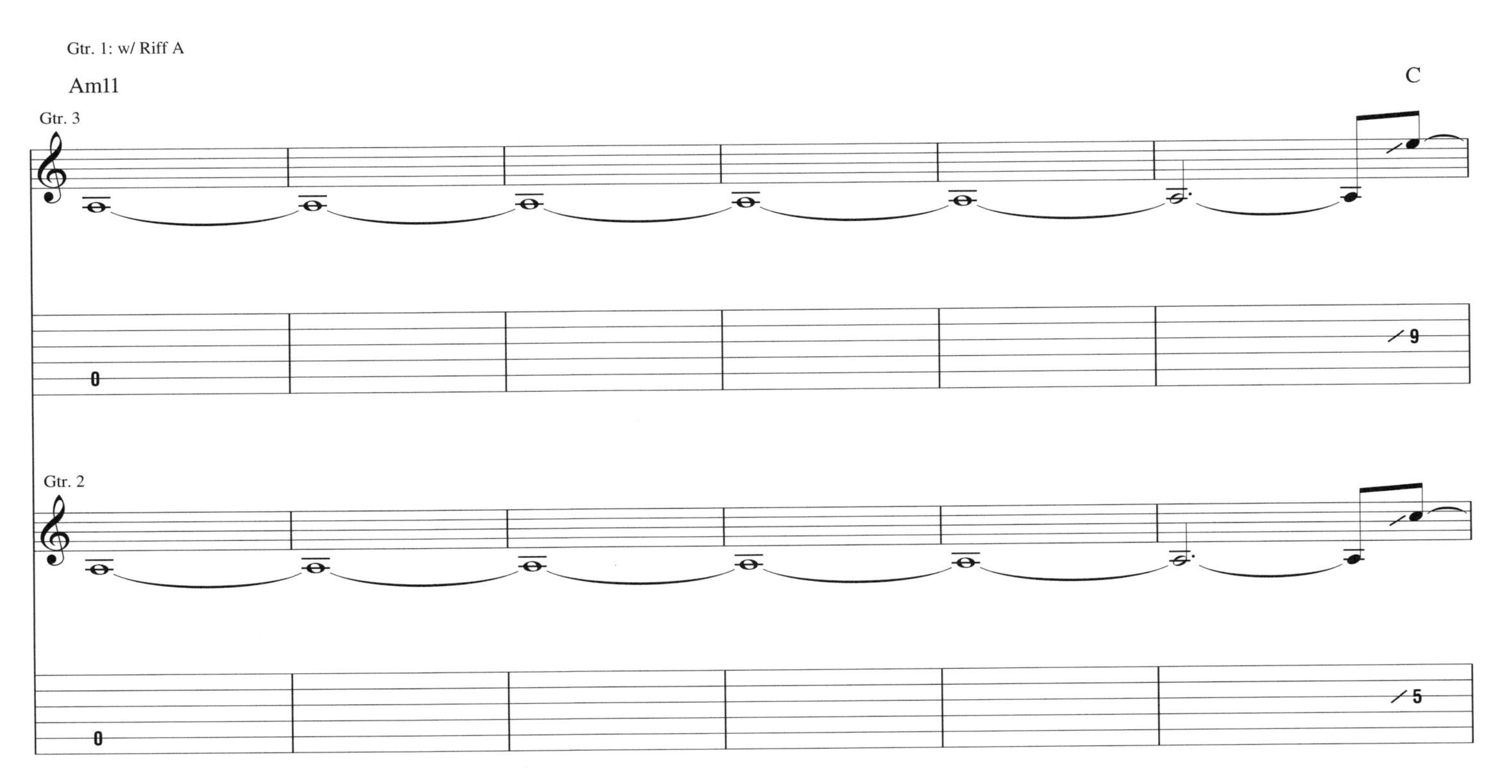
Gtr. 1: w/ Riff A
Am11
C
Gtr. 3
Gtr. 2

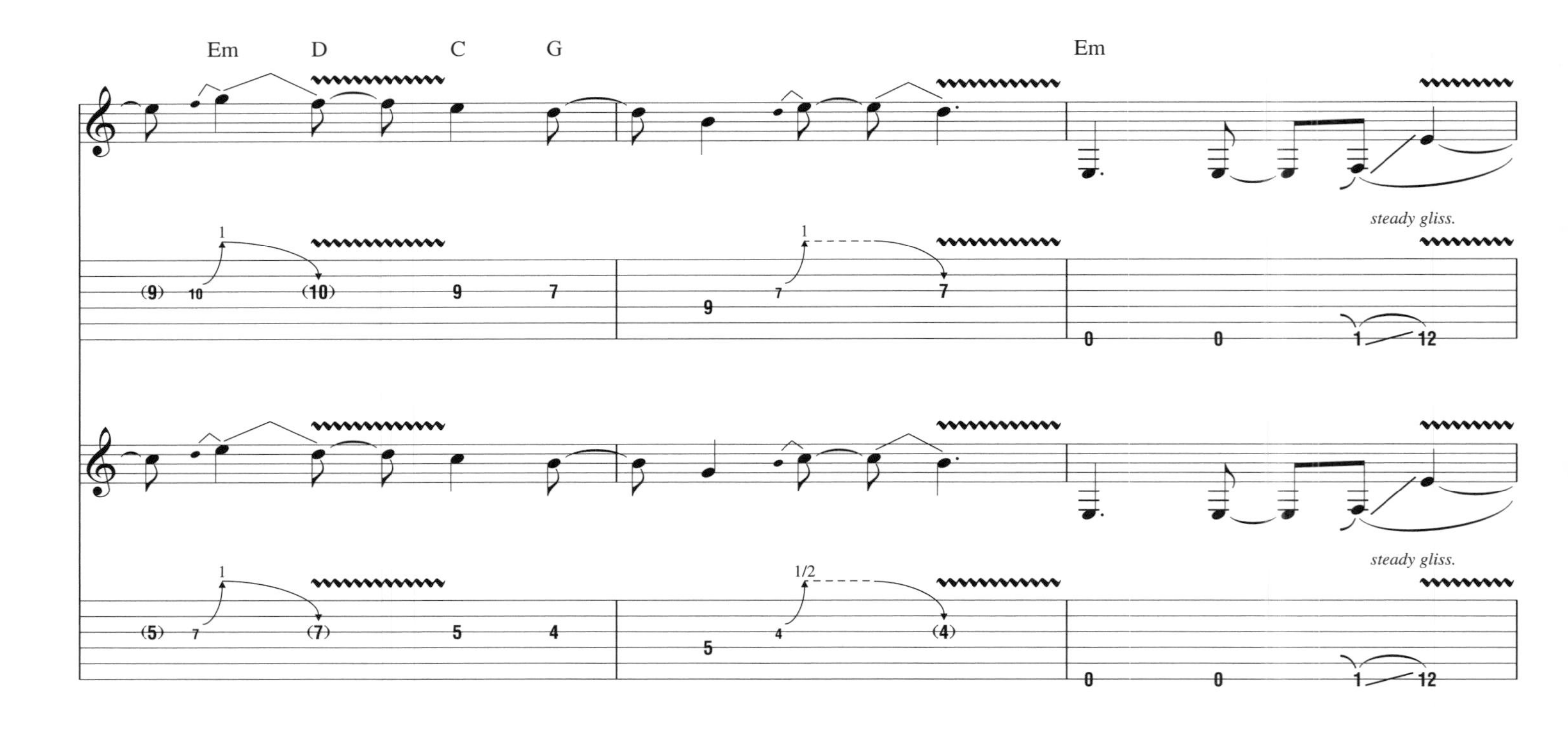
Em
D
C
G
Em
steady gliss.
steady gliss.

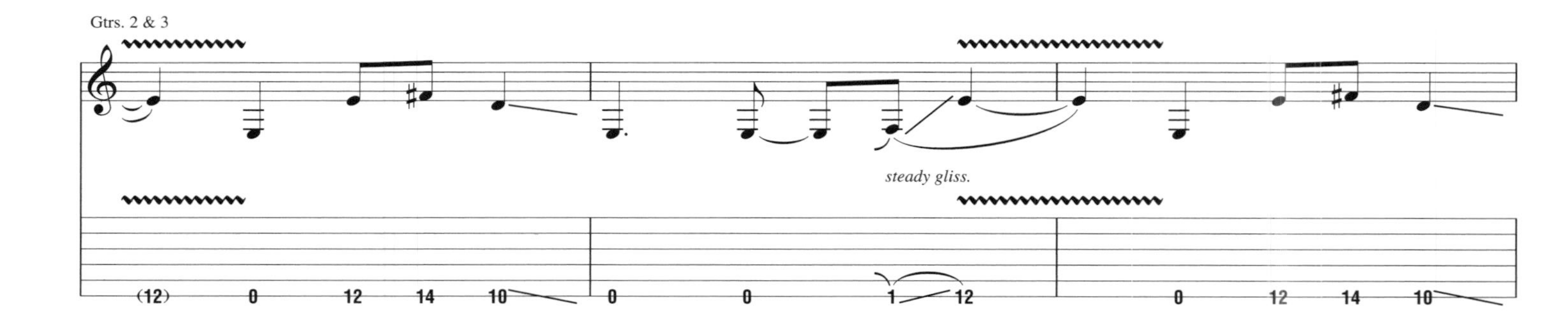
Gtrs. 2 & 3
steady gliss.

D.S. al Coda
(take 1st ending)
Gtr. 6 (elec.)
mf
w/ dist.
steady gliss.
steady gliss.
Gtrs. 2 & 3
steady gliss.
steady gliss.

Coda
Gtr. 1: w/ Riff D
A5
C5/G
G5
of me.
We hide be - hind the crim - son door while the sum -
Gtrs. 2 & 3

D5/A
A5
C5/G
G5
- mer's killed by the fall. A - live be - hind the crim - son door while the win -

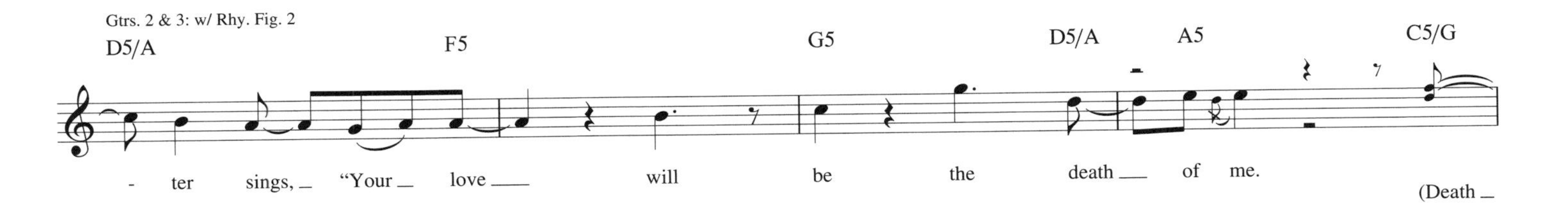
Gtrs. 2 & 3: w/ Rhy. Fig. 2
D5/A
F5
G5
D5/A
A5
C5/G
- ter sings, "Your love will be the death of me.
(Death

Outro

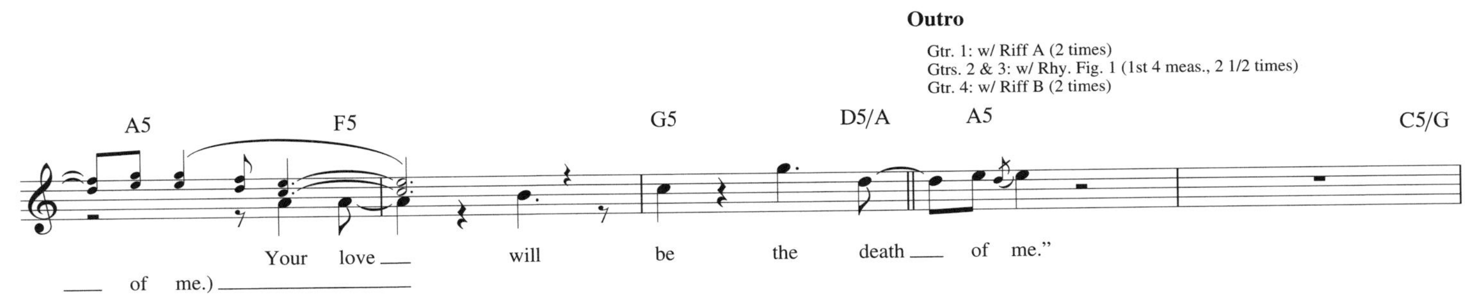
Gtr. 1: w/ Riff A (2 times)
Gtrs. 2 & 3: w/ Rhy. Fig. 1 (1st 4 meas., 2 1/2 times)
Gtr. 4: w/ Riff B (2 times)
A5
F5
G5
D5/A
A5
C5/G
Your love will be the death of me."
of me.)

E5/B D5/A C5/G G G5 Gsus4 G D5/A A5 C5/G
We hide be - hind the crim - son door.
E5/B D5/A C5/G G G5 Gsus4 G D5/A A5 C5/G
We hide be - hind the crim - son door.
E5/B D5/A C5/G G G5 Gsus4 G D5/A A5
We hide be - hind the crim - son door.
Gtrs. 2 & 3
C5/G E5/B D5/A C5/G G G5 Gsus4 G D5/A A5
We hide be - hind the crim - son door.

The Face of God

Words and Music by Ville Valo

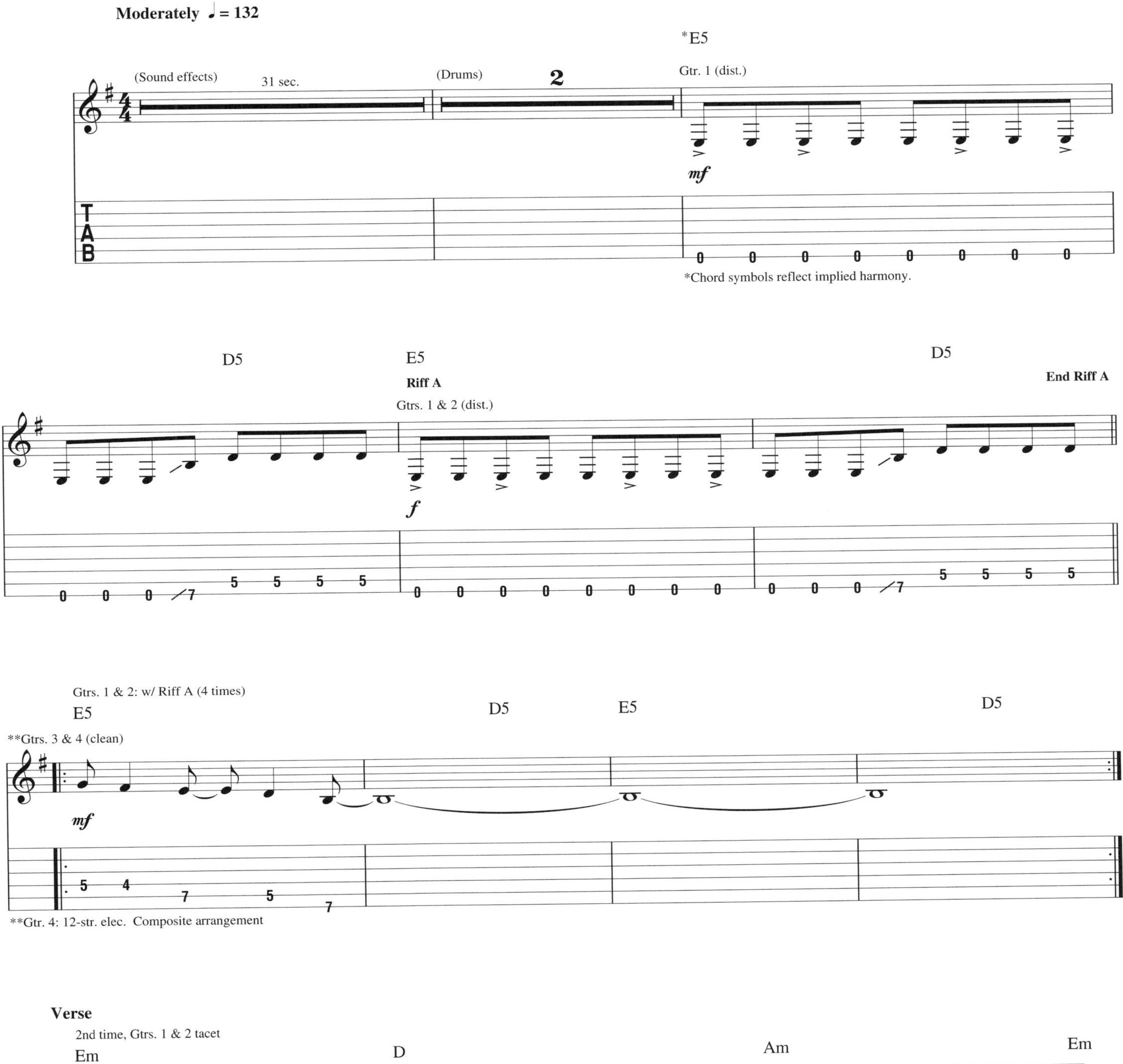

G
D5
is read - ing the words of the sad - dest po - em to be en -
on stum - bling in the gar - den of with - er - ing trust with -
let ring
2nd time, Gtrs. 3 & 4: w/ Fill 1
D
E5
D5/A
Pre-Chorus
Half-time feel
Gtrs. 3 & 4 tacet
A5
graved on the stone on my grave. I'd kill to share
out the cour - age to leave. Oh, I'd take my life
Gtrs. 3 & 4
let ring
Gtrs. 1 & 2
Rhy. Fig. 1

Fill 1
Gtrs. 3 & 4
let ring

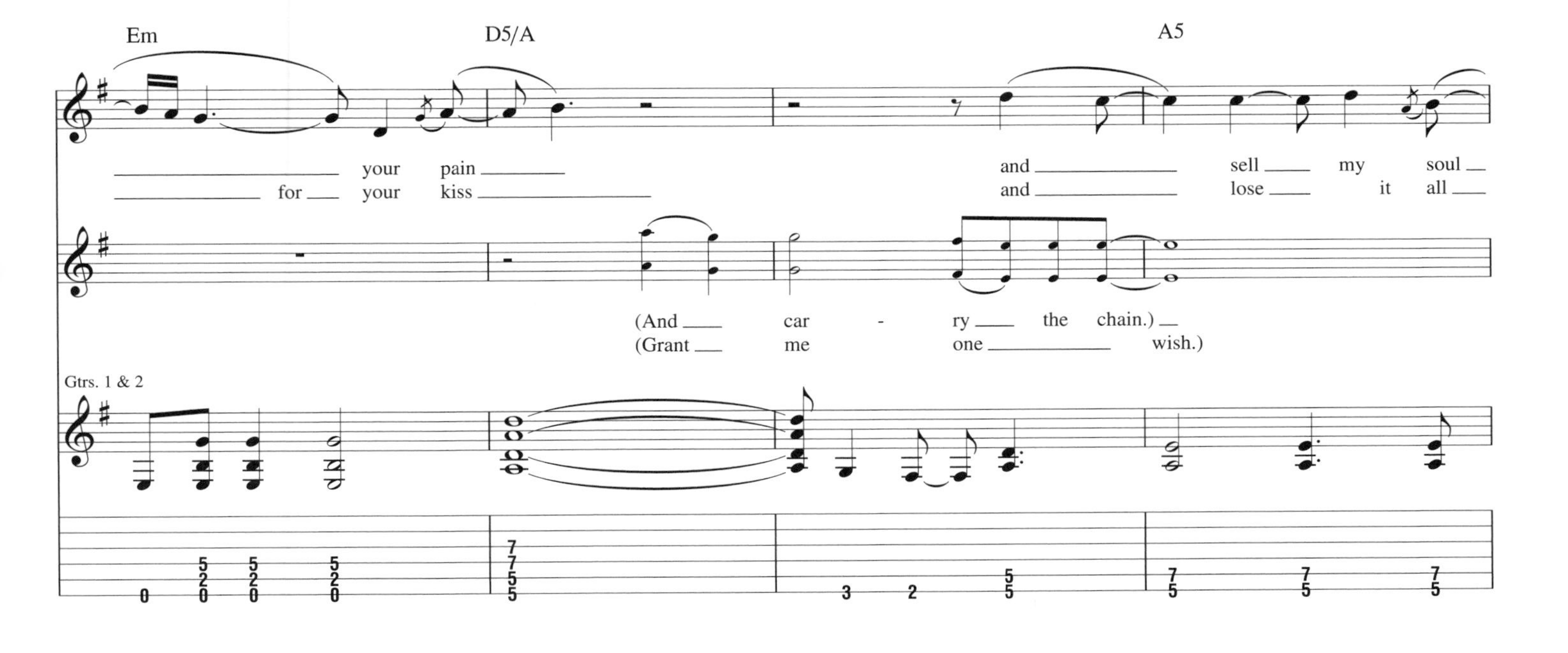
Em
D5/A
A5
your pain
for your kiss
and sell my soul
and lose it all
(And carry the chain.)
(Grant me one wish.)
Gtrs. 1 & 2

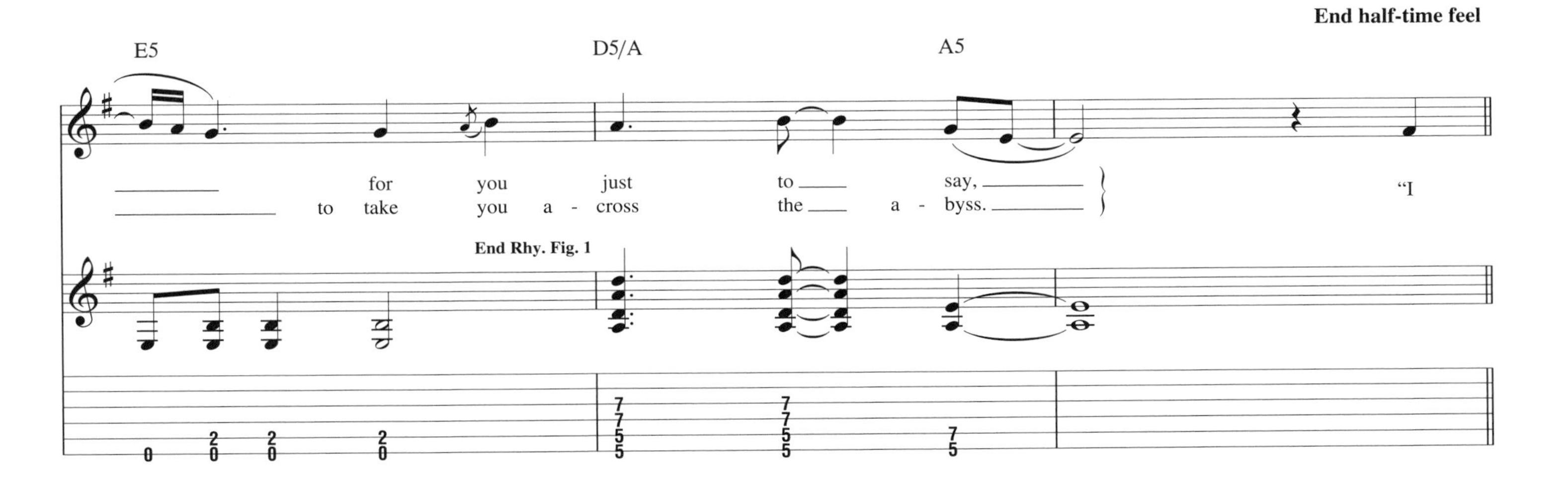
End half-time feel
E5
D5/A
A5
for you just to say,
to take you a-cross the a-byss.
"I
End Rhy. Fig. 1

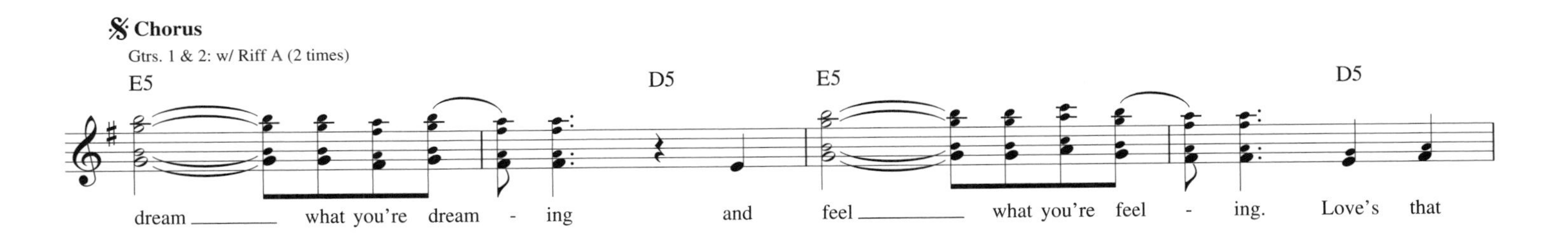
Chorus
Gtrs. 1 & 2: w/ Riff A (2 times)
E5
D5
E5
D5
dream what you're dream-ing and feel what you're feel-ing. Love's that

1.
C5/G
G5
D5/A
shad-ow on the wall with the face of
Gtrs. 1 & 2

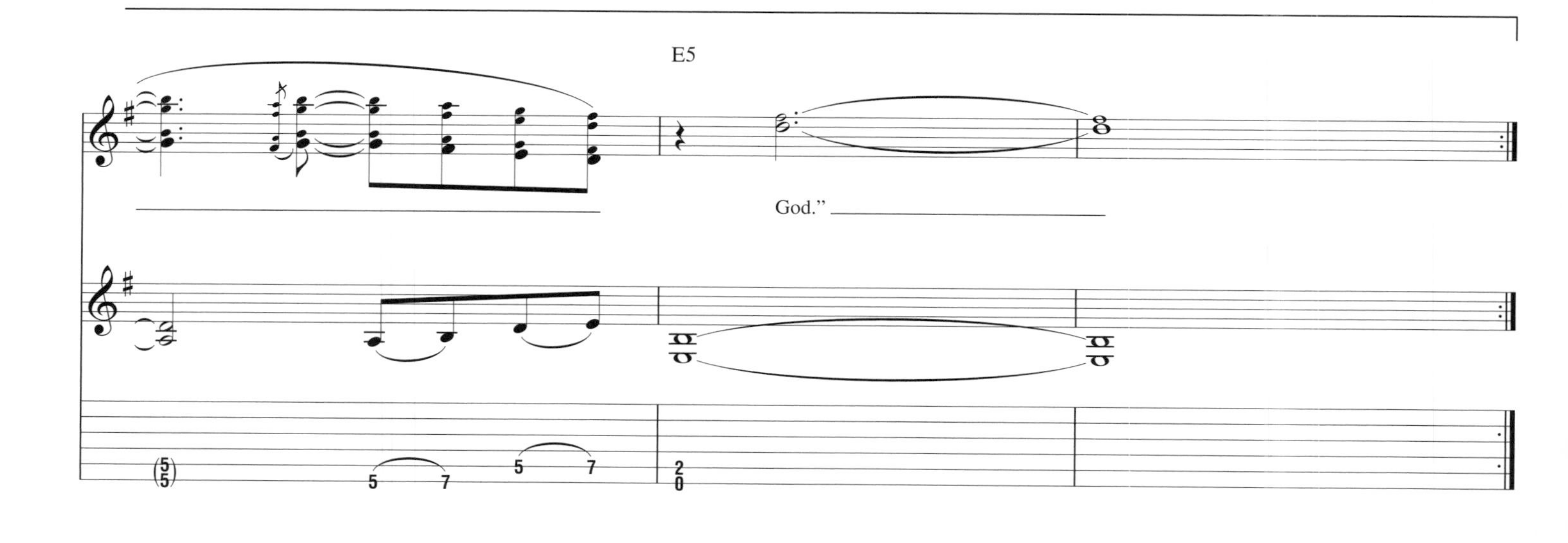
E5
God."

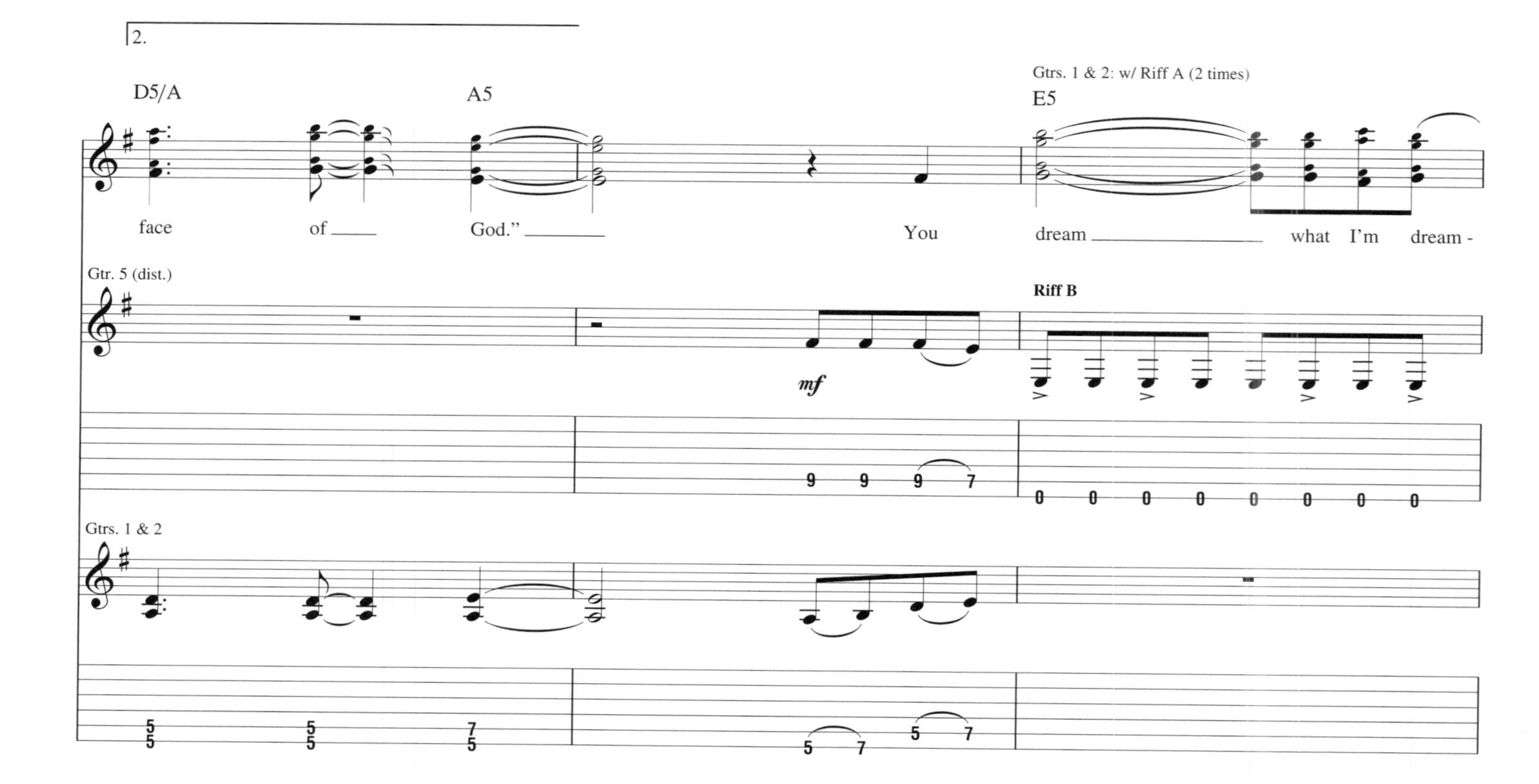
2.
D5/A
A5
Gtrs. 1 & 2: w/ Riff A (2 times)
E5
face of God." You dream what I'm dream -
Gtr. 5 (dist.)
Riff B
mf
Gtrs. 1 & 2

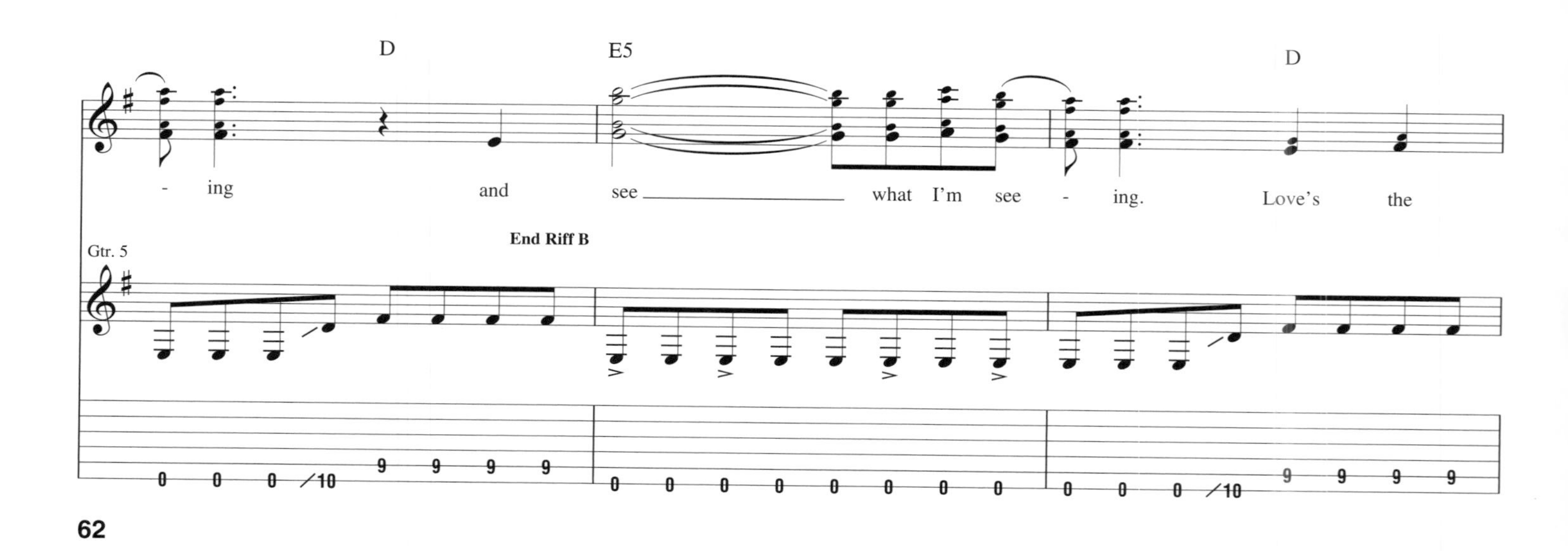
D
E5
D
- ing and see what I'm see - ing. Love's the
Gtr. 5
End Riff B

To Coda
Gtr. 5 tacet
C5/G
G5
D5/A
shad - ow on the wall with the face of
Gtrs. 1 & 2

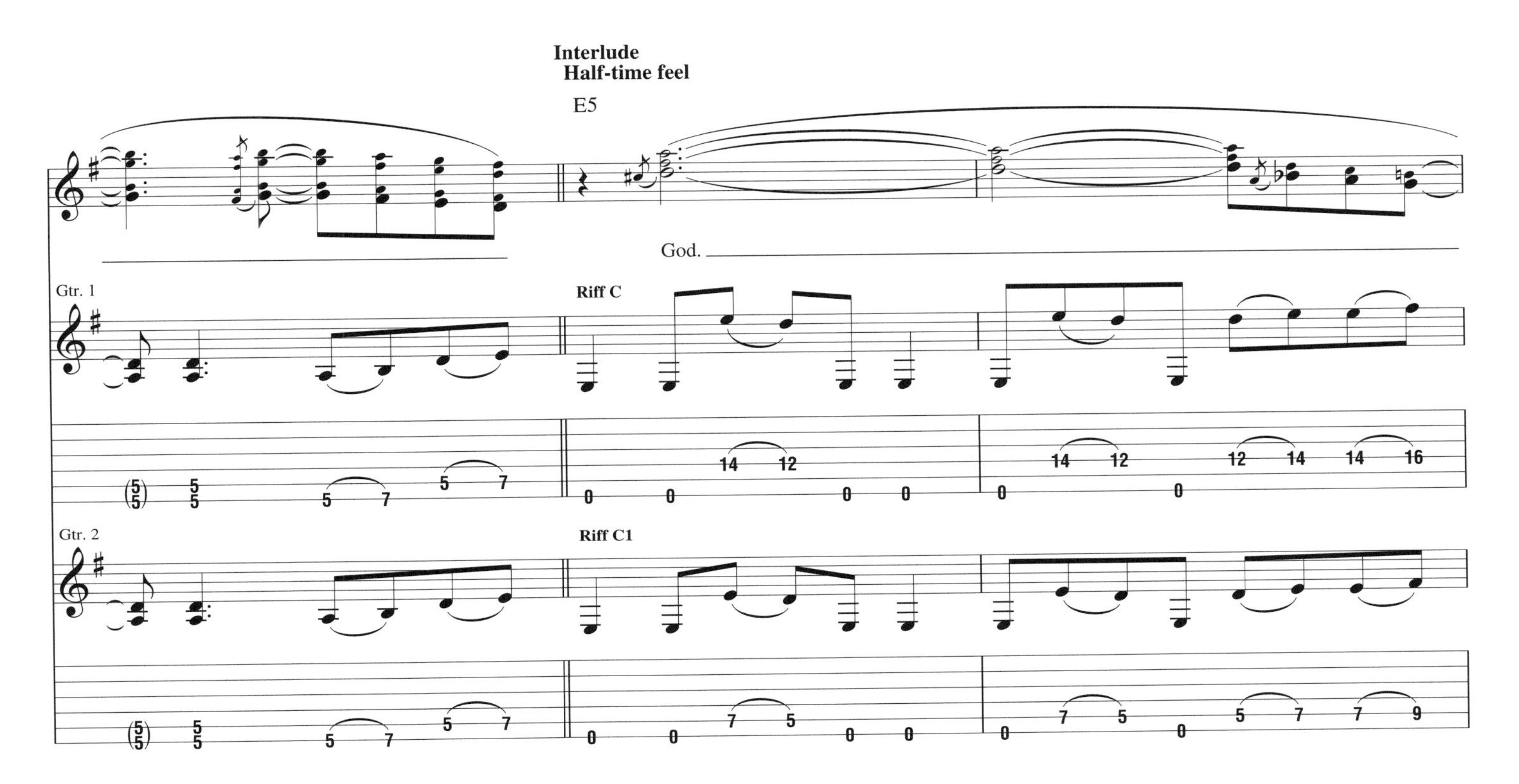
Interlude
Half-time feel
E5
God.
Gtr. 1
Riff C
Gtr. 2
Riff C1

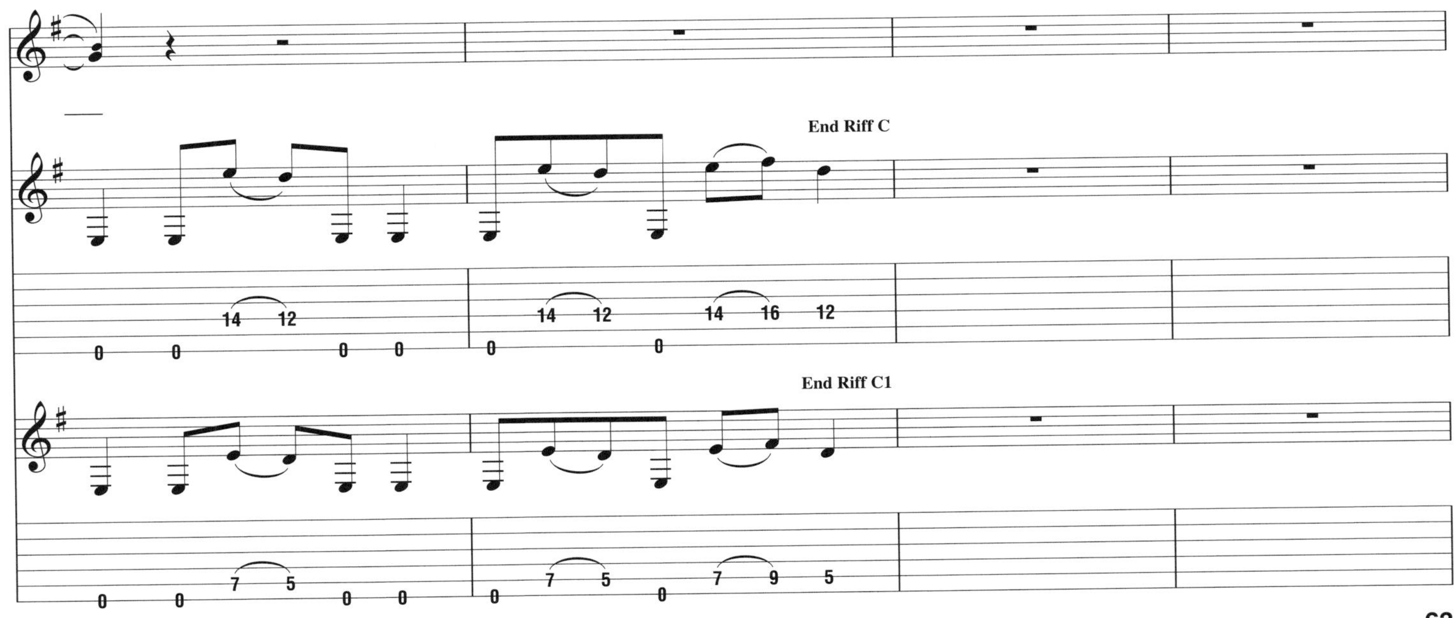
Gtrs. 1 & 2: w/ Riffs C & C1
End Riff C
End Riff C1

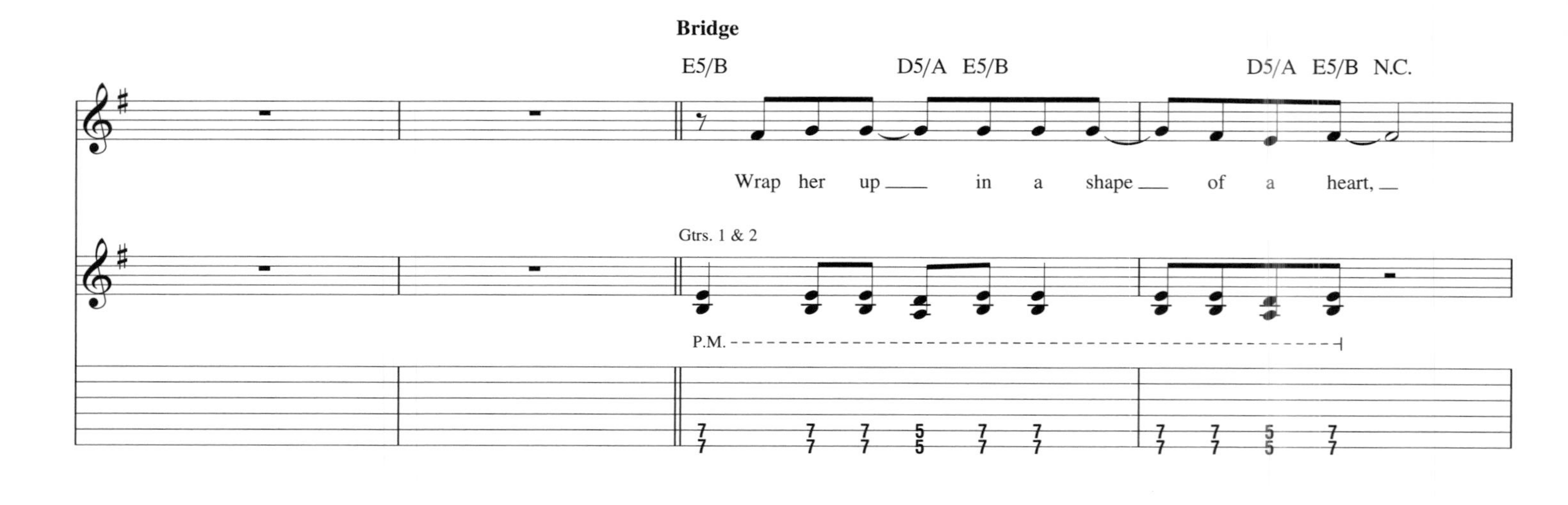
Bridge
E5/B D5/A E5/B D5/A E5/B N.C.
Wrap her up in a shape of a heart,
Gtrs. 1 & 2
P.M.

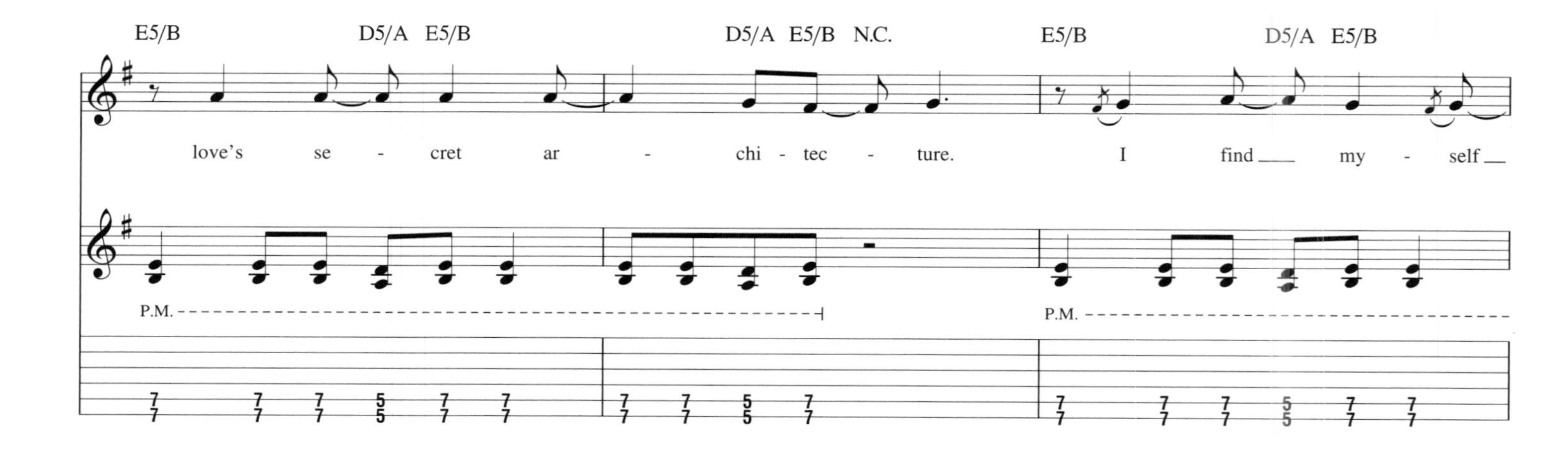
E5/B D5/A E5/B D5/A E5/B N.C. E5/B D5/A E5/B
love's se - cret ar - chi - tec - ture. I find my - self
P.M.
P.M.

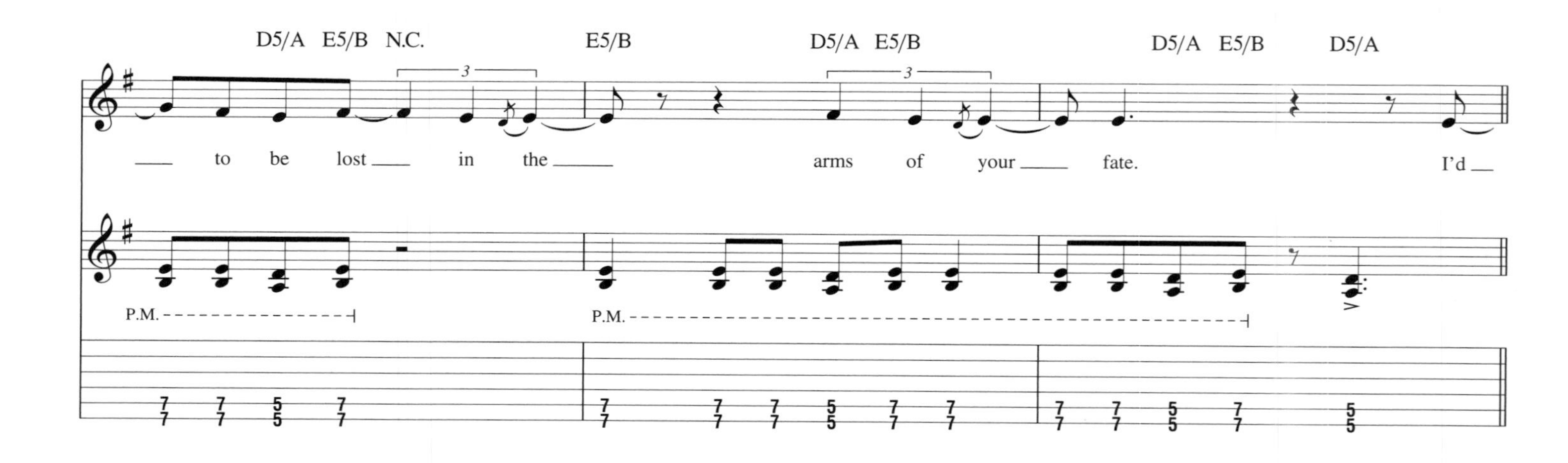
D5/A E5/B N.C. E5/B D5/A E5/B D5/A E5/B D5/A
to be lost in the arms of your fate. I'd
P.M.
P.M.

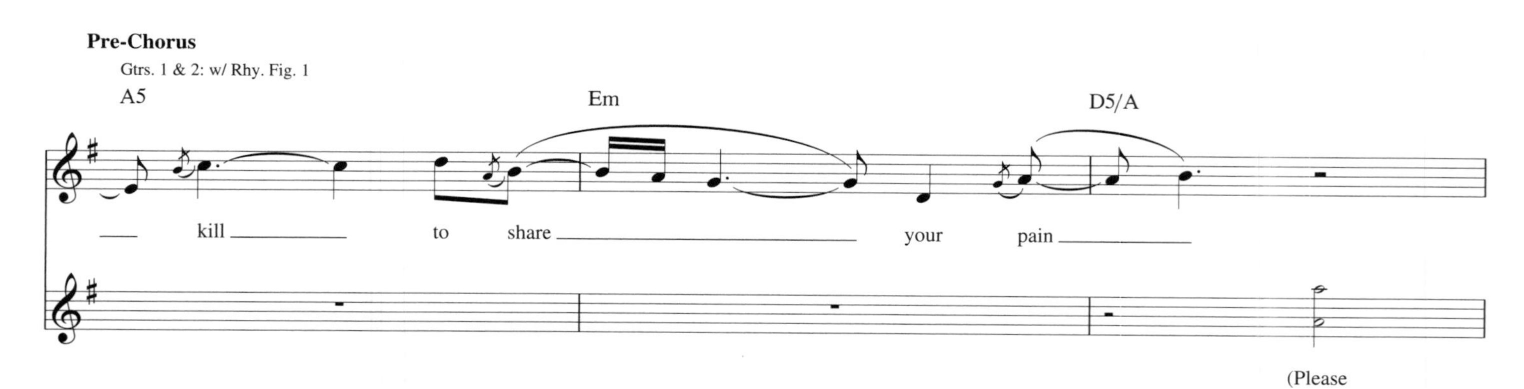
Pre-Chorus
Gtrs. 1 & 2: w/ Rhy. Fig. 1
A5 Em D5/A
kill to share your pain
(Please

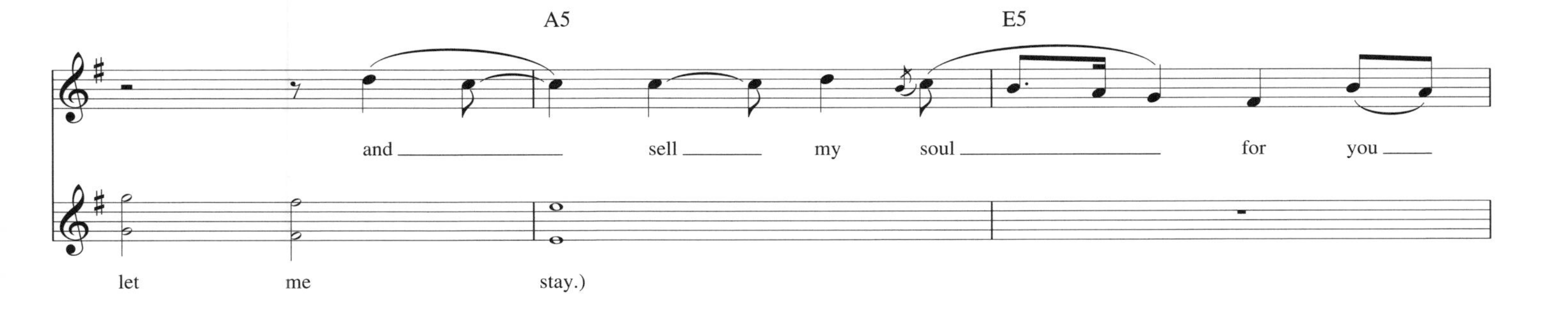

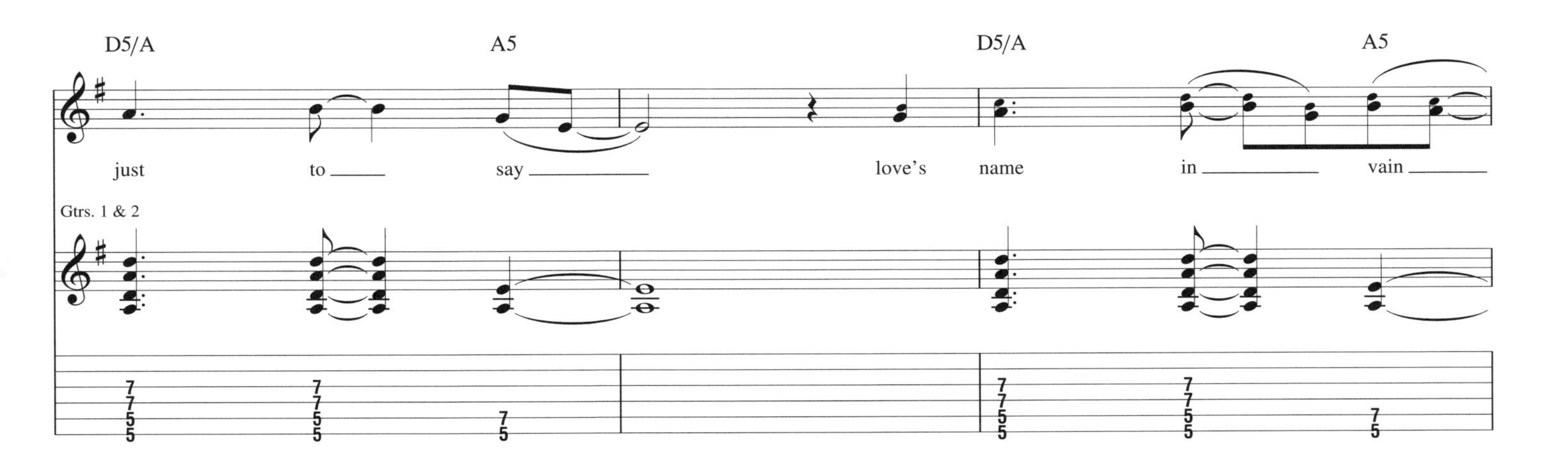

D.S. al Coda
(take 2nd ending)

End half-time feel

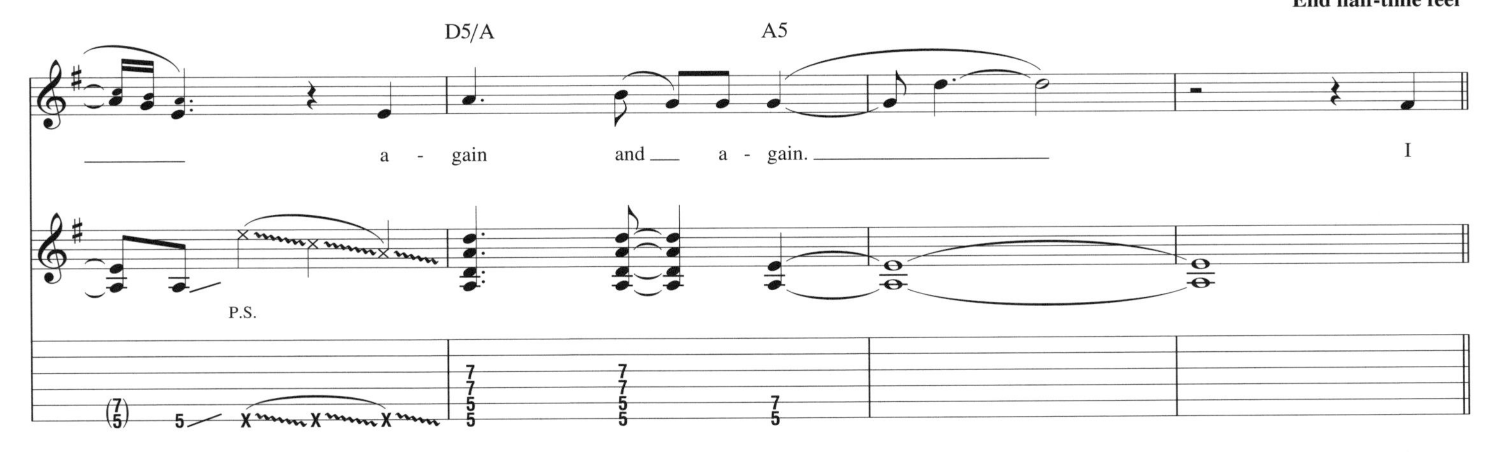

Coda

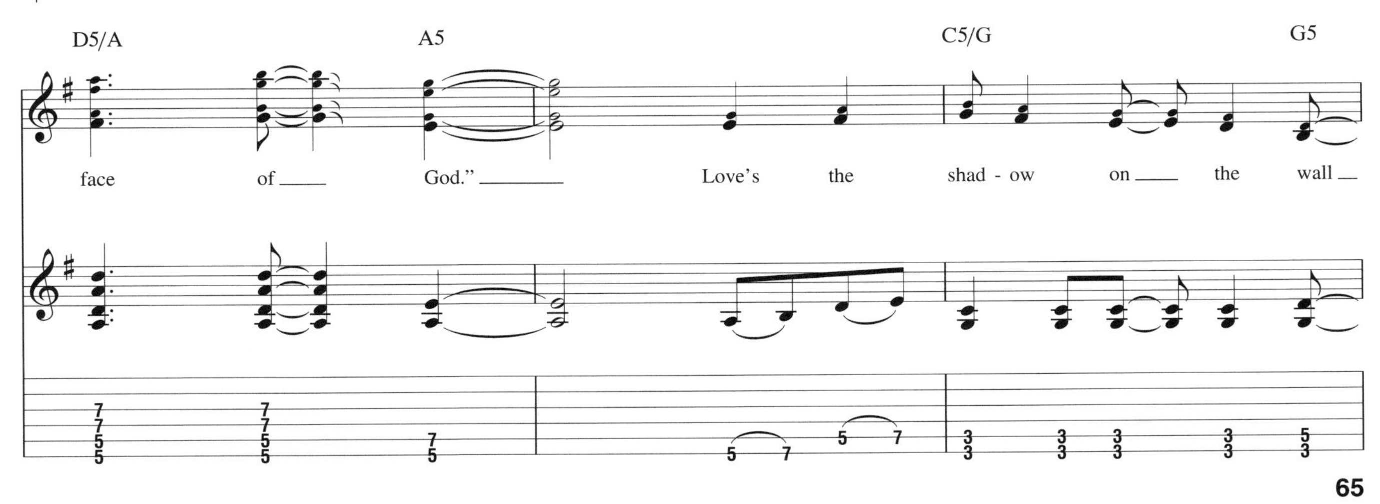

D5/A
with the face of, the
(Face of,
Outro
Gtrs. 1 & 2: w/ Riff A (4 times)
Gtr. 5: w/ Riff B (4 times)
D5
E5
D
face of
God.
face of...)

E5
D
E5
D

E5
D
N.C.
Face of
God.

Drunk on Shadows

Words and Music by Ville Valo

Gtr. 5: Tuning:
(low to high) C♯-A-D-G-B-E

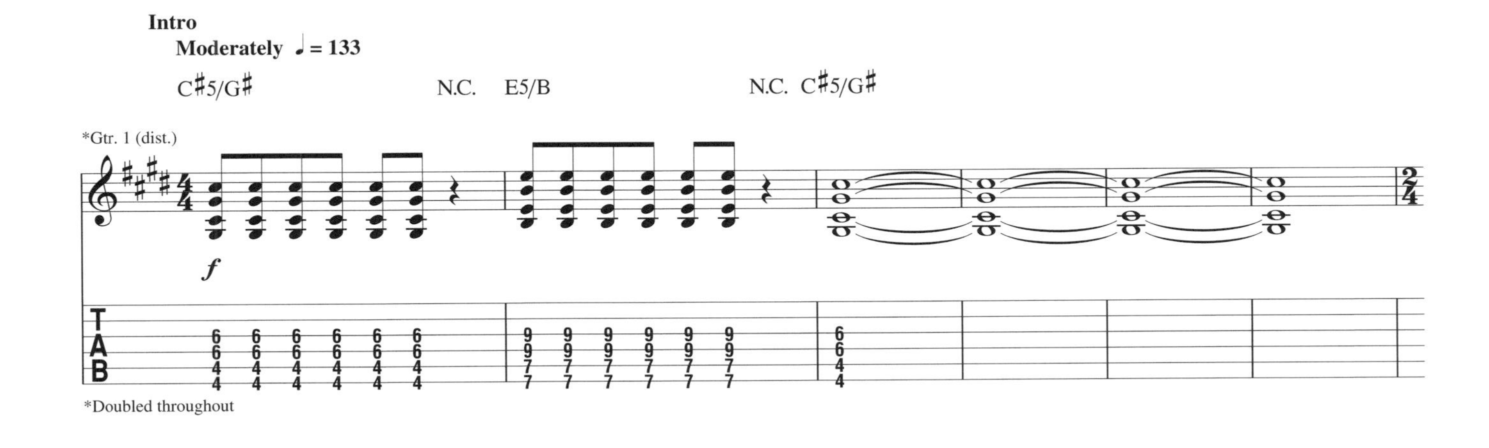

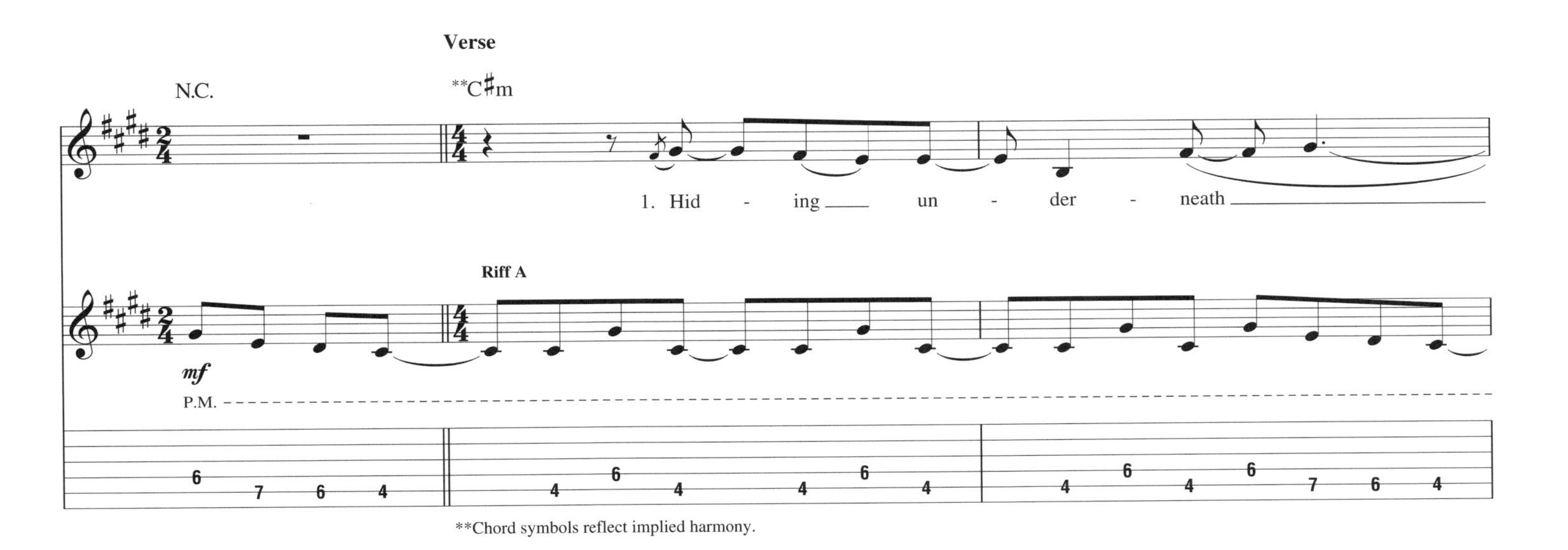

Gtr. 2 tacet
A(add♯4)
C♯m
her weep - ing.
Rhy. Fig. 1
Gtr. 2 (dist.)
End Rhy. Fig. 1
mf
Gtr. 1
P.M.
Gtr. 1: w/ Riff A (1st 3 meas.)
On her once white wings, she will
Gtr. 2: w/ Rhy. Fig. 1
Aadd♯4
be car'y - ing the weight of our deeds
Gtr. 1
Riff B
P.M.
Half-time feel
E5/B
B5/F♯
End half-time feel
as she bleeds for love for - ev - er gone.
End Riff B
Rhy. Fig. 2
End Rhy. Fig. 2
P.M.
f

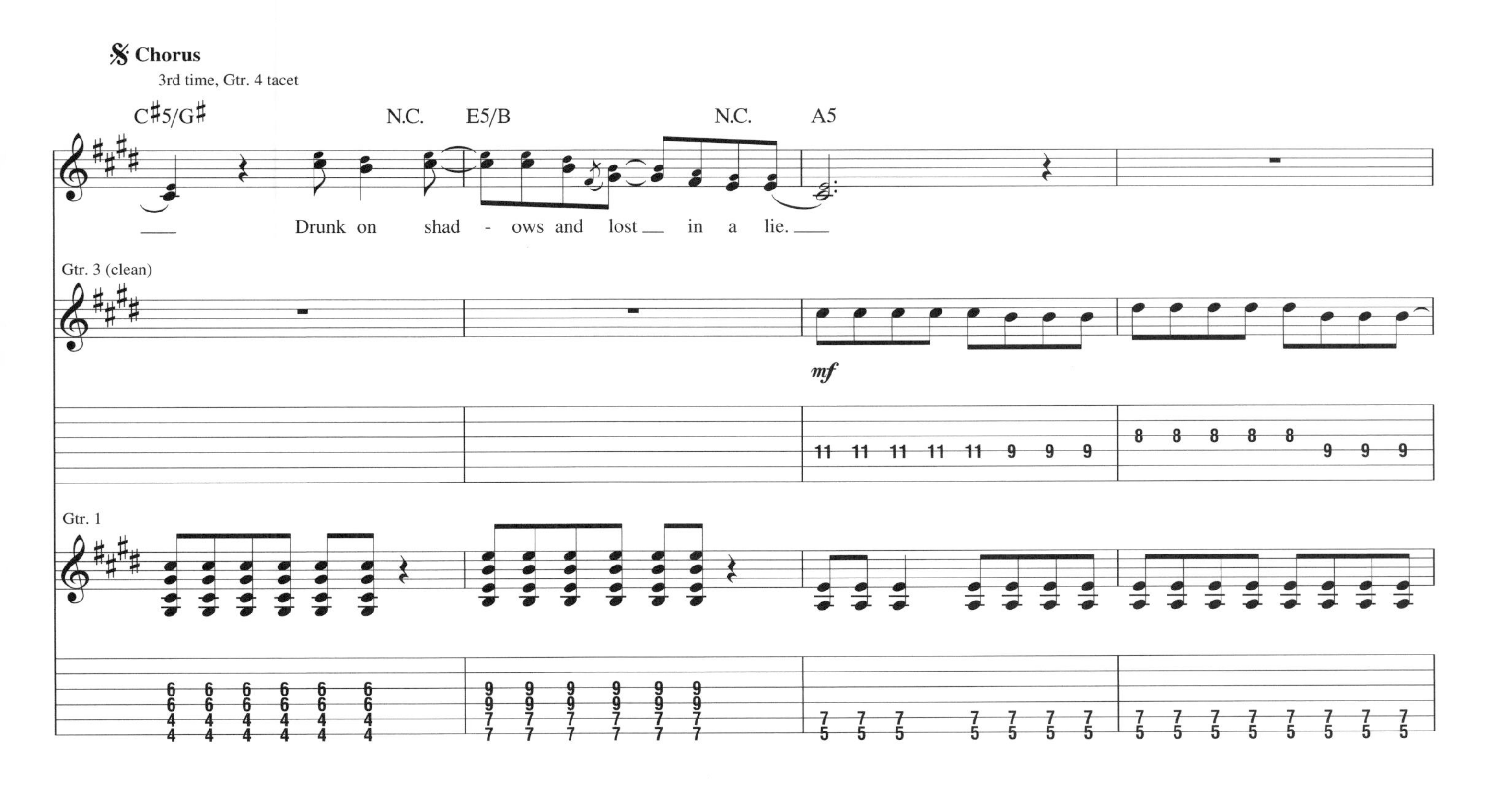
Chorus
3rd time, Gtr. 4 tacet
C#5/G#
N.C.
E5/B
N.C.
A5
Drunk on shad - ows and lost in a lie.
Gtr. 3 (clean)
mf
Gtr. 1

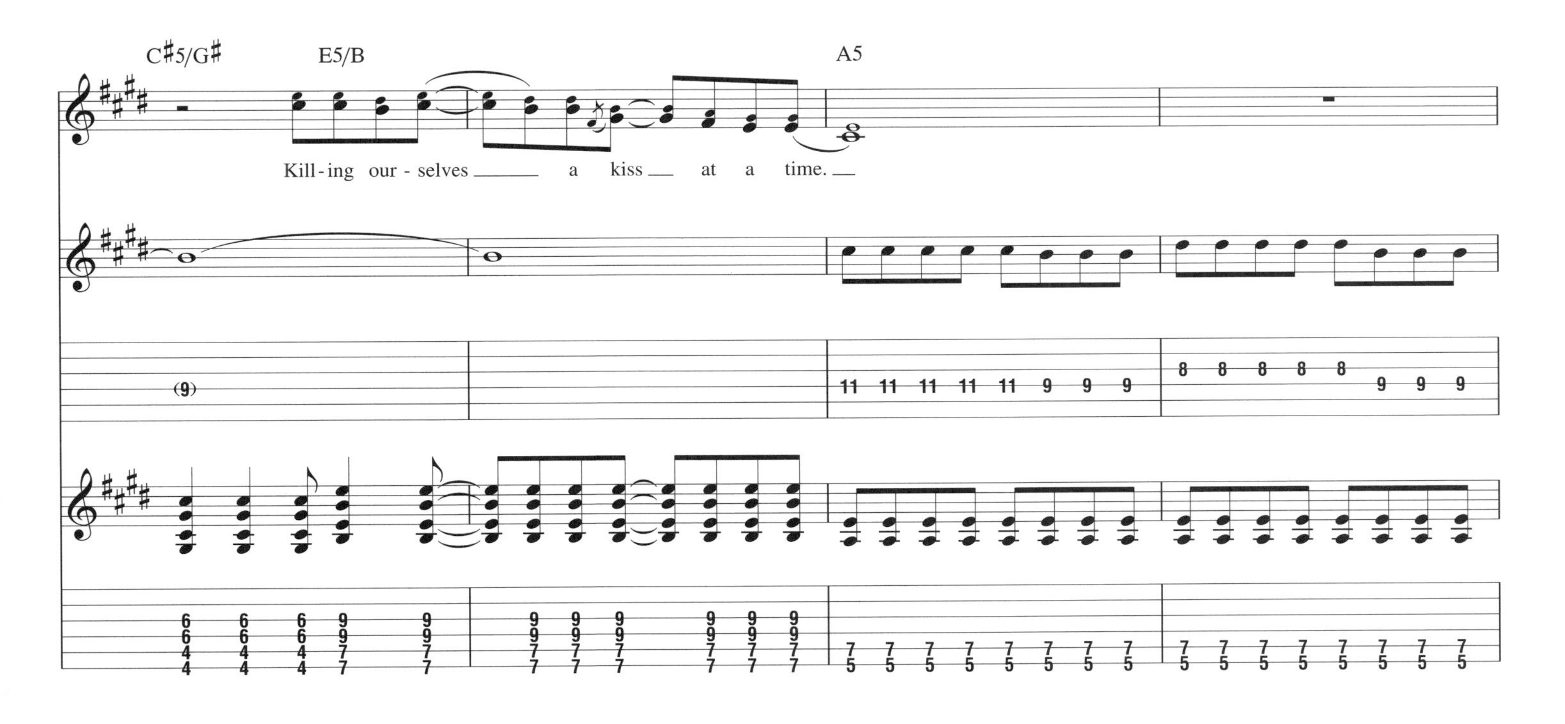
C#5/G#
E5/B
A5
Kill-ing our-selves a kiss at a time.

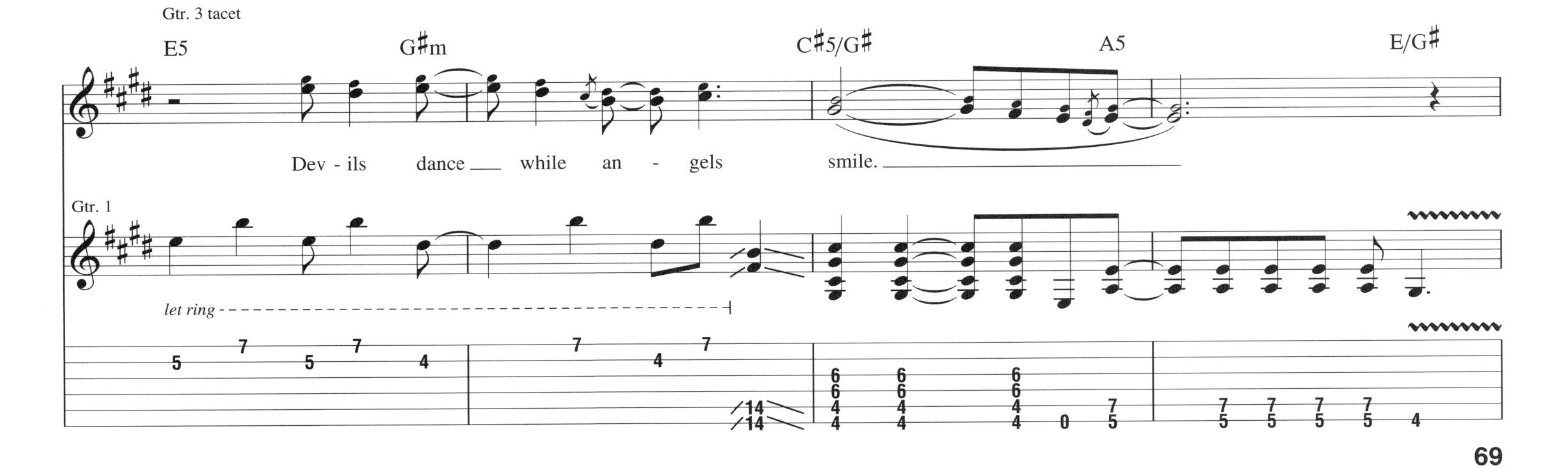
Gtr. 3 tacet
E5
G#m
C#5/G#
A5
E/G#
Dev - ils dance while an - gels smile.
Gtr. 1
let ring

To Coda 1
To Coda 2
C#5/G#
N.C.
E5/B
N.C.
A5
Drunk on shad - ows and lost in a lie.
mf
P.M.
Verse
Gtr. 1: w/ Riff A
C#m
2. Find - ing souls to feed the night - side
Gtr. 1: w/ Riff B
Gtr. 2: w/ Rhy. Fig. 1
Aadd#4
of E - den, we see her strug - gling
D.S. al Coda 1
Half-time feel
End half-time feel
Gtr. 1: w/ Rhy. Fig. 2
E5/B
B5/F#
for her love's last breath and walk off.
Coda 1
Interlude
C#m/G#
*Gtr. 4
mf
*Synth. strings arr. for gtr.
Gtr. 1
f
pp

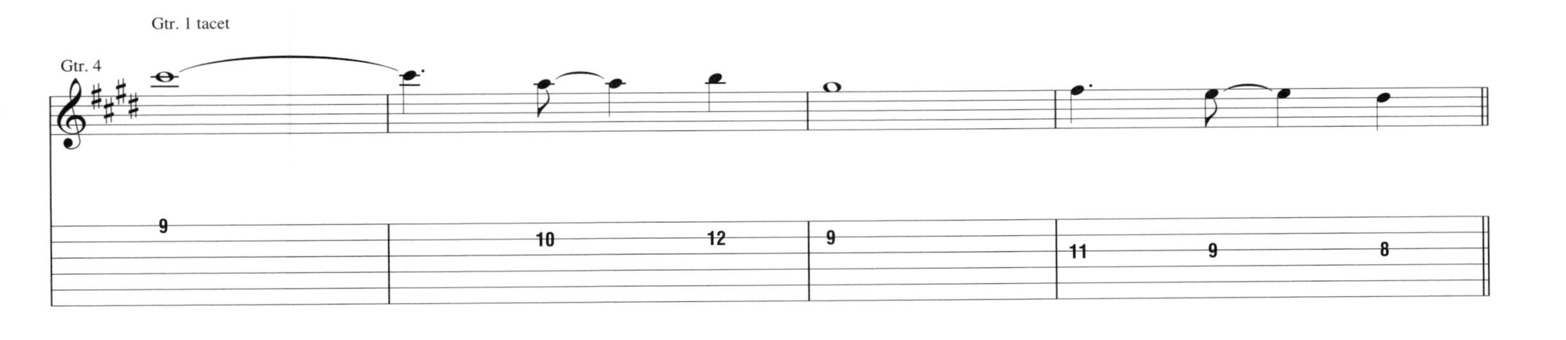
Gtr. 1 tacet
Gtr. 4

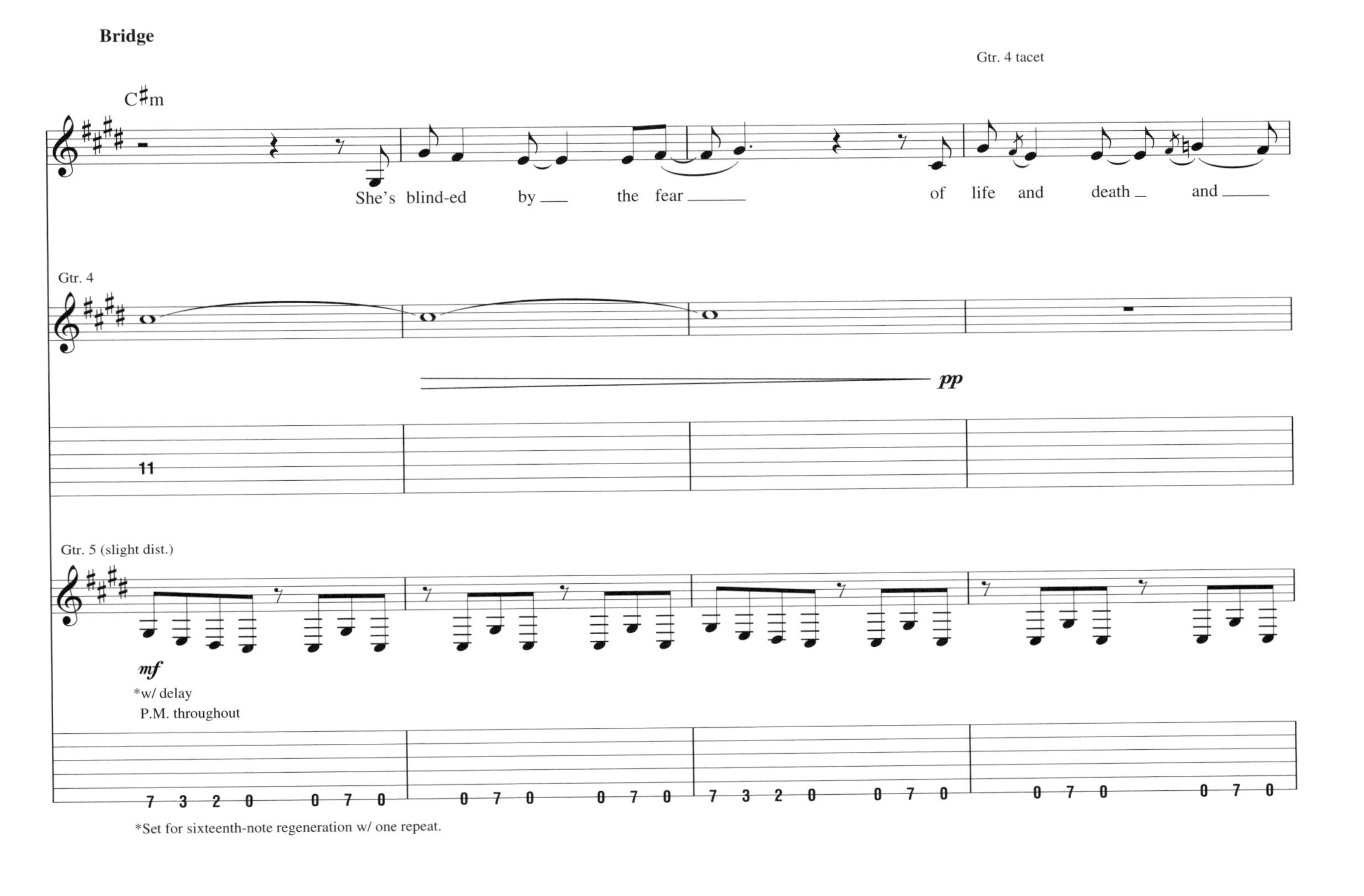
Bridge
Gtr. 4 tacet
C♯m
She's blind-ed by the fear of life and death and
Gtr. 4
pp
Gtr. 5 (slight dist.)
mf
*w/ delay
P.M. throughout
*Set for sixteenth-note regeneration w/ one repeat.

Aadd♯4
ev - 'ry - thing in be - tween. We smile when she cries
Gtr. 5

Half-time feel
Gtr. 5 tacet
E
B
E
B
a riv - er of tears, a mir - ror where we see
Gtr. 4
mf
w/ fingers
let ring throughout

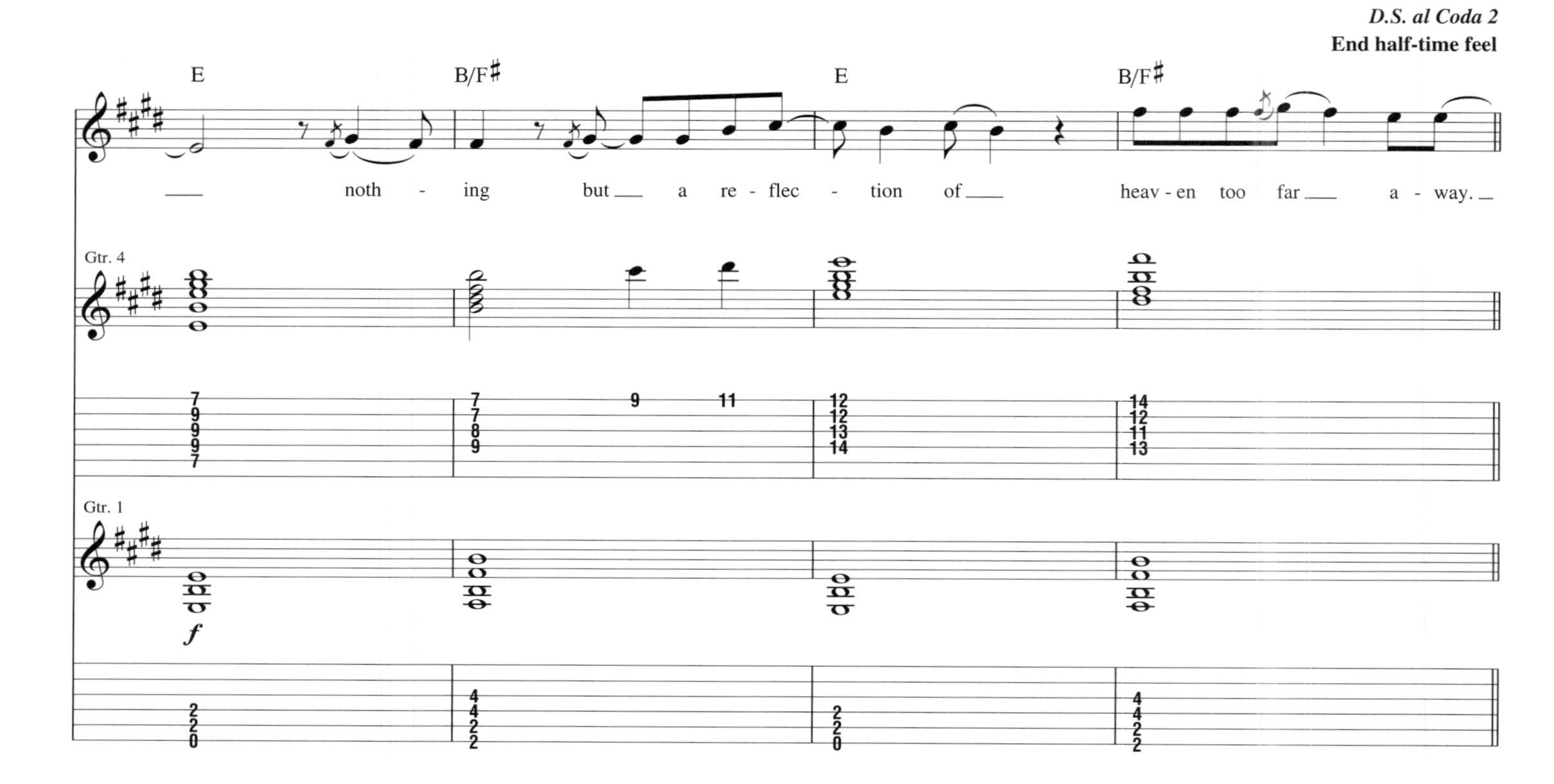
D.S. al Coda 2
End half-time feel
E
B/F♯
E
B/F♯
noth - ing but a re - flec - tion of heav - en too far a - way.
Gtr. 4
Gtr. 1
f

Coda 2
Outro
A5
E5
B5/F♯
So a - live,
Rhy. Fig. 3

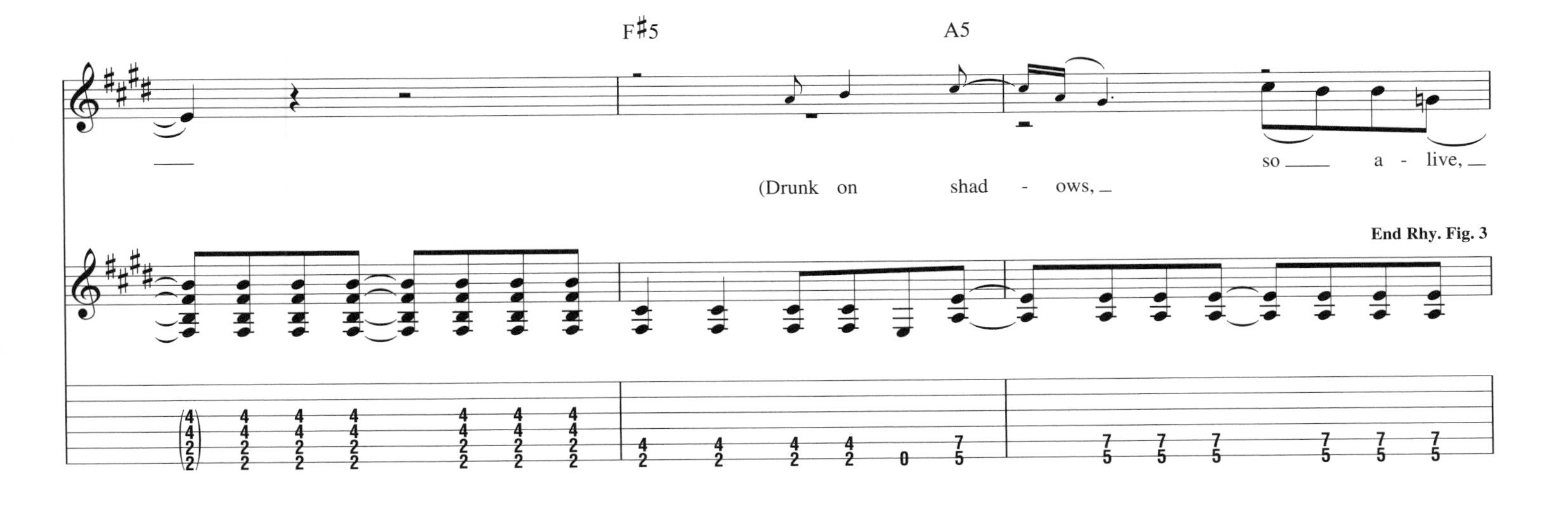
F♯5
A5
so a - live,
(Drunk on shad - ows,
End Rhy. Fig. 3

Gtr. 1: w/ Rhy. Fig. 3 (2 times)
E5
B5/F♯
F♯5
A5
so a - live,
(drunk on shad - ows,

E5
B5/F♯
F♯5
A5
so a - live.
drunk on shad - ows,
drunk on shad - ows,

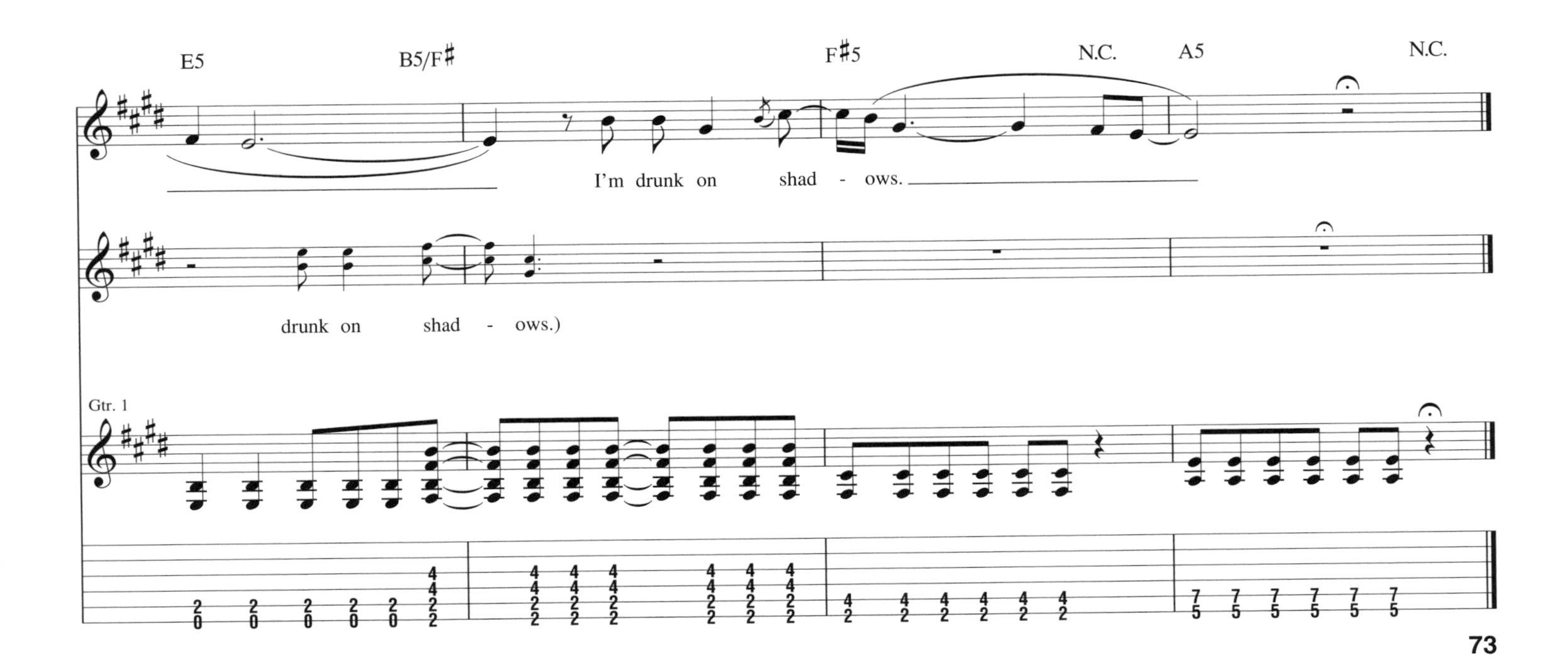
E5
B5/F♯
F♯5
N.C.
A5
N.C.
I'm drunk on shad - ows.
drunk on shad - ows.)
Gtr. 1

Play Dead

Words and Music by Ville Valo

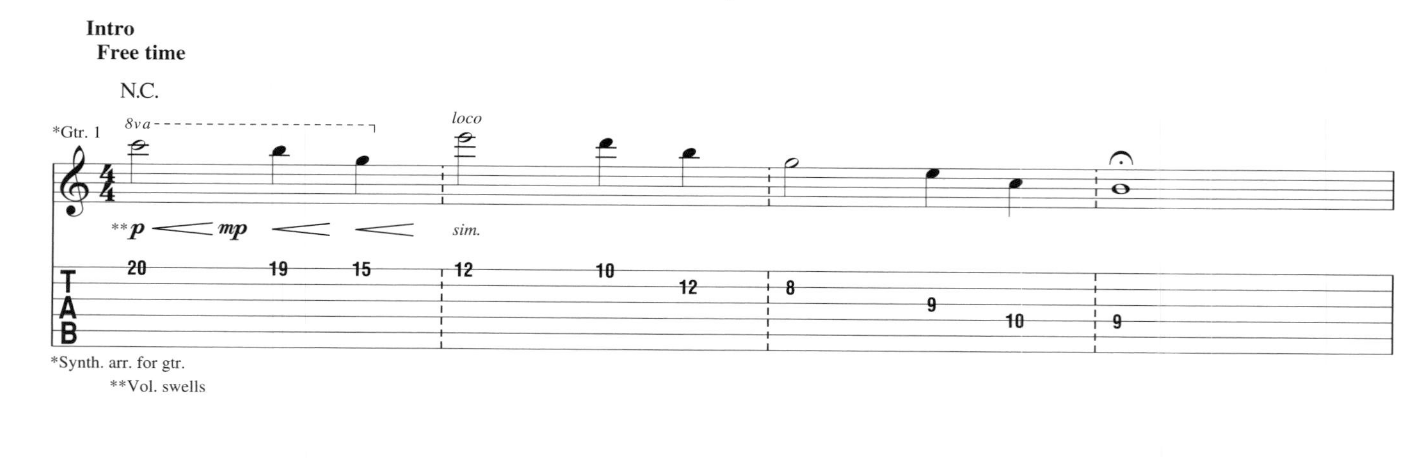

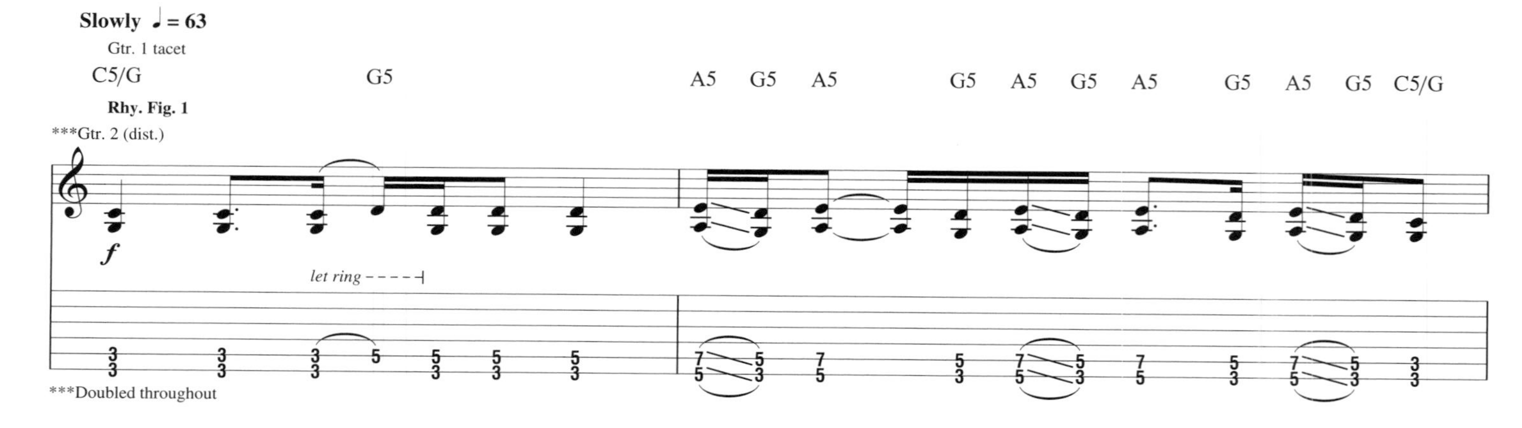

Verse

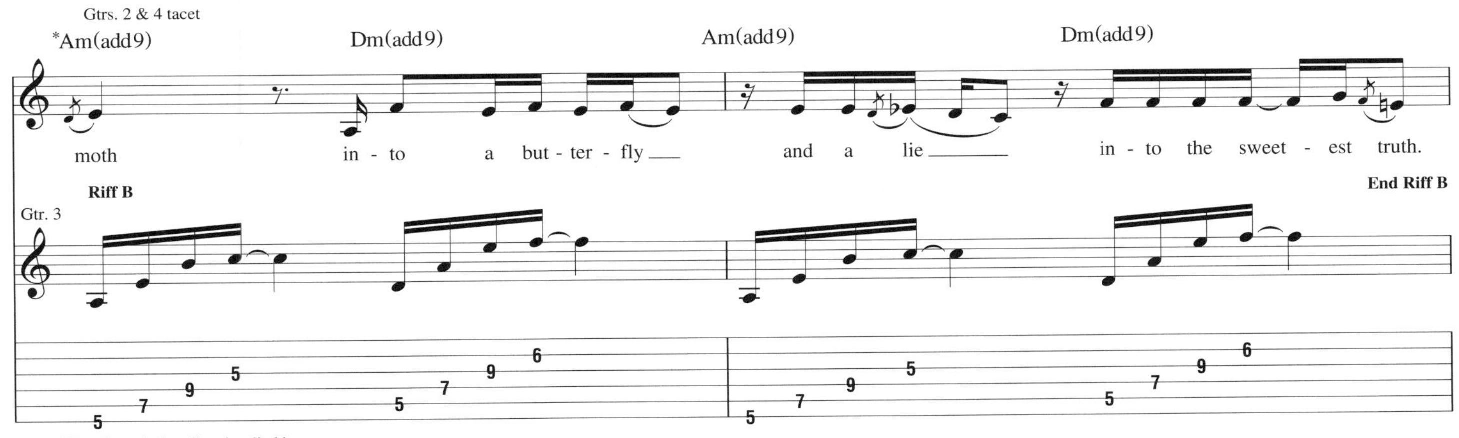

*Chord symbols reflect implied harmony.

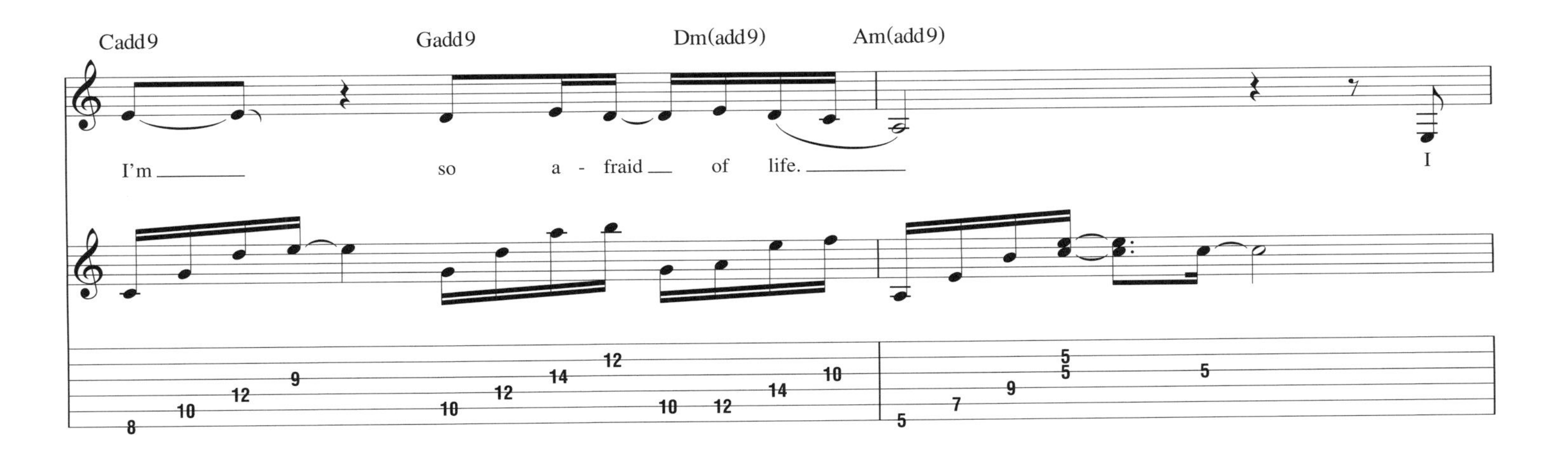

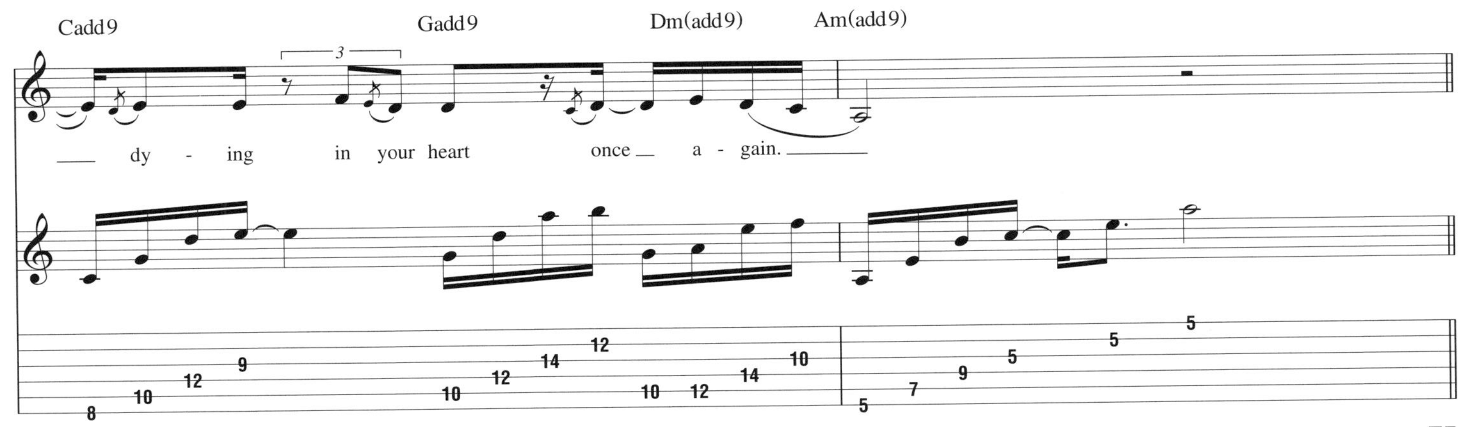

Pre-Chorus

Gtr. 3 tacet
Fsus2
Am7
Fsus2
Am7
I see the sea - sons chang - ing and in the heart of this au - tumn I fall
I see the rea - sons chang - ing and in the warmth of the past I crawl,
Riff C
Gtr. 2
let ring
Riff C1
Gtr. 5 (slight dist.)
mf
w/ chorus
let ring throughout

G5
F5
Gtr. 5 tacet
G
Am
G/B
G
with the leaves from the trees.
scorched by the shame.
End Riff C
End Riff C1
Chorus
Gtr. 2: w/ Rhy. Fig. 1
C5/G
G5
A5 G5 A5
G5 A5 G5 A5
G5 A5 G5 C5/G
I play dead to

To Coda

Gtr. 3: w/ Riff A
D5/A
E5
F5
hide my heart 'til the world gone dark fades a - way.
A5
E5
A5
B5
E5
2. I cry
Gtr. 4
Riff D1
End Riff D1
Gtr. 2
Riff D
End Riff D

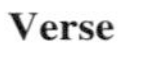
Verse

Gtrs. 2 & 4 tacet
Gtr. 3: w/ Riff B
Am(add9)
Dm(add9)
Am(add9)
Dm(add9)
like God cries the rain, and I'm just one step a -
Gtr. 6 (clean)
mf
let ring throughout

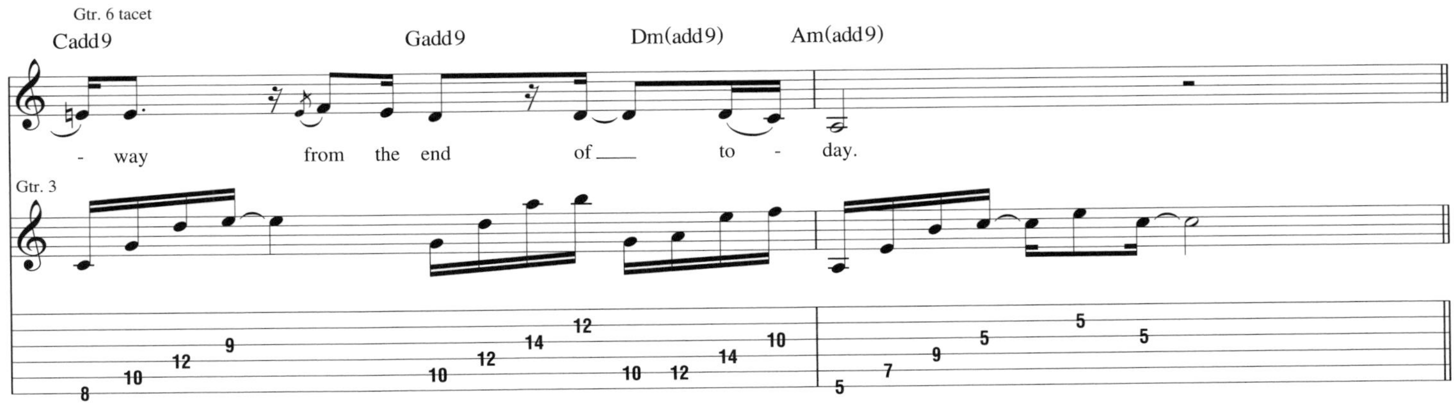
D.S. al Coda
Gtr. 6 tacet
Cadd9
Gadd9
Dm(add9)
Am(add9)
- way from the end of to - day.
Gtr. 3

Coda

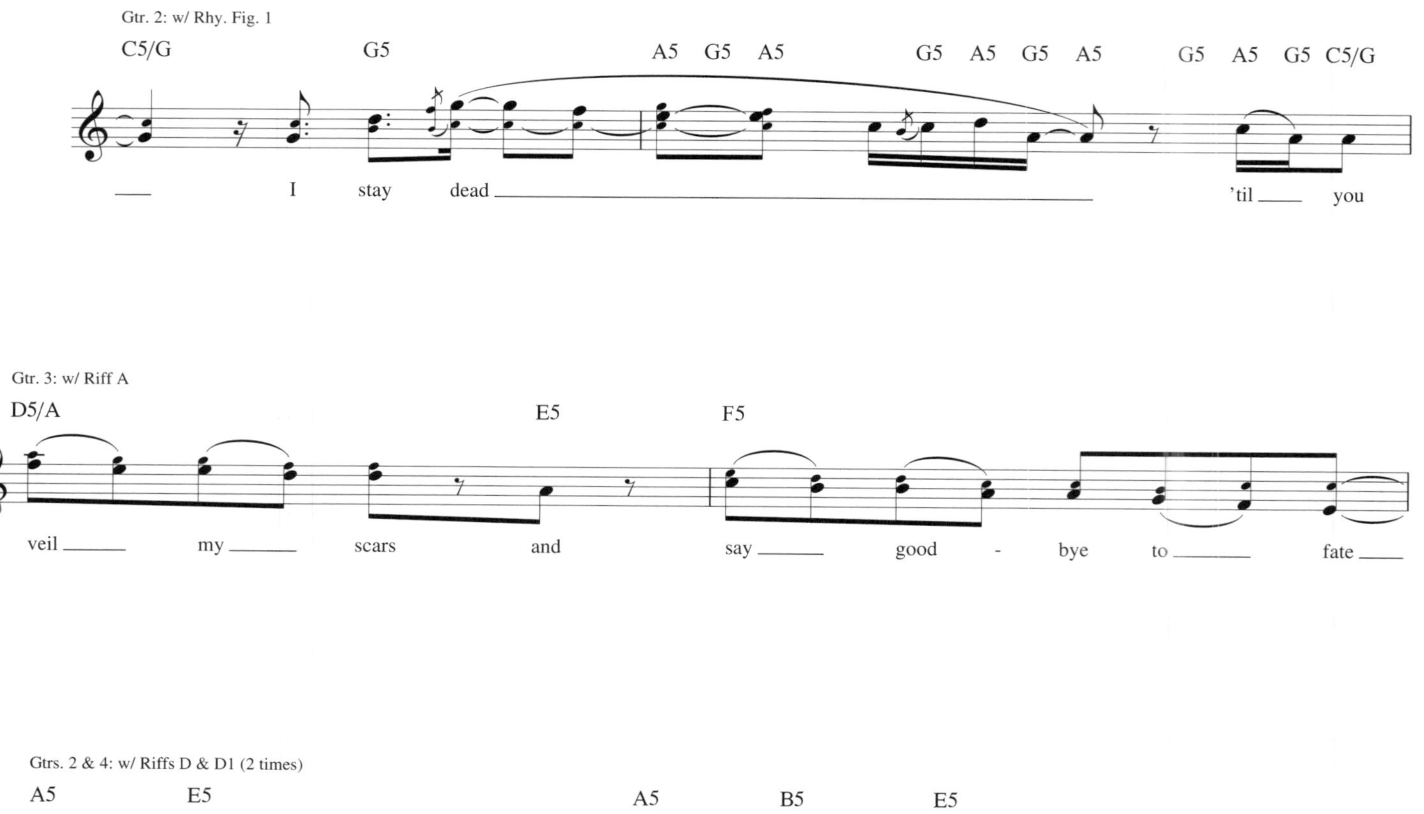

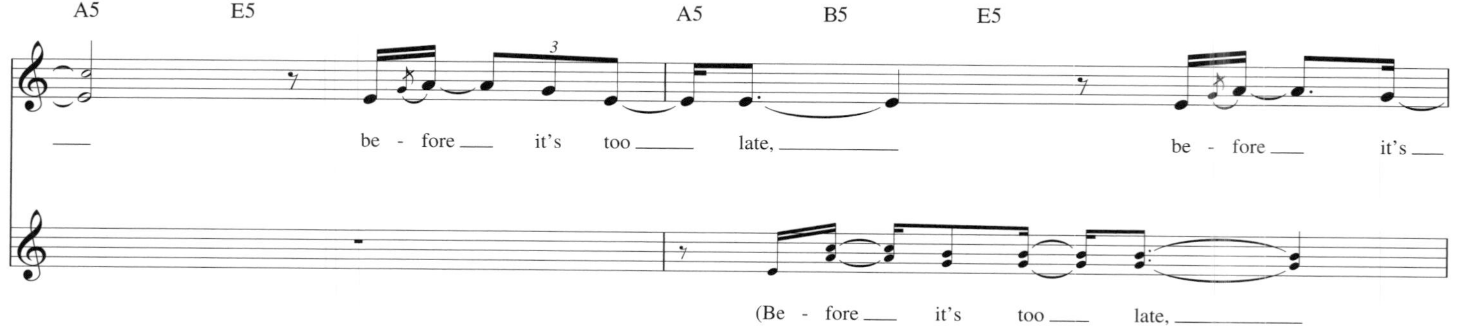

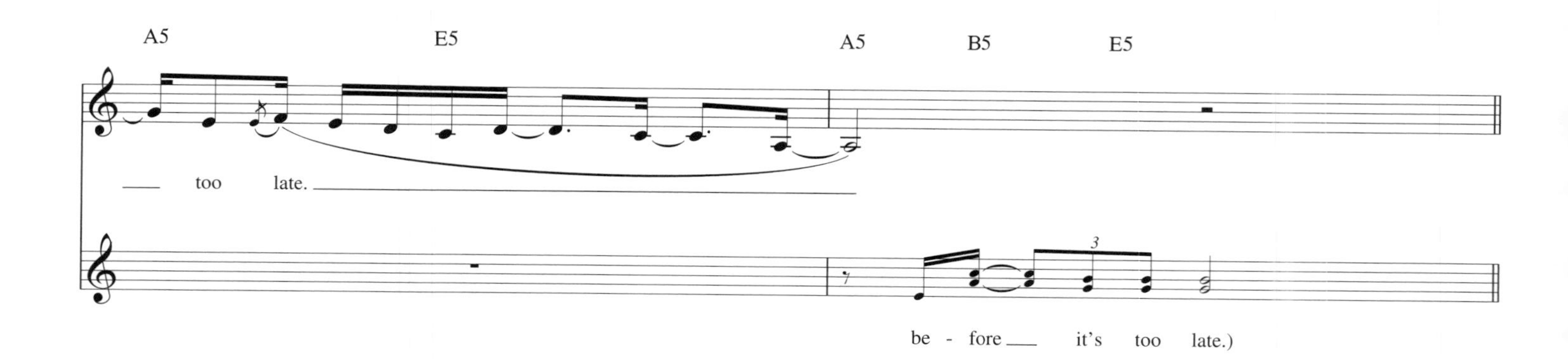

Interlude

Gtrs. 2 & 5: w/ Riffs C & C1

Fsus2 Am7 Fsus2 Am7 G5 F5 G Am G/B G

Chorus
C5/G
*G
A5 G5 A5
G5 A5 G5 A5
G5 A5 G5
I play dead ___ to
Gtr. 2
*Piano plays chord.
Gtr. 2: w/ Rhy. Fig. 1 (last 2 meas.)
Gtr. 3: w/ Riff A
D5/A
E5
F5
hide ___ my ___ heart 'til the world gone ___ dark fades a - way. ___
Gtr. 2: w/ Rhy. Fig. 1 (2 times)
C5/G
G5
A5 G5 A5
G5 A5 G5 A5
G5 A5 G5 C5/G
___ I stay dead ___ 'til ___ you
Gtr. 3: w/ Riff A
D5/A
E5
F5
veil ___ my ___ scars and say ___ good - bye to ___ fate. ___
C5/G
G5
A5 G5 A5
G5 A5 G5 A5
G5 A5 G5 C5/G
___ I play dead ___ to
D5/A
E5
F5
hide ___ my ___ heart 'til the world gone ___ dark fades a - way ___
Gtr. 3

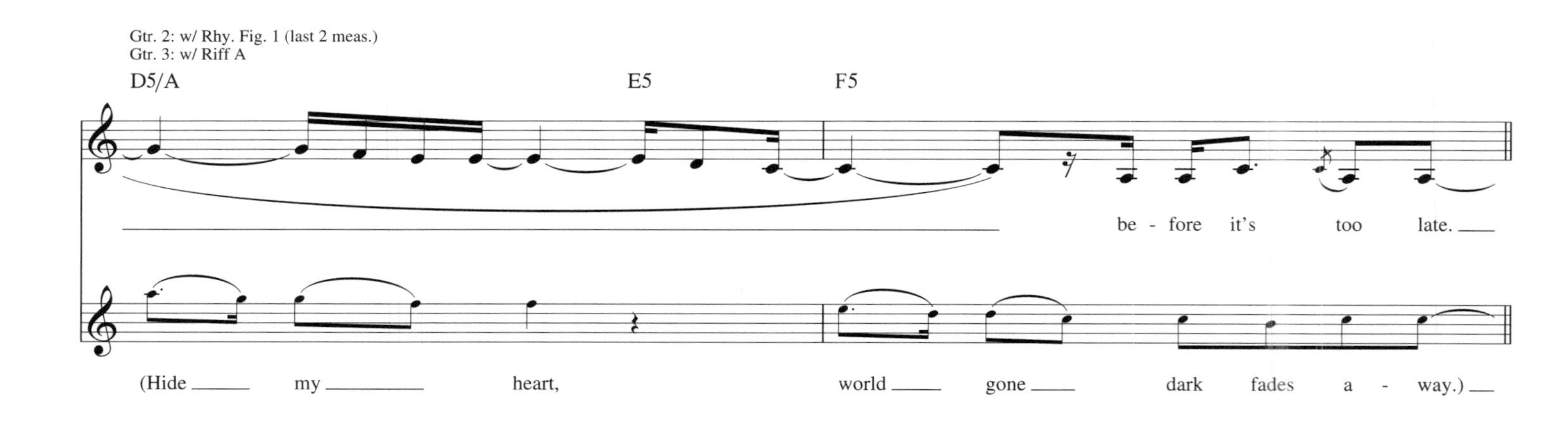
Gtr. 2: w/ Rhy. Fig. 1 (last 2 meas.)
Gtr. 3: w/ Riff A
D5/A
E5
F5
be - fore it's too late.
(Hide my heart, world gone dark fades a - way.)

Outro

Free time
Am
Em
N.C.
Gtr. 1
8va
loco
*p mp
sim.
*Vol. swells
Gtr. 4
pp
Gtr. 7 (dist.)
f
pp
Gtr. 2
pp

In the Nightside of Eden

Words and Music by Ville Valo

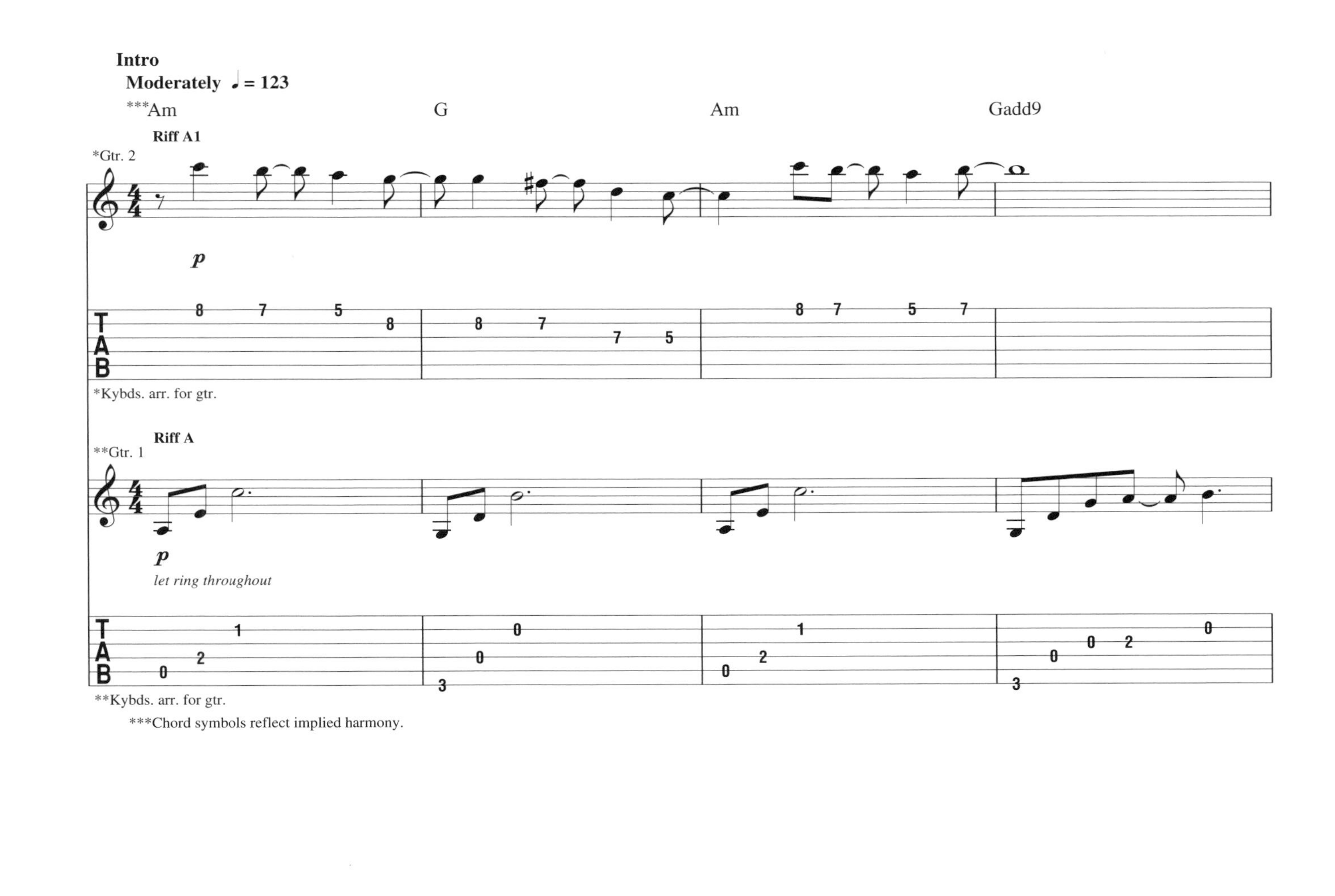

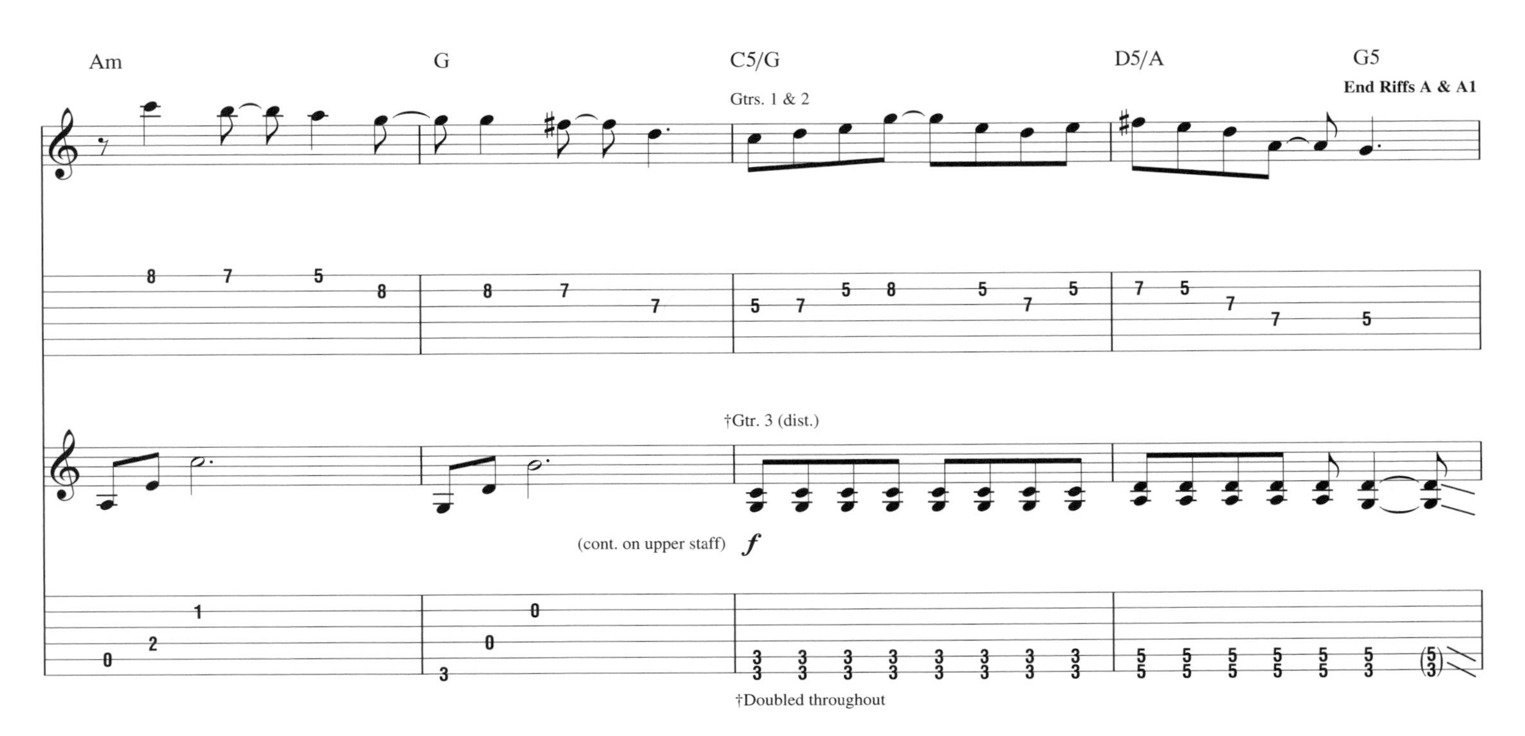

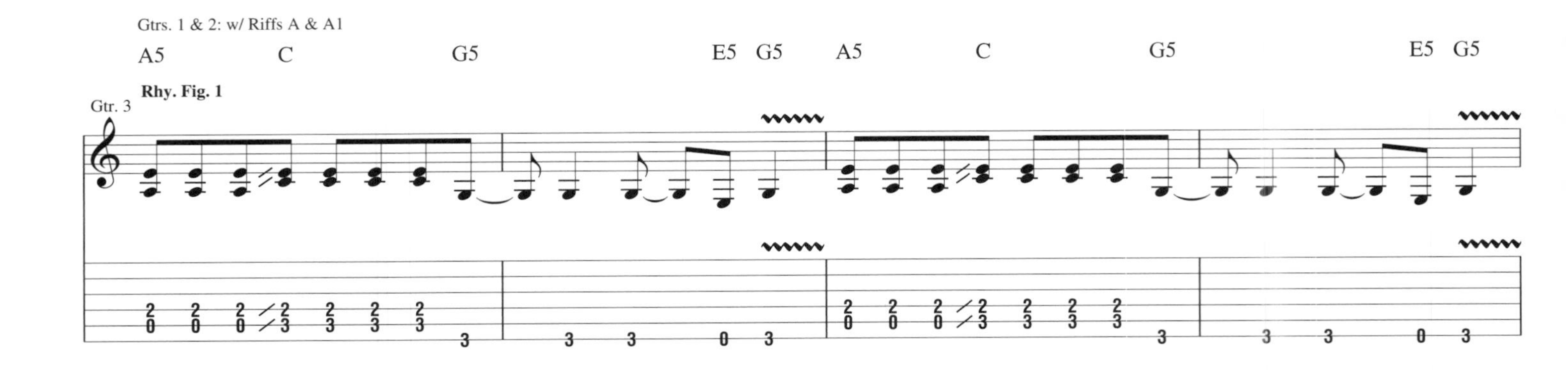
Gtrs. 1 & 2: w/ Riffs A & A1
A5 C G5 E5 G5 A5 C G5 E5 G5
Rhy. Fig. 1
Gtr. 3

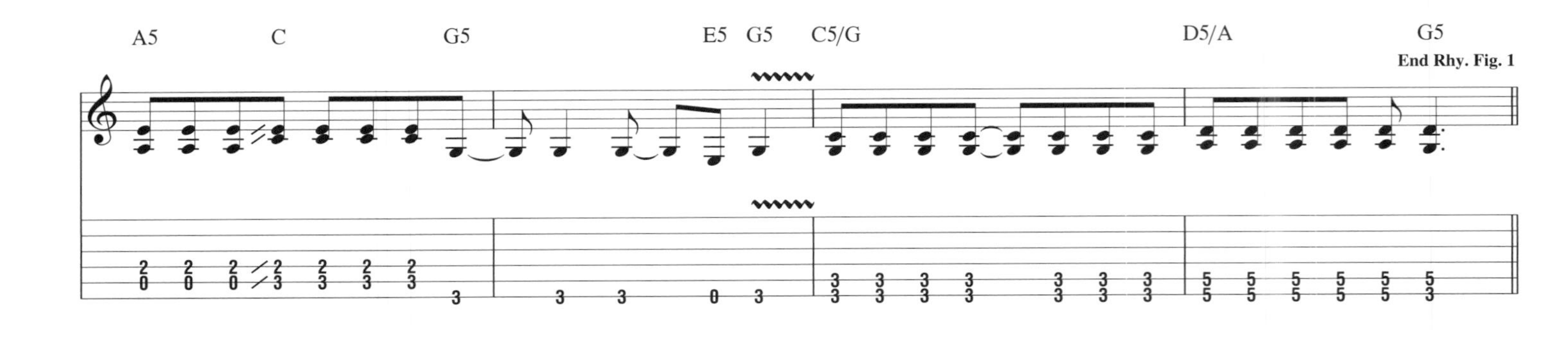
A5 C G5 E5 G5 C5/G D5/A G5
End Rhy. Fig. 1

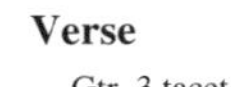
Verse

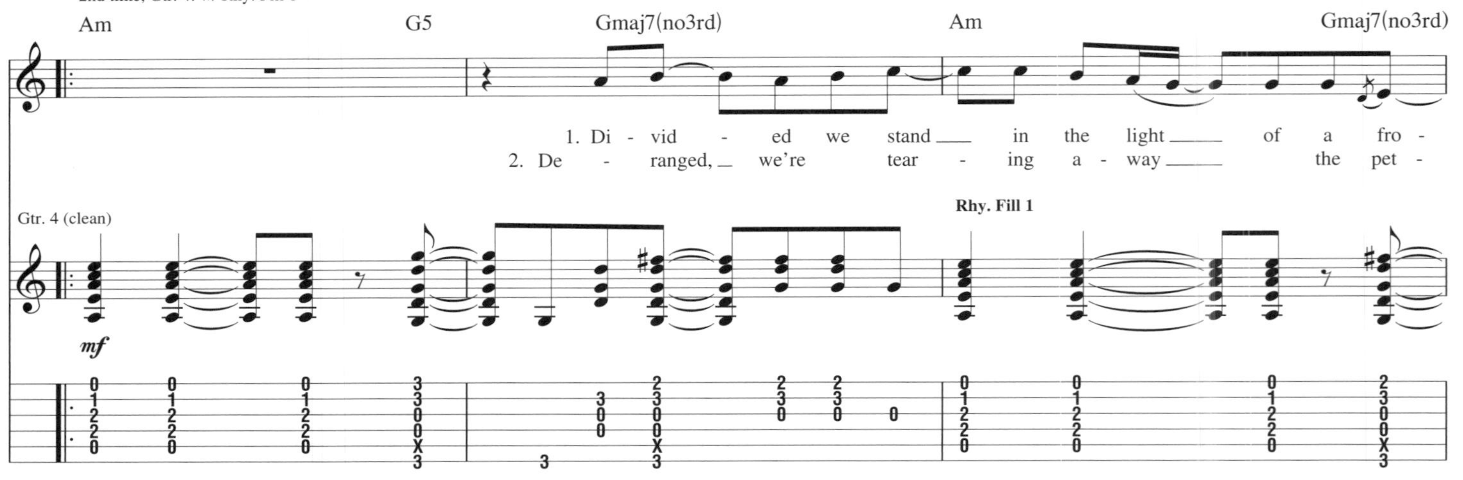
Gtr. 3 tacet
2nd time, Gtr. 4: w/ Rhy. Fill 1
Am G5 Gmaj7(no3rd) Am Gmaj7(no3rd)
1. Di - vid - ed we stand in the light of a fro -
2. De - ranged, we're tear - ing a - way the pet -
Gtr. 4 (clean)
Rhy. Fill 1
mf

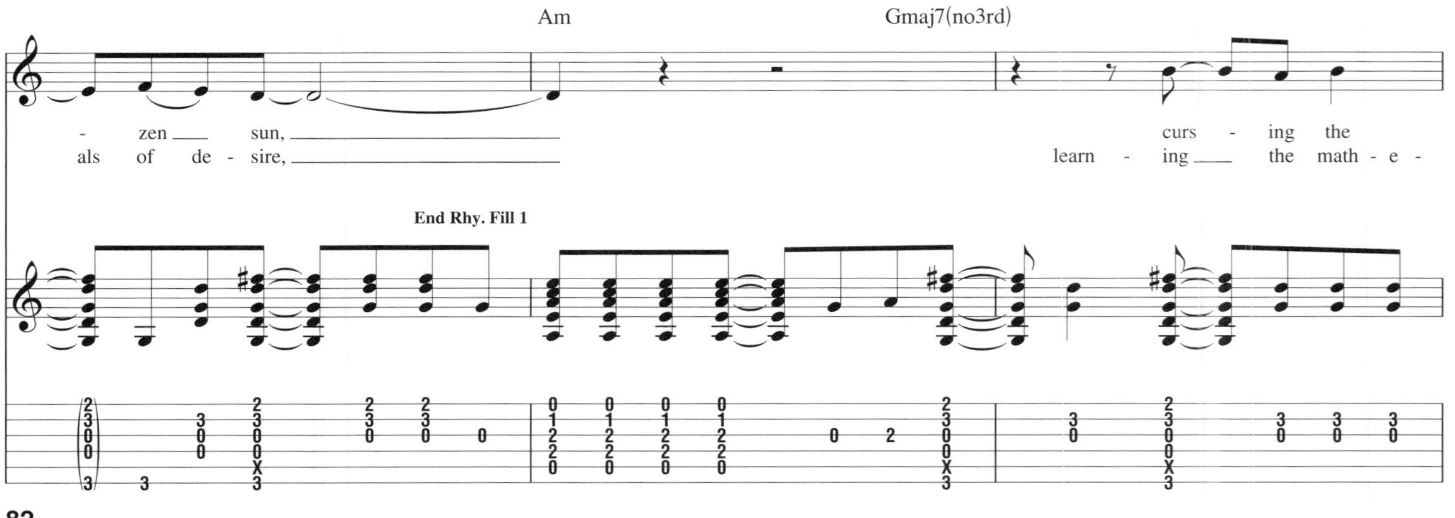
Am Gmaj7(no3rd)
- zen sun, curs - ing the
als of de - sire, learn - ing the math - e -
End Rhy. Fill 1

Gtr. 4 tacet
C
D
Gmaj7(no3rd)
A5
E5
G5
gods we have be - come.
We steal the fire
mat - ics of e - vil by heart.
We de - ceive our - selves
Gtr. 4
Gtr. 3
P.M.

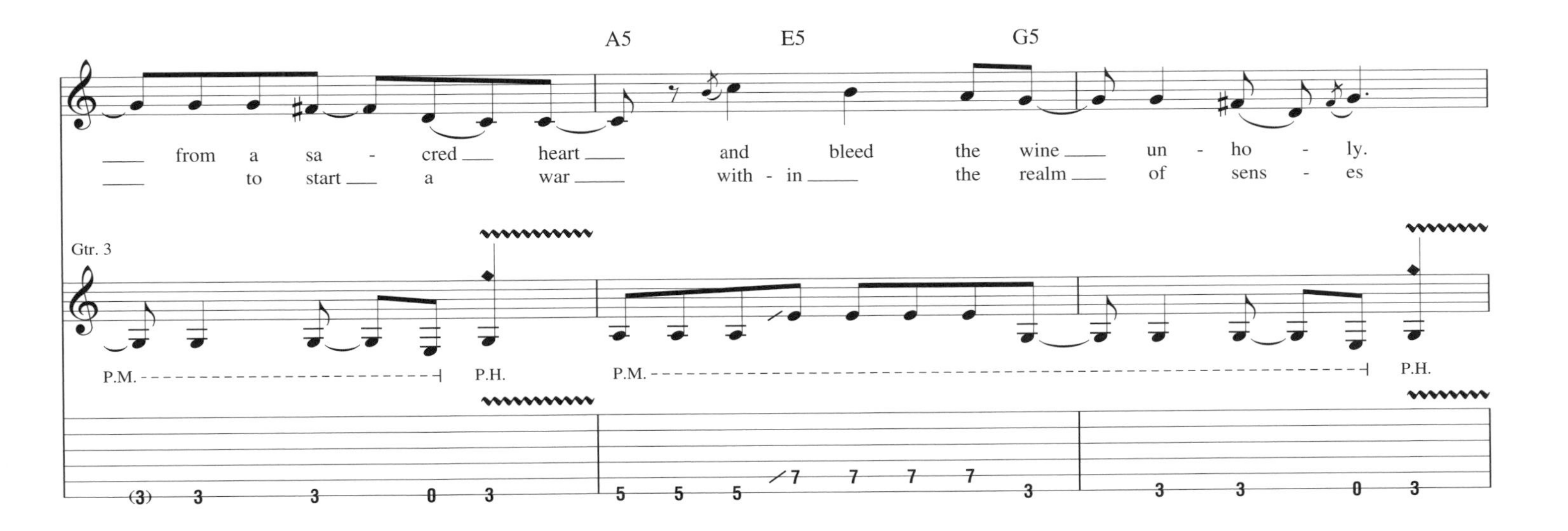
A5
E5
G5
from a sa - cred heart and bleed the wine un - ho - ly.
to start a war with - in the realm of sens - es
Gtr. 3
P.M.
P.H.
P.M.
P.H.

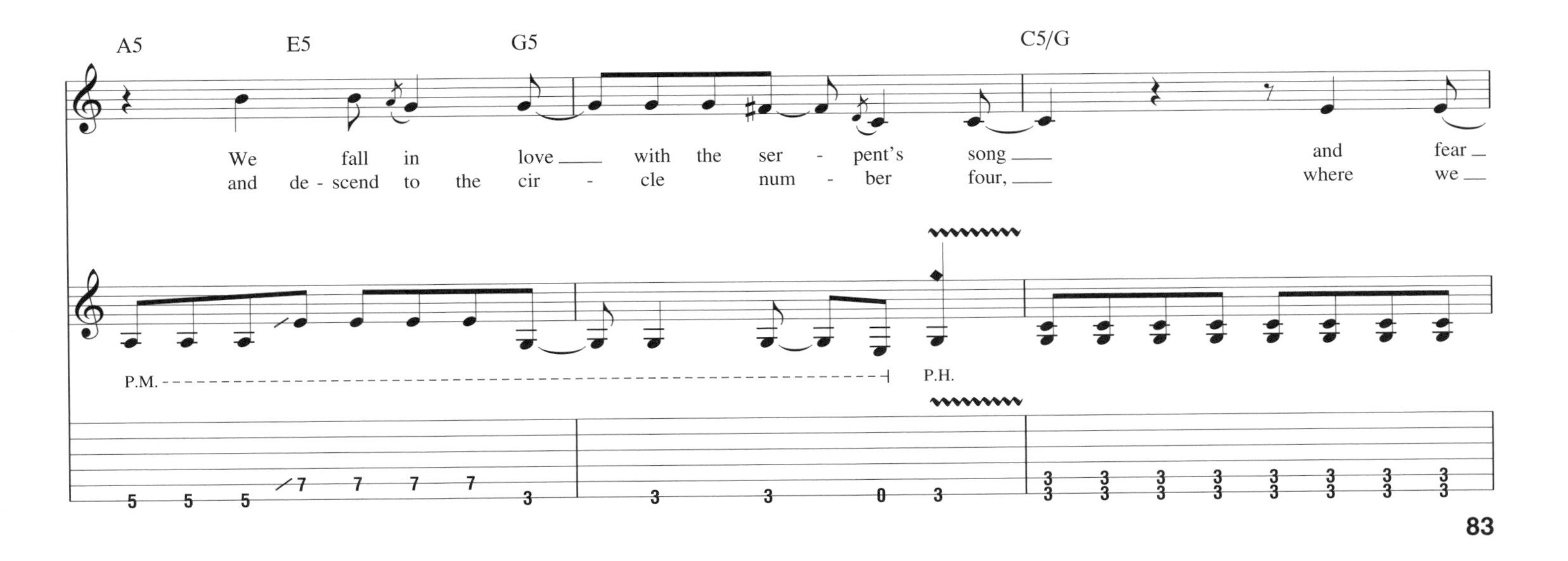
A5
E5
G5
C5/G
We fall in love with the ser - pent's song and fear
and de - scend to the cir - cle num - ber four, where we
P.M.
P.H.

D5/A G5 D/F♯ E5
nothing.
are nothing.
In the night-side of E-
Pre-Chorus
*Half-time feel
B5 A5 B5 A5 B5 A5 C♯5 A5
-den we're born again,
Gtr. 3
Rhy. Fig. 2
*1st & 2nd times only.
E5
dead.
End Rhy. Fig. 2
P.M.
Chorus
Gtr. 3: w/ Rhy. Fig. 2
To Coda
B5 A5 B5 A5 B5 A5 C♯5 A5
For-ever we are, for-ever we've been. For-ever we'll be crucified to a
Riff B
**Gtrs. 5 & 6 (clean)
mf
let ring throughout
End Riff B
**Gtr. 6: 12-str. elec.

1.
End half-time feel
E5
G5
dream
in the night-side of E - den.
Gtr. 3
Rhy. Fig. 3
End Rhy. Fig. 3
Riff C
Gtrs. 5 & 6
End Riff C
Interlude
Gtrs. 1 & 2: w/ Riffs A & A1
Gtr. 3: w/ Rhy. Fig. 1
Gtrs. 5 & 6 tacet
A5 C G5 E5 G5 A5 C G5 E5 G5 A5 C G5 E5 G5
2.
C5/G D5/A G5
G5
in the night-side of E - den.
(In the night-side of E - den.
Gtr. 3
Gtrs. 5 & 6

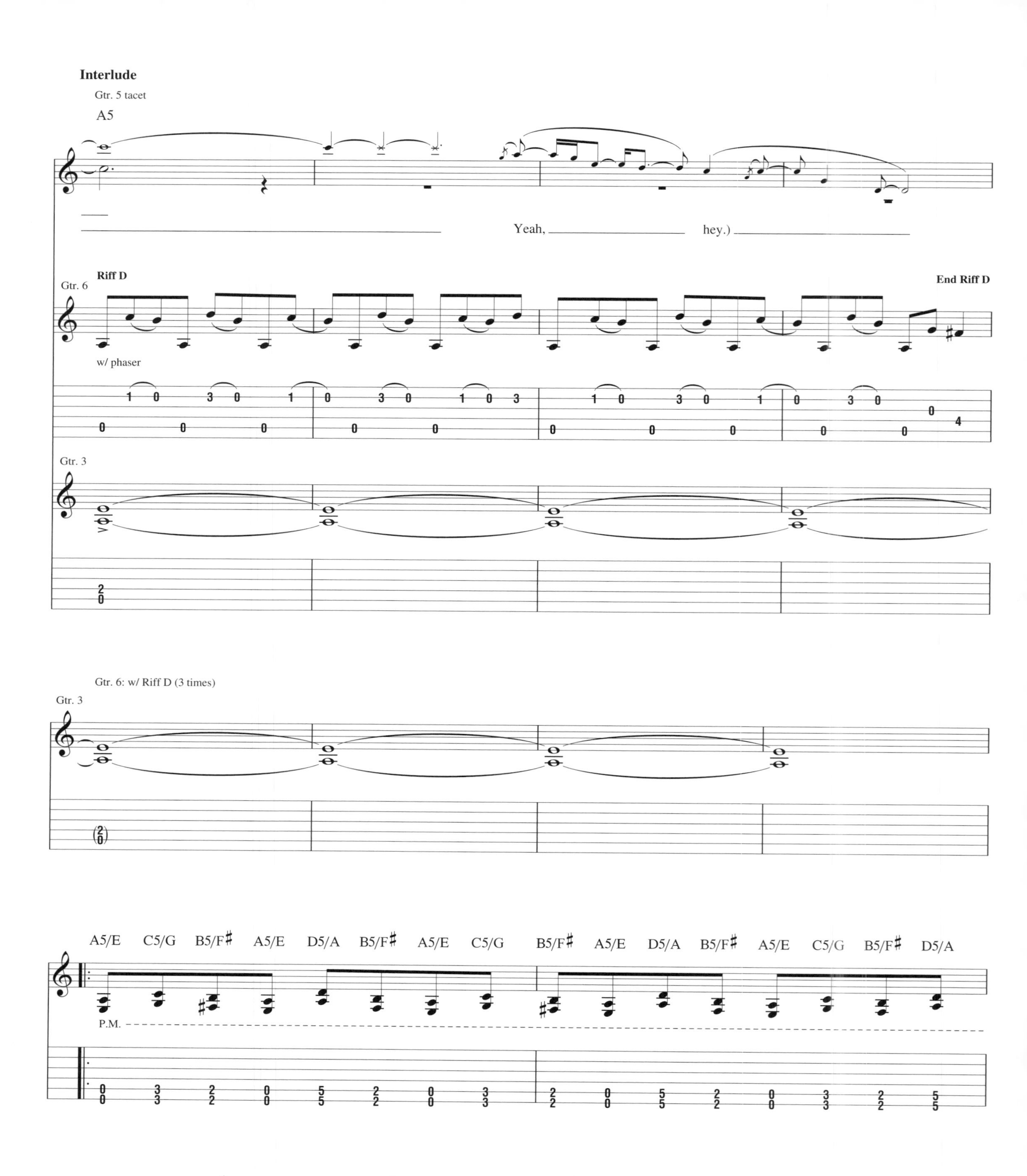
Interlude
Gtr. 5 tacet
A5
Yeah, hey.)
Riff D
Gtr. 6
End Riff D
w/ phaser
Gtr. 3
Gtr. 6: w/ Riff D (3 times)
Gtr. 3
A5/E C5/G B5/F♯ A5/E D5/A B5/F♯ A5/E C5/G B5/F♯ A5/E D5/A B5/F♯ A5/E C5/G B5/F♯ D5/A
P.M.

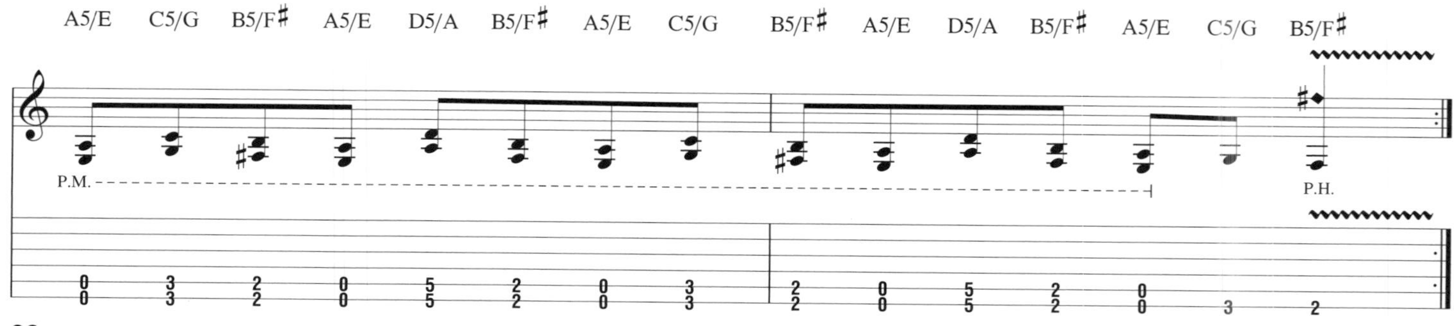
A5/E C5/G B5/F♯ A5/E D5/A B5/F♯ A5/E C5/G B5/F♯ A5/E D5/A B5/F♯ A5/E C5/G B5/F♯
P.M.
P.H.

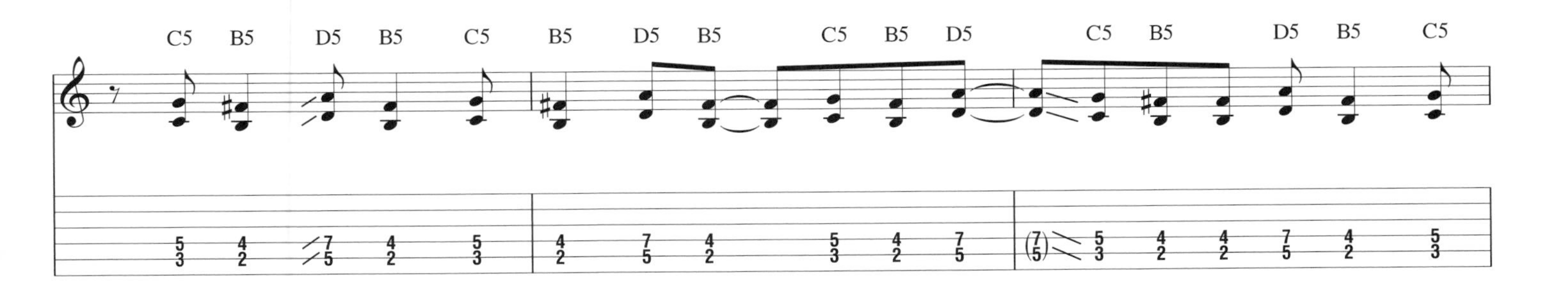

Coda

E5

dream.

In the night - side of E - den

Chorus

Gtr. 3: w/ Rhy. Fig. 2
Gtrs. 5 & 6: w/ Riff B

B5 A5 B5 A5

(For - ev - er we are,

Gtr. 3

Gtrs. 5 & 6

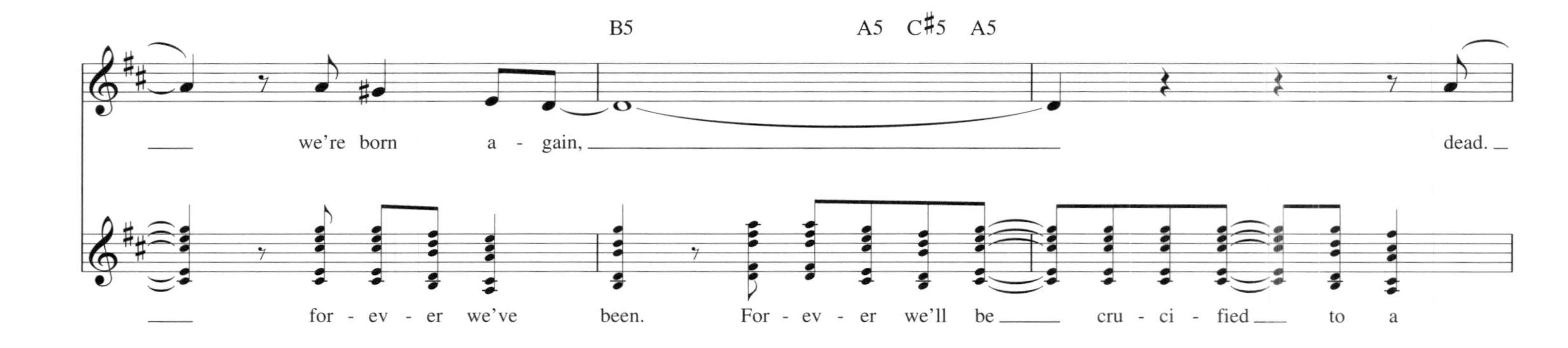

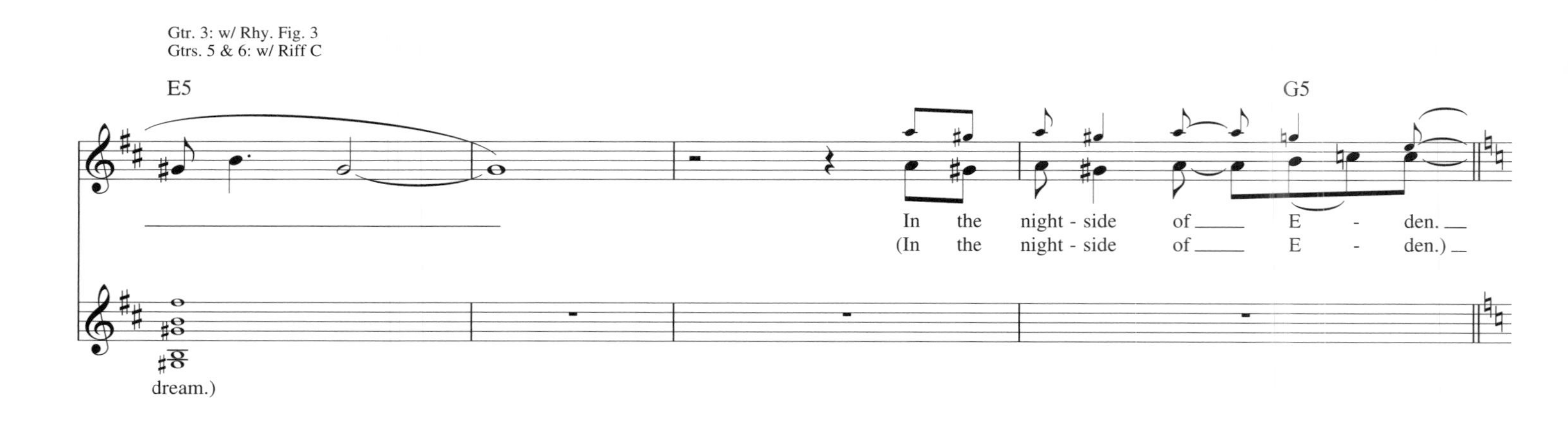

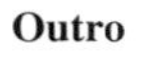

Gtr. 3: w/ Riff E

Am G Am G5 D/F♯

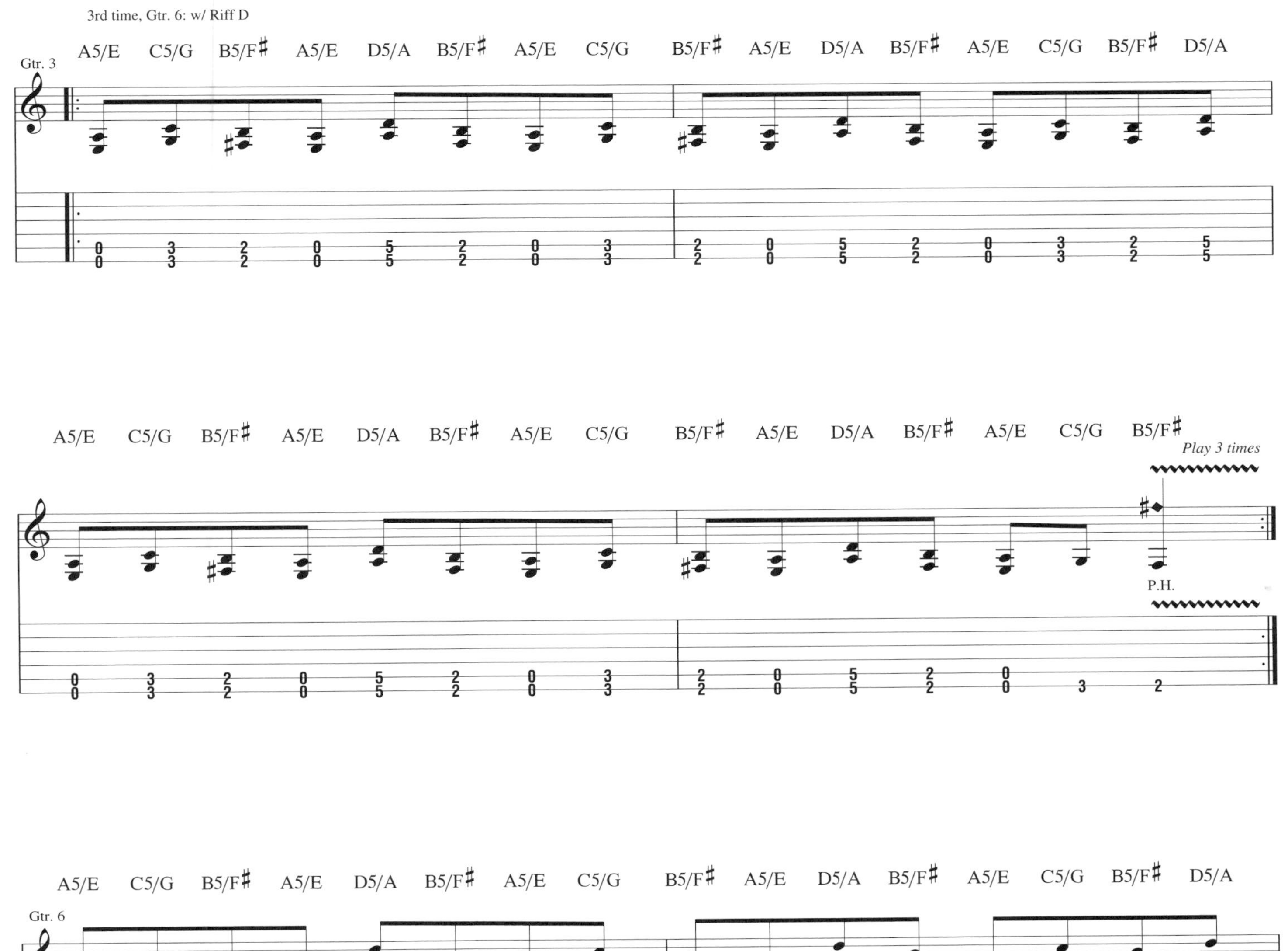

*Doubled throughout

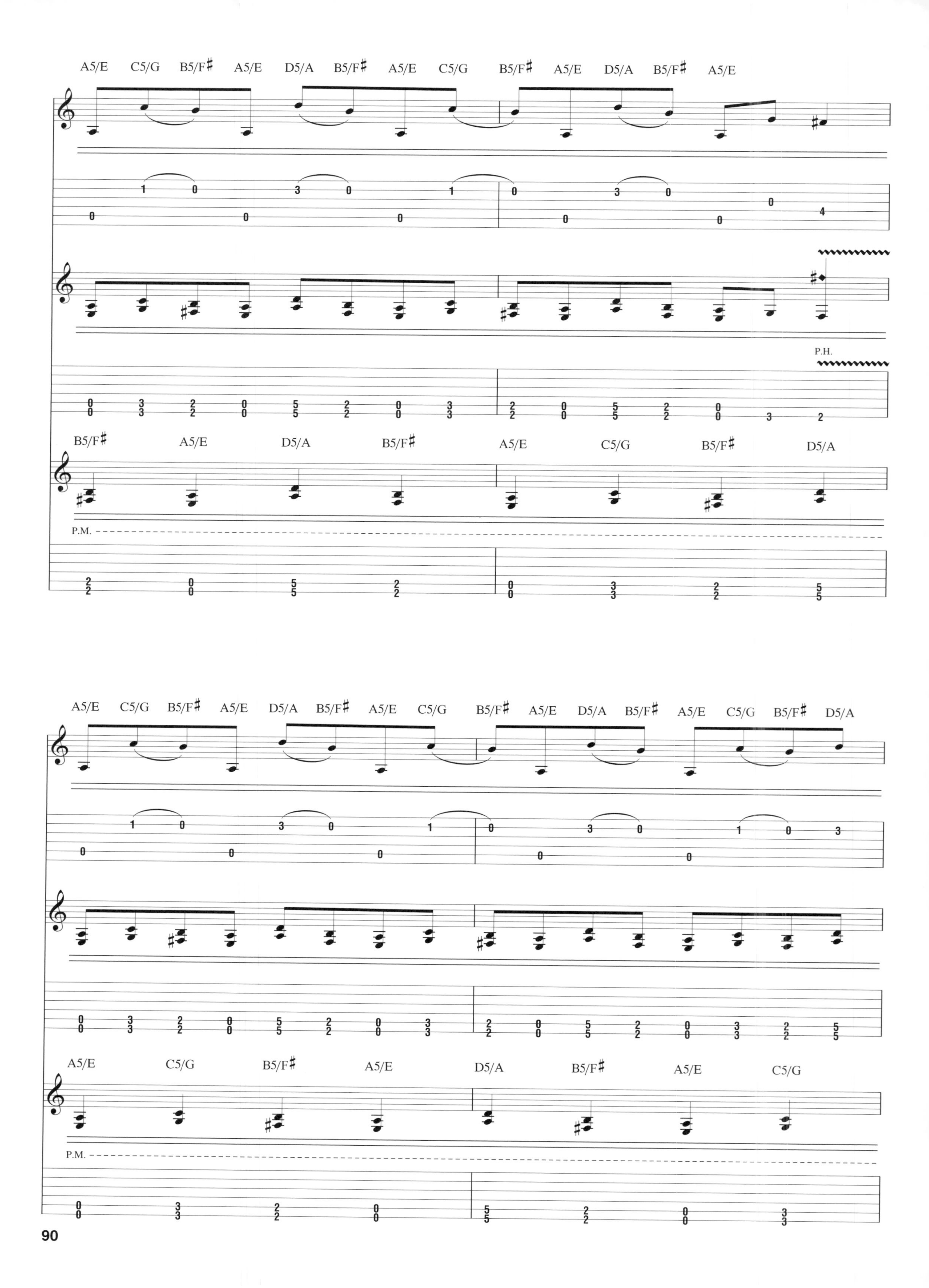
A5/E C5/G B5/F♯ A5/E D5/A B5/F♯ A5/E C5/G B5/F♯ A5/E D5/A B5/F♯ A5/E
P.H.
B5/F♯ A5/E D5/A B5/F♯ A5/E C5/G B5/F♯ D5/A
P.M.
A5/E C5/G B5/F♯ A5/E D5/A B5/F♯ A5/E C5/G B5/F♯ A5/E D5/A B5/F♯ A5/E C5/G B5/F♯ D5/A
A5/E C5/G B5/F♯ A5/E D5/A B5/F♯ A5/E C5/G
P.M.

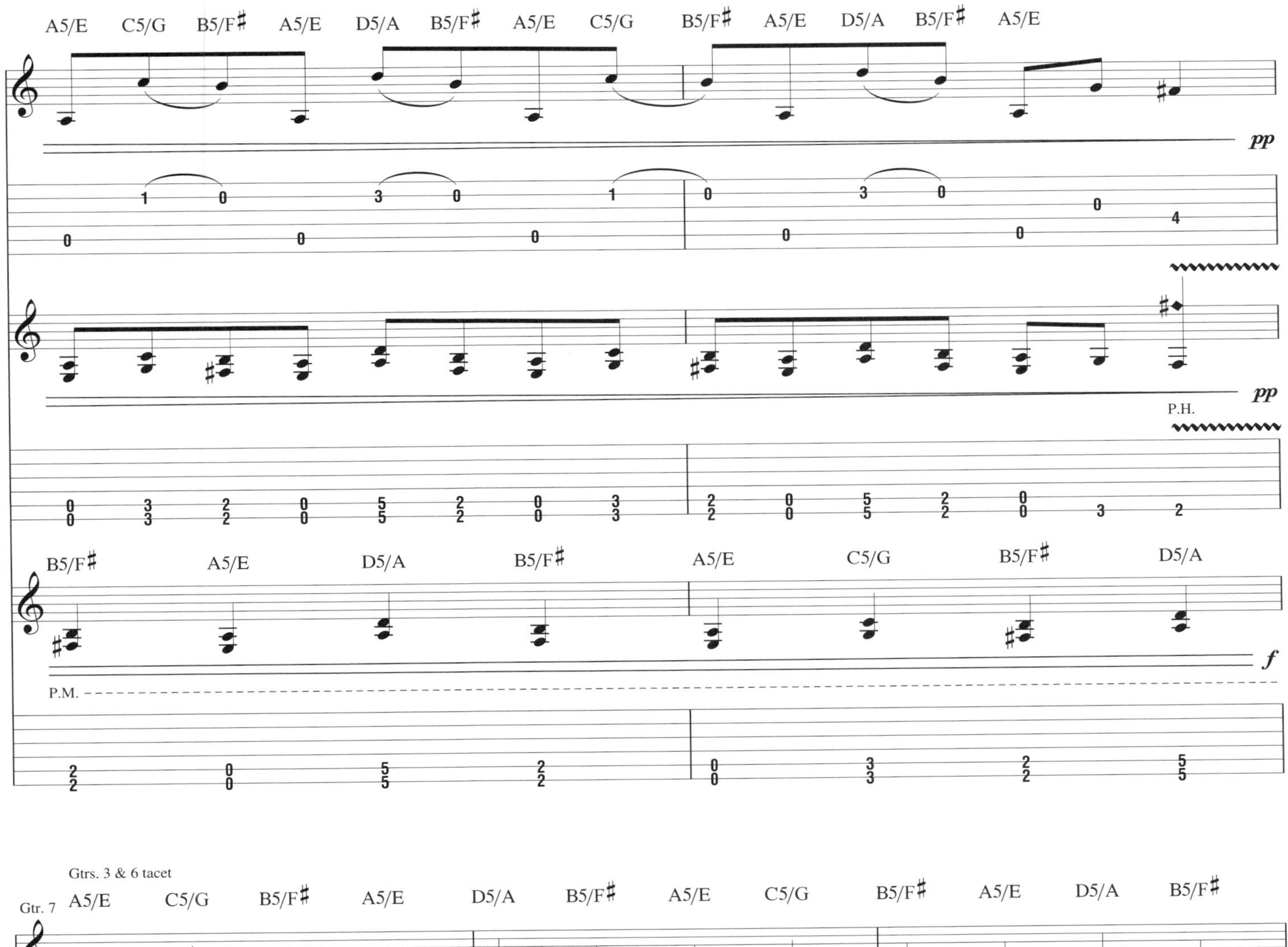
A5/E C5/G B5/F♯ A5/E D5/A B5/F♯ A5/E C5/G B5/F♯ A5/E D5/A B5/F♯ A5/E
pp
pp
P.H.
B5/F♯ A5/E D5/A B5/F♯ A5/E C5/G B5/F♯ D5/A
f
P.M.

Gtrs. 3 & 6 tacet
Gtr. 7
A5/E C5/G B5/F♯ A5/E D5/A B5/F♯ A5/E C5/G B5/F♯ A5/E D5/A B5/F♯
P.M.

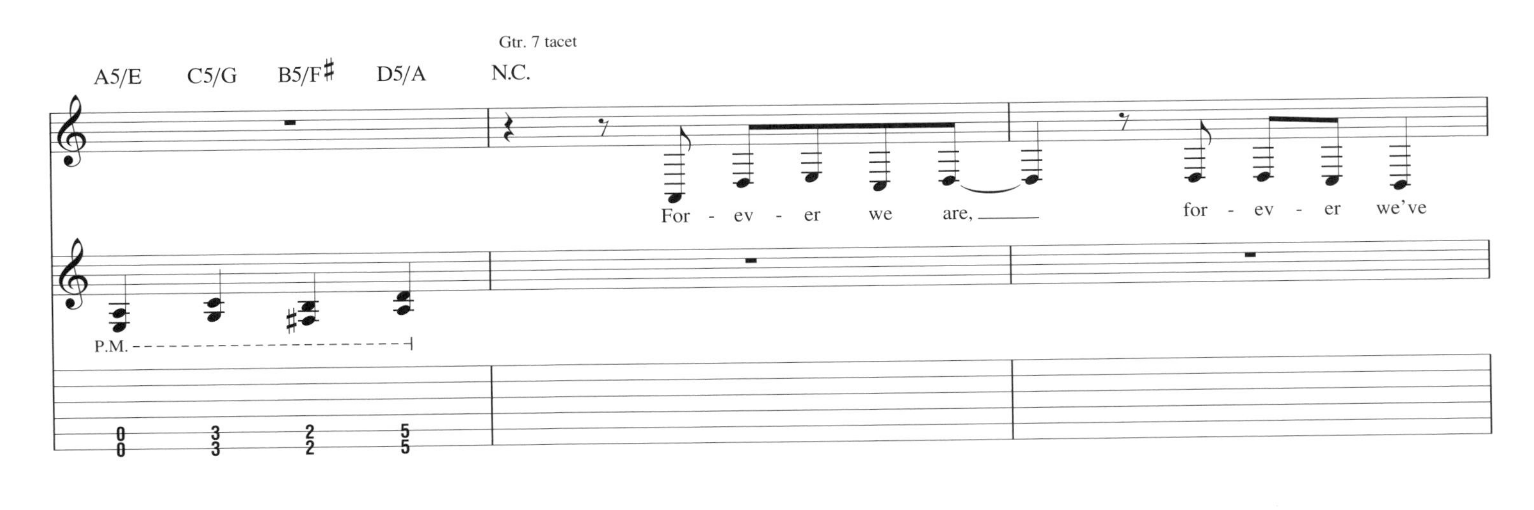
Gtr. 7 tacet
A5/E C5/G B5/F♯ D5/A N.C.
For - ev - er we are,
for - ev - er we've
P.M.

been. For - ev - er we'll be cru - ci - fied to a dream.

Guitar Notation Legend

Guitar Music can be notated three different ways: on a *musical staff*, in *tablature*, and in *rhythm slashes*.

RHYTHM SLASHES are written above the staff. Strum chords in the rhythm indicated. Use the chord diagrams found at the top of the first page of the transcription for the appropriate chord voicings. Round noteheads indicate single notes.

THE MUSICAL STAFF shows pitches and rhythms and is divided by bar lines into measures. Pitches are named after the first seven letters of the alphabet.

TABLATURE graphically represents the guitar fingerboard. Each horizontal line represents a a string, and each number represents a fret.

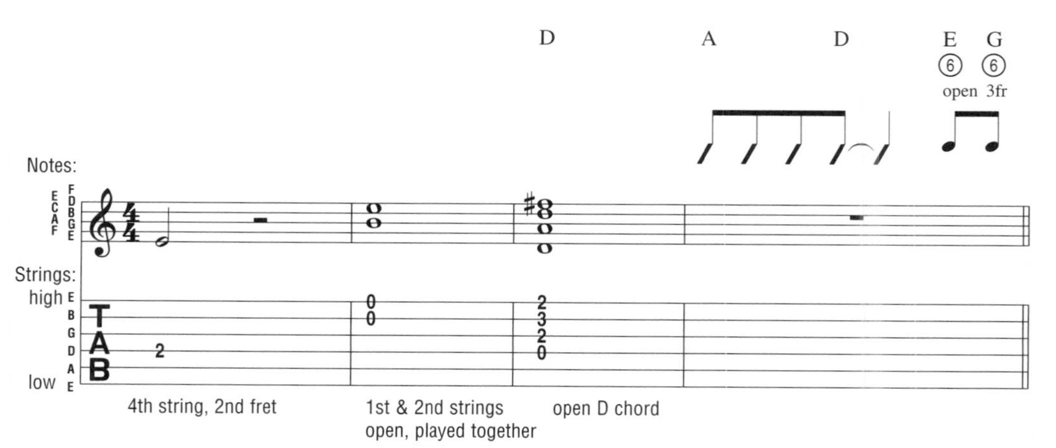

Definitions for Special Guitar Notation

HALF-STEP BEND: Strike the note and bend up 1/2 step.

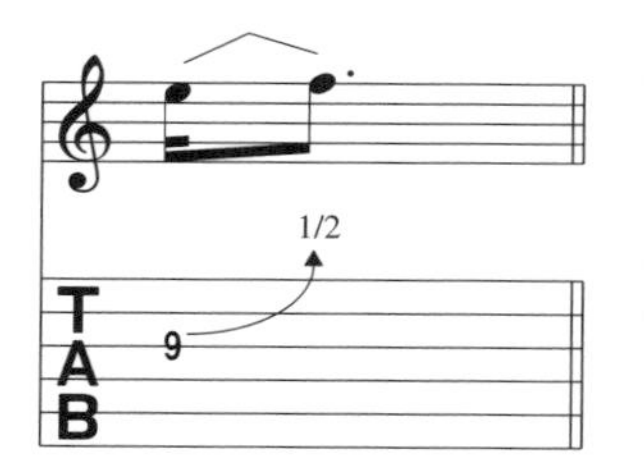

WHOLE-STEP BEND: Strike the note and bend up one step.

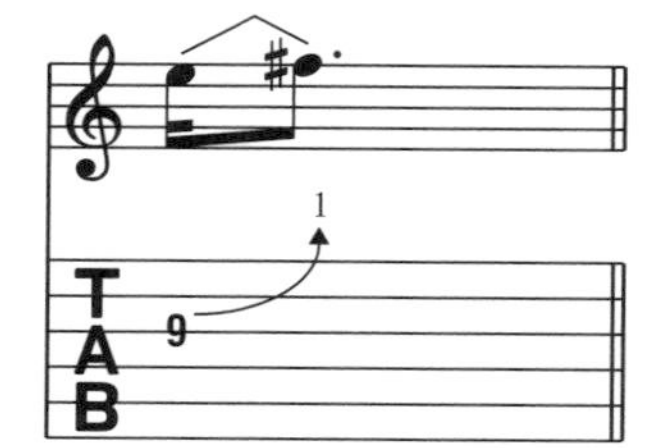

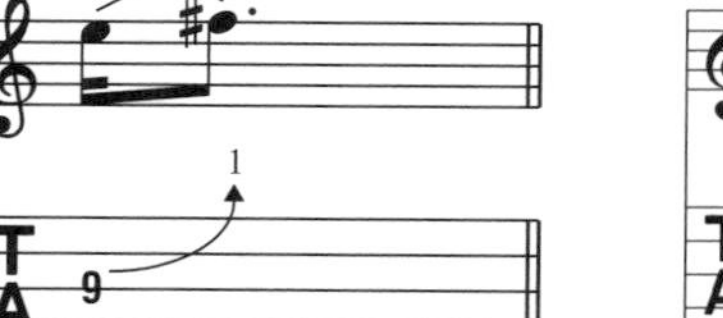

GRACE NOTE BEND: Strike the note and immediately bend up as indicated.

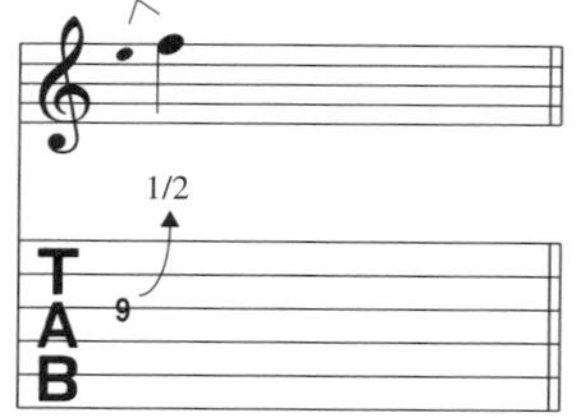

SLIGHT (MICROTONE) BEND: Strike the note and bend up 1/4 step.

BEND AND RELEASE: Strike the note and bend up as indicated, then release back to the original note. Only the first note is struck.

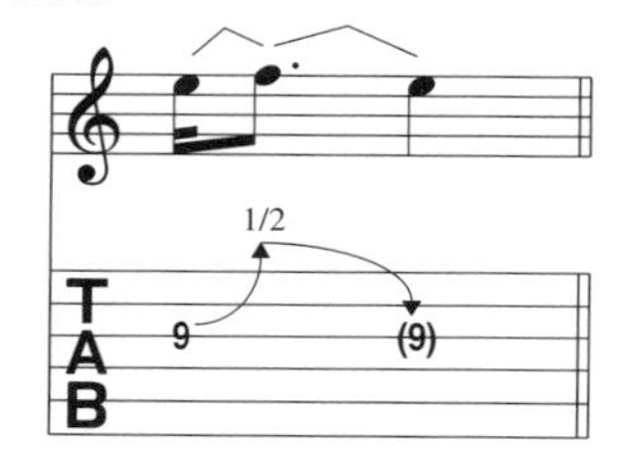

PRE-BEND: Bend the note as indicated, then strike it.

PRE-BEND AND RELEASE: Bend the note as indicated. Strike it and release the bend back to the original note.

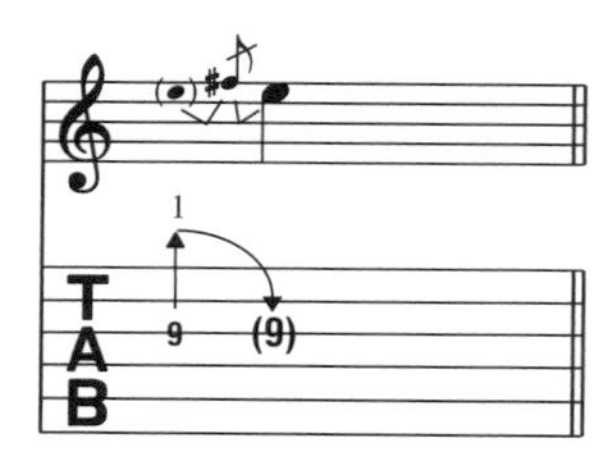

UNISON BEND: Strike the two notes simultaneously and bend the lower note up to the pitch of the higher.

VIBRATO: The string is vibrated by rapidly bending and releasing the note with the fretting hand.

WIDE VIBRATO: The pitch is varied to a greater degree by vibrating with the fretting hand.

HAMMER-ON: Strike the first (lower) note with one finger, then sound the higher note (on the same string) with another finger by fretting it without picking.

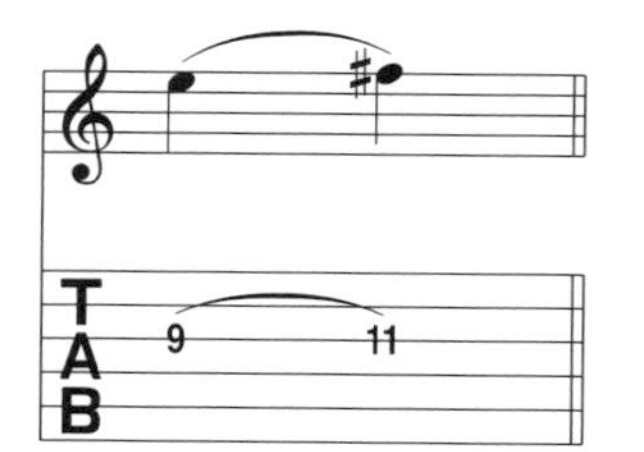

PULL-OFF: Place both fingers on the notes to be sounded. Strike the first note and without picking, pull the finger off to sound the second (lower) note.

LEGATO SLIDE: Strike the first note and then slide the same fret-hand finger up or down to the second note. The second note is not struck.

SHIFT SLIDE: Same as legato slide, except the second note is struck.

TRILL: Very rapidly alternate between the notes indicated by continuously hammering on and pulling off.

TAPPING: Hammer ("tap") the fret indicated with the pick-hand index or middle finger and pull off to the note fretted by the fret hand.

NATURAL HARMONIC: Strike the note while the fret-hand lightly touches the string directly over the fret indicated.

PINCH HARMONIC: The note is fretted normally and a harmonic is produced by adding the edge of the thumb or the tip of the index finger of the pick hand to the normal pick attack.

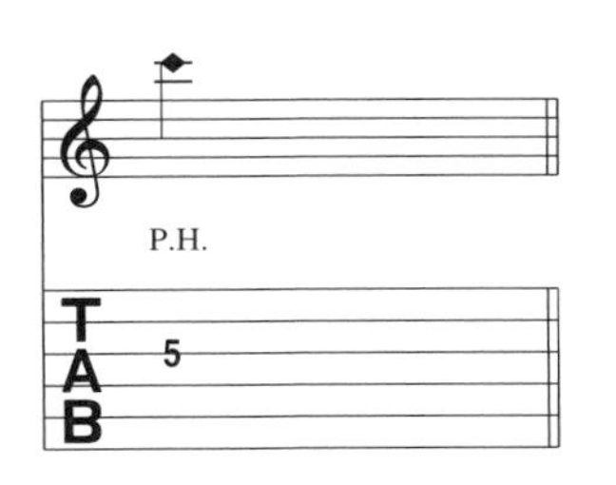

HARP HARMONIC: The note is fretted normally and a harmonic is produced by gently resting the pick hand's index finger directly above the indicated fret (in parentheses) while the pick hand's thumb or pick assists by plucking the appropriate string.

PICK SCRAPE: The edge of the pick is rubbed down (or up) the string, producing a scratchy sound.

MUFFLED STRINGS: A percussive sound is produced by laying the fret hand across the string(s) without depressing, and striking them with the pick hand.

PALM MUTING: The note is partially muted by the pick hand lightly touching the string(s) just before the bridge.

RAKE: Drag the pick across the strings indicated with a single motion.

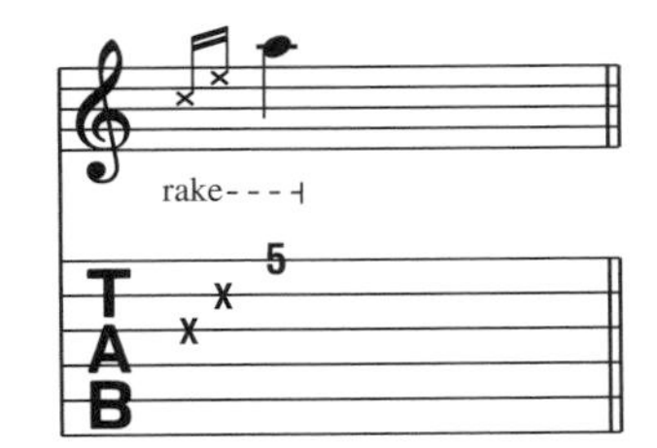

TREMOLO PICKING: The note is picked as rapidly and continuously as possible.

ARPEGGIATE: Play the notes of the chord indicated by quickly rolling them from bottom to top.

VIBRATO BAR DIVE AND RETURN: The pitch of the note or chord is dropped a specified number of steps (in rhythm) then returned to the original pitch.

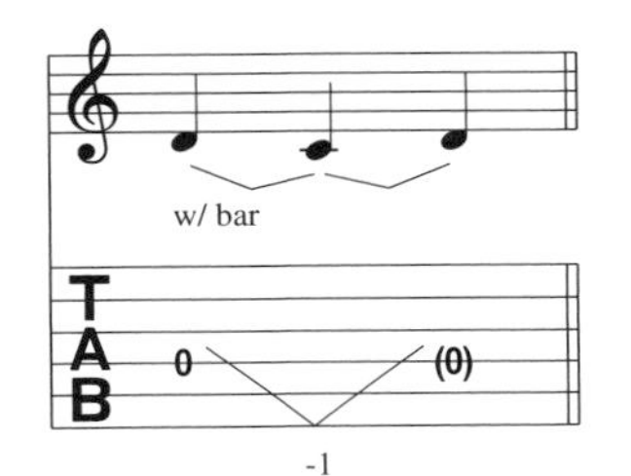

VIBRATO BAR SCOOP: Depress the bar just before striking the note, then quickly release the bar.

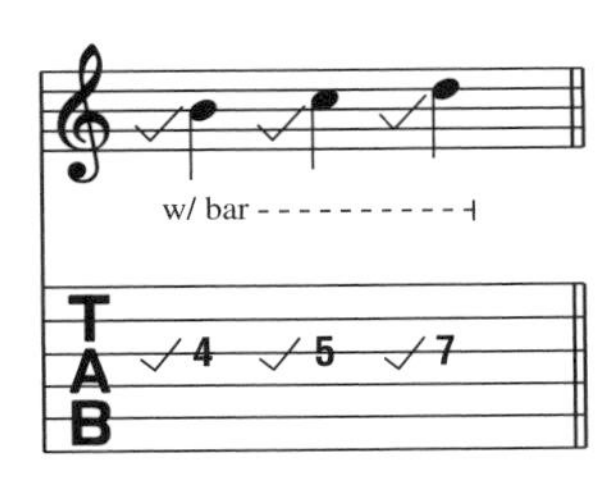

VIBRATO BAR DIP: Strike the note and then immediately drop a specified number of steps, then release back to the original pitch.

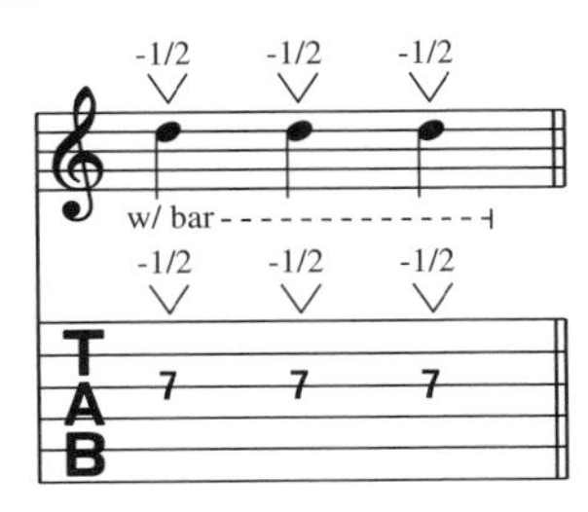

Additional Musical Definitions

(accent)	• Accentuate note (play it louder)
(accent)	• Accentuate note with great intensity
(staccato)	• Play the note short
⊓	• Downstroke
V	• Upstroke
D.S. al Coda	• Go back to the sign (𝄋), then play until the measure marked "***To Coda,***" then skip to the section labelled "**Coda.**"
D.C. al Fine	• Go back to the beginning of the song and play until the measure marked "***Fine***" (end).

Rhy. Fig.	• Label used to recall a recurring accompaniment pattern (usually chordal).
Riff	• Label used to recall composed, melodic lines (usually single notes) which recur.
Fill	• Label used to identify a brief melodic figure which is to be inserted into the arrangement.
Rhy. Fill	• A chordal version of a Fill.
tacet	• Instrument is silent (drops out).
(repeat signs)	• Repeat measures between signs.
1. 2.	• When a repeated section has different endings, play the first ending only the first time and the second ending only the second time.

NOTE: Tablature numbers in parentheses mean:
1. The note is being sustained over a system (note in standard notation is tied), or
2. The note is sustained, but a new articulation (such as a hammer-on, pull-off, slide or vibrato begins), or
3. The note is a barely audible "ghost" note (note in standard notation is also in parentheses).

AUTHENTIC TRANSCRIPTIONS WITH NOTES AND TABLATURE

GUITAR RECORDED VERSIONS®

Guitar Recorded Versions® are note-for-note transcriptions of guitar music taken directly off recordings. This series, one of the most popular in print today, features some of the greatest guitar players and groups from blues and rock to country and jazz.

Guitar Recorded Versions are transcribed by the best transcribers in the business. Every book contains notes and tablature.

Item	Title	Price
00690016	Will Ackerman Collection	$19.95
00690501	Bryan Adams – Greatest Hits	$19.95
00690002	Aerosmith – Big Ones	$24.95
00692015	Aerosmith – Greatest Hits	$22.95
00690603	Aerosmith – O Yeah! (Ultimate Hits)	$24.95
00690147	Aerosmith – Rocks	$19.95
00690146	Aerosmith – Toys in the Attic	$19.95
00690139	Alice in Chains	$19.95
00690178	Alice in Chains – Acoustic	$19.95
00694865	Alice in Chains – Dirt	$19.95
00660225	Alice in Chains – Facelift	$19.95
00694925	Alice in Chains – Jar of Flies/Sap	$19.95
00690387	Alice in Chains – Nothing Safe: Best of the Box	$19.95
00690812	All American Rejects – Move Along	$19.95
00694932	Allman Brothers Band – Definitive Collection for Guitar Volume 1	$24.95
00694933	Allman Brothers Band – Definitive Collection for Guitar Volume 2	$24.95
00694934	Allman Brothers Band – Definitive Collection for Guitar Volume 3	$24.95
00690755	Alter Bridge – One Day Remains	$19.95
00690571	Trey Anastasio	$19.95
00690158	Chet Atkins – Almost Alone	$19.95
00694876	Chet Atkins – Contemporary Styles	$19.95
00694878	Chet Atkins – Vintage Fingerstyle	$19.95
00690418	Best of Audio Adrenaline	$17.95
00690609	Audioslave	$19.95
00690804	Audioslave – Out of Exile	$19.95
00694918	Randy Bachman Collection	$22.95
00690366	Bad Company – Original Anthology – Book 1	$19.95
00690367	Bad Company – Original Anthology – Book 2	$19.95
00690503	Beach Boys – Very Best of	$19.95
00694929	Beatles: 1962-1966	$24.95
00694930	Beatles: 1967-1970	$24.95
00690489	Beatles – 1	$24.95
00694880	Beatles – Abbey Road	$19.95
00690110	Beatles – Book 1 (White Album)	$19.95
00690111	Beatles – Book 2 (White Album)	$19.95
00694832	Beatles – For Acoustic Guitar	$22.95
00690137	Beatles – A Hard Day's Night	$16.95
00690482	Beatles – Let It Be	$16.95
00694891	Beatles – Revolver	$19.95
00694914	Beatles – Rubber Soul	$19.95
00694863	Beatles – Sgt. Pepper's Lonely Hearts Club Band	$19.95
00690383	Beatles – Yellow Submarine	$19.95
00690792	Beck – Guero	$19.95
00690175	Beck – Odelay	$17.95
00690346	Beck – Mutations	$19.95
00690632	Beck – Sea Change	$19.95
00694884	Best of George Benson	$19.95
00692385	Chuck Berry	$19.95
00690149	Black Sabbath	$14.95
00690148	Black Sabbath – Master of Reality	$14.95
00690142	Black Sabbath – Paranoid	$14.95
00692200	Black Sabbath – We Sold Our Soul for Rock 'N' Roll	$19.95
00690115	Blind Melon – Soup	$19.95
00690674	Blink-182	$19.95
00690305	Blink-182 – Dude Ranch	$19.95
00690389	Blink-182 – Enema of the State	$19.95
00690523	Blink-182 – Take Off Your Pants and Jacket	$19.95
00690028	Blue Oyster Cult – Cult Classics	$19.95
00690008	Bon Jovi – Cross Road	$19.95
00690491	Best of David Bowie	$19.95
00690583	Box Car Racer	$19.95
00690764	Breaking Benjamin – We Are Not Alone	$19.95
00690451	Jeff Buckley Collection	$24.95
00690364	Cake – Songbook	$19.95
00690564	The Calling – Camino Palmero	$19.95
00690261	Carter Family Collection	$19.95
00690293	Best of Steven Curtis Chapman	$19.95
00690043	Best of Cheap Trick	$19.95
00690171	Chicago – The Definitive Guitar Collection	$22.95
00690567	Charlie Christian – The Definitive Collection	$19.95
00690590	Eric Clapton – Anthology	$29.95
00692391	Best of Eric Clapton – 2nd Edition	$22.95
00690393	Eric Clapton – Selections from Blues	$19.95
00690074	Eric Clapton – Cream of Clapton	$24.95
00690265	Eric Clapton – E.C. Was Here	$19.95
00690010	Eric Clapton – From the Cradle	$19.95
00690716	Eric Clapton – Me and Mr. Johnson	$19.95
00690263	Eric Clapton – Slowhand	$19.95
00694873	Eric Clapton – Timepieces	$19.95
00694869	Eric Clapton – Unplugged	$22.95
00690415	Clapton Chronicles – Best of Eric Clapton	$18.95
00694896	John Mayall/Eric Clapton – Bluesbreakers	$19.95
00690162	Best of The Clash	$19.95
00690682	Coldplay – Live in 2003	$19.95
00690494	Coldplay – Parachutes	$19.95
00690593	Coldplay – A Rush of Blood to the Head	$19.95
00690806	Coldplay – X & Y	$19.95
00694940	Counting Crows – August & Everything After	$19.95
00690197	Counting Crows – Recovering the Satellites	$19.95
00690405	Counting Crows – This Desert Life	$19.95
00694840	Cream – Disraeli Gears	$19.95
00690285	Cream – Those Were the Days	$17.95
00690401	Creed – Human Clay	$19.95
00690352	Creed – My Own Prison	$19.95
00690551	Creed – Weathered	$19.95
00690648	Very Best of Jim Croce	$19.95
00690572	Steve Cropper – Soul Man	$19.95
00690613	Best of Crosby, Stills & Nash	$19.95
00690777	Crossfade	$19.95
00699521	The Cure – Greatest Hits	$24.95
00690637	Best of Dick Dale	$19.95
00690184	dc Talk – Jesus Freak	$19.95
00690289	Best of Deep Purple	$17.95
00694831	Derek and The Dominos – Layla & Other Assorted Love Songs	$19.95
00690384	Best of Ani DiFranco	$19.95
00690322	Ani DiFranco – Little Plastic Castle	$19.95
00690380	Ani DiFranco – Up Up Up Up Up Up	$19.95
00690191	Dire Straits – Money for Nothing	$24.95
00695382	Very Best of Dire Straits – Sultans of Swing	$19.95
00660178	Willie Dixon – Master Blues Composer	$24.95
00690347	The Doors – Anthology	$22.95
00690348	The Doors – Essential Guitar Collection	$16.95
00690250	Best of Duane Eddy	$16.95
00690533	Electric Light Orchestra Guitar Collection	$19.95
00690555	Best of Melissa Etheridge	$19.95
00690524	Melissa Etheridge – Skin	$19.95
00690496	Best of Everclear	$19.95
00690515	Extreme II – Pornograffitti	$19.95
00690810	Fall Out Boy – From Under the Cork Tree	$19.95
00690664	Best of Fleetwood Mac	$19.95
00690734	Franz Ferdinand	$19.95
00694920	Best of Free	$19.95
00690257	John Fogerty – Blue Moon Swamp	$19.95
00690089	Foo Fighters	$19.95
00690235	Foo Fighters – The Colour and the Shape	$19.95
00690808	Foo Fighters – In Your Honor	$19.95
00690595	Foo Fighters – One by One	$19.95
00690394	Foo Fighters – There Is Nothing Left to Lose	$19.95
00690222	G3 Live – Joe Satriani, Steve Vai, and Eric Johnson	$22.95
00694807	Danny Gatton – 88 Elmira St	$19.95
00690438	Genesis Guitar Anthology	$19.95
00120167	Godsmack	$19.95
00690753	Best of Godsmack	$19.95
00690127	Goo Goo Dolls – A Boy Named Goo	$19.95
00690338	Goo Goo Dolls – Dizzy Up the Girl	$19.95
00690576	Goo Goo Dolls – Gutterflower	$19.95
00690773	Good Charlotte – Chronicles of Life and Death	$19.95
00690601	Good Charlotte – The Young and the Hopeless	$19.95
00690117	John Gorka Collection	$19.95
00690591	Patty Griffin – Guitar Collection	$19.95
00690114	Buddy Guy Collection Vol. A-J	$22.95
00690193	Buddy Guy Collection Vol. L-Y	$22.95
00690697	Best of Jim Hall	$19.95
00694798	George Harrison Anthology	$19.95
00690778	Hawk Nelson – Letters to the President	$19.95
00690068	Return of the Hellecasters	$19.95
00692930	Jimi Hendrix – Are You Experienced?	$24.95
00692931	Jimi Hendrix – Axis: Bold As Love	$22.95
00690304	Jimi Hendrix – Band of Gypsys	$19.95
00690321	Jimi Hendrix – BBC Sessions	$22.95
00690608	Jimi Hendrix – Blue Wild Angel	$24.95
00694944	Jimi Hendrix – Blues	$24.95
00692932	Jimi Hendrix – Electric Ladyland	$24.95
00690218	Jimi Hendrix – First Rays of the Rising Sun	$27.95
00660099	Jimi Hendrix – Radio One	$24.95
00690280	Jimi Hendrix – South Saturn Delta	$24.95
00690602	Jimi Hendrix – Smash Hits	$19.95
00690017	Jimi Hendrix – Woodstock	$24.95
00660029	Buddy Holly	$19.95
00660169	John Lee Hooker – A Blues Legend	$19.95
00694905	Howlin' Wolf	$19.95
00690692	Very Best of Billy Idol	$19.95
00690688	Incubus – A Crow Left of the Murder	$19.95
00690457	Incubus – Make Yourself	$19.95
00690544	Incubus – Morningview	$19.95
00690136	Indigo Girls – 1200 Curfews	$22.95
00690730	Alan Jackson – Guitar Collection	$19.95
00694938	Elmore James – Master Electric Slide Guitar	$19.95
00690652	Best of Jane's Addiction	$19.95
00690721	Jet – Get Born	$19.95
00690684	Jethro Tull – Aqualung	$19.95
00690647	Best of Jewel	$19.95
00694833	Billy Joel for Guitar	$19.95
00690751	John5 – Vertigo	$19.95
00660147	Eric Johnson	$19.95
00694912	Eric Johnson – Ah Via Musicom	$19.95
00690660	Best of Eric Johnson	$19.95
00690169	Eric Johnson – Venus Isle	$22.95
00690271	Robert Johnson – The New Transcriptions	$24.95
00699131	Best of Janis Joplin	$19.95
00690427	Best of Judas Priest	$19.95
00690651	Juanes – Exitos de Juanes	$19.95
00690277	Best of Kansas	$19.95
00690742	The Killers – Hot Fuss	$19.95
00690504	Very Best of Albert King	$19.95
00690073	B. B. King – 1950-1957	$24.95
00690444	B.B. King & Eric Clapton – Riding with the King	$19.95
00690134	Freddie King Collection	$19.95
00690339	Best of the Kinks	$19.95
00690156	Kiss	$17.95
00690157	Kiss – Alive!	$19.95
00694903	Best of Kiss for Guitar	$24.95
00690188	Mark Knopfler – Golden Heart	$19.95
00690164	Mark Knopfler Guitar – Vol. 1	$19.95
00690165	Mark Knopfler Guitar – Vol. 2	$19.95
00690163	Mark Knopfler/Chet Atkins – Neck and Neck	$19.95
00690780	Korn – Greatest Hits, Volume 1	$22.95
00690377	Kris Kristofferson Collection	$17.95
00690658	Johnny Lang – Long Time Coming	$19.95
00690614	Avril Lavigne – Let Go	$19.95
00690726	Avril Lavigne – Under My Skin	$19.95
00690679	John Lennon – Guitar Collection	$19.95
00690279	Ottmar Liebert + Luna Negra – Opium Highlights	$19.95
00690785	Best of Limp Bizkit	$19.95
00690781	Linkin Park – Hybrid Theory	$22.95
00690782	Linkin Park – Meteora	$22.95
00690783	Best of Live	$19.95
00699623	Best of Chuck Loeb	$19.95
00690743	Los Lonely Boys	$19.95
00690720	Lostprophets – Start Something	$19.95
00690525	Best of George Lynch	$19.95
00694954	New Best of Lynyrd Skynyrd	$19.95
00690577	Yngwie Malmsteen – Anthology	$24.95
00694845	Yngwie Malmsteen – Fire and Ice	$19.95
00694755	Yngwie Malmsteen's Rising Force	$19.95

AUTHENTIC TRANSCRIPTIONS WITH NOTES AND TABLATURE

00694757 Yngwie Malmsteen – Trilogy $19.95
00690754 Marilyn Manson – Lest We Forget $19.95
00694956 Bob Marley – Legend $19.95
00690075 Bob Marley – Natural Mystic $19.95
00690548 Very Best of Bob Marley & The Wailers – One Love $19.95
00694945 Bob Marley – Songs of Freedom $24.95
00690748 Maroon5 – 1.22.03 Acoustic $19.95
00690657 Maroon5 – Songs About Jane $19.95
00690442 Matchbox 20 – Mad Season $19.95
00690616 Matchbox 20 – More Than You Think You Are $19.95
00690239 Matchbox 20 – Yourself or Someone Like You $19.95
00690283 Best of Sarah McLachlan $19.95
00690382 Sarah McLachlan – Mirrorball $19.95
00690354 Sarah McLachlan – Surfacing $19.95
00120080 Don McLean Songbook $19.95
00694952 Megadeth – Countdown to Extinction $19.95
00690244 Megadeth – Cryptic Writings $19.95
00694951 Megadeth – Rust in Peace $22.95
00694953 Megadeth – Selections from Peace Sells...But Who's Buying? & So Far, So Good...So What! $22.95
00690768 Megadeth – The System Has Failed $19.95
00690495 Megadeth – The World Needs a Hero $19.95
00690011 Megadeth – Youthanasia $19.95
00690505 John Mellencamp Guitar Collection $19.95
00690562 Pat Metheny – Bright Size Life $19.95
00690646 Pat Metheny – One Quiet Night $19.95
00690559 Pat Metheny – Question & Answer $19.95
00690565 Pat Metheny – Rejoicing $19.95
00690558 Pat Metheny Trio – 99>00 $19.95
00690561 Pat Metheny Trio – Live $22.95
00690040 Steve Miller Band Greatest Hits $19.95
00690769 Modest Mouse – Good News for People Who Love Bad News $19.95
00694802 Gary Moore – Still Got the Blues $19.95
00690103 Alanis Morissette – Jagged Little Pill $19.95
00690786 Mudvayne – The End of All Things to Come $22.95
00690787 Mudvayne – L.D. 50 $22.95
00690794 Mudvayne – Lost and Found $19.95
00690448 MxPx – The Ever Passing Moment $19.95
00690500 Ricky Nelson Guitar Collection $17.95
00690722 New Found Glory – Catalyst $19.95
00690345 Best of Newsboys $17.95
00690611 Nirvana $22.95
00694895 Nirvana – Bleach $19.95
00690189 Nirvana – From the Muddy Banks of the Wishkah $19.95
00694913 Nirvana – In Utero $19.95
00694901 Nirvana – Incesticide $19.95
00694883 Nirvana – Nevermind $19.95
00690026 Nirvana – Unplugged in York $19.95
00690739 No Doubt – Rock Steady $22.95
00120112 No Doubt – Tragic Kingdom $22.95
00690273 Oasis – Be Here Now $19.95
00690159 Oasis – Definitely Maybe $19.95
00690121 Oasis – (What's the Story) Morning Glory $19.95
00690226 Oasis – The Other Side of Oasis $19.95
00690358 The Offspring – Americana $19.95
00690485 The Offspring – Conspiracy of One $19.95
00690807 The Offspring – Greatest Hits $19.95
00690204 The Offspring – Ixnay on the Hombre $17.95
00690203 The Offspring – Smash $18.95
00690663 The Offspring – Splinter $19.95
00694847 Best of Ozzy Osbourne $22.95
00694830 Ozzy Osbourne – No More Tears $19.95
00690399 Ozzy Osbourne – The Ozzman Cometh $19.95
00690129 Ozzy Osbourne – Ozzmosis $22.95
00690594 Best of Les Paul $19.95
00690546 P.O.D. – Satellite $19.95
00694855 Pearl Jam – Ten $19.95
00690439 A Perfect Circle – Mer De Noms $19.95
00690661 A Perfect Circle – Thirteenth Step $19.95
00690499 Tom Petty – Definitive Guitar Collection $19.95
00690176 Phish – Billy Breathes $22.95
00690424 Phish – Farmhouse $19.95
00690240 Phish – Hoist $19.95
00690331 Phish – Story of the Ghost $19.95
00690642 Pillar – Fireproof $19.95
00690731 Pillar – Where Do We Go from Here $19.95
00690428 Pink Floyd – Dark Side of the Moon $19.95
00693864 Best of The Police $19.95
00690299 Best of Elvis: The King of Rock 'n' Roll $19.95
00692535 Elvis Presley $18.95
00690003 Classic Queen $24.95
00694975 Queen – Greatest Hits $24.95
00690670 Very Best of Queensryche $19.95
00694910 Rage Against the Machine $19.95
00690145 Rage Against the Machine – Evil Empire $19.95
00690179 Rancid – And Out Come the Wolves $22.95
00690426 Best of Ratt $19.95
00690055 Red Hot Chili Peppers – Bloodsugarsexmagik $19.95
00690584 Red Hot Chili Peppers – By the Way $19.95
00690379 Red Hot Chili Peppers – Californication $19.95
00690673 Red Hot Chili Peppers – Greatest Hits $19.95
00690255 Red Hot Chili Peppers – Mother's Milk $19.95
00690090 Red Hot Chili Peppers – One Hot Minute $22.95
00690511 Django Reinhardt – The Definitive Collection $19.95
00690779 Relient K – MMHMM $19.95
00690643 Relient K – Two Lefts Don't Make a Right ... But Three Do $19.95
00694899 R.E.M. – Automatic for the People $19.95
00690260 Jimmie Rodgers Guitar Collection $19.95
00690014 Rolling Stones – Exile on Main Street $24.95
00690631 Rolling Stones – Guitar Anthology $24.95
00690186 Rolling Stones – Rock & Roll Circus $19.95
00690685 David Lee Roth – Eat 'Em and Smile $19.95
00690694 David Lee Roth – Guitar Anthology $24.95
00690749 Saliva – Survival of the Sickest $19.95
00690031 Santana's Greatest Hits $19.95
00690796 Very Best of Michael Schenker $19.95
00690566 Best of Scorpions $19.95
00690604 Bob Seger – Guitar Anthology $19.95
00690659 Bob Seger and the Silver Bullet Band – Greatest Hits, Volume 2 $17.95
00120105 Kenny Wayne Shepherd – Ledbetter Heights $19.95
00690750 Kenny Wayne Shepherd – The Place You're In $19.95
00120123 Kenny Wayne Shepherd – Trouble Is $19.95
00690196 Silverchair – Freak Show $19.95
00690130 Silverchair – Frogstomp $19.95
00690357 Silverchair – Neon Ballroom $19.95
00690419 Slipknot $19.95
00690530 Slipknot – Iowa $19.95
00690733 Slipknot – Volume 3 (The Subliminal Verses) $19.95
00690691 Smashing Pumpkins Anthology $19.95
00690330 Social Distortion – Live at the Roxy $19.95
00120004 Best of Steely Dan $24.95
00694921 Best of Steppenwolf $22.95
00690655 Best of Mike Stern $19.95
00694801 Best of Rod Stewart $22.95
00694957 Rod Stewart – Unplugged...And Seated $22.95
00690021 Sting – Fields of Gold $19.95
00694955 Sting for Guitar Tab $19.95
00690597 Stone Sour $19.95
00690689 Story of the Year – Page Avenue $19.95
00690520 Styx Guitar Collection $19.95
00120081 Sublime $19.95
00690519 SUM 41 – All Killer No Filler $19.95
00690771 SUM 41 – Chuck $19.95
00690612 SUM 41 – Does This Look Infected? $19.95
00690767 Switchfoot – The Beautiful Letdown $19.95
00690815 Switchfoot – Nothing Is Sound $19.95
00690425 System of a Down $19.95
00690799 System of a Down – Mezmerize $19.95
00690606 System of a Down – Steal This Album $19.95
00690531 System of a Down – Toxicity $19.95
00694824 Best of James Taylor $16.95
00694887 Best of Thin Lizzy $19.95
00690238 Third Eye Blind $19.95
00690671 Three Days Grace $19.95
00690738 3 Doors Down – Away from the Sun $22.95
00690737 3 Doors Down – The Better Life $22.95
00690776 3 Doors Down – Seventeen Days $19.95
00690267 311 $19.95
00690580 311 – From Chaos $19.95
00690269 311 – Grass Roots $19.95
00690268 311 – Music $19.95
00690665 Thursday – War All the Time $19.95
00690030 Toad the Wet Sprocket $19.95
00690654 Best of Train $19.95
00690233 Merle Travis Collection $19.95
00690683 Robin Trower – Bridge of Sighs $19.95
00690740 Shania Twain – Guitar Collection $19.95
00699191 U2 – Best of: 1980-1990 $19.95
00690732 U2 – Best of: 1990-2000 $19.95
00690775 U2 – How to Dismantle an Atomic Bomb $22.95
00694411 U2 – The Joshua Tree $19.95
00690039 Steve Vai – Alien Love Secrets $24.95
00690172 Steve Vai – Fire Garden $24.95
00690343 Steve Vai – Flex-able Leftovers $19.95
00660137 Steve Vai – Passion & Warfare $24.95
00690605 Steve Vai – Selections from the Elusive Light and Sound, Volume 1 $24.95
00694904 Steve Vai – Sex and Religion $24.95
00690392 Steve Vai – The Ultra Zone $22.95
00690023 Jimmie Vaughan – Strange Pleasures $19.95
00690455 Stevie Ray Vaughan – Blues at Sunrise $19.95
00690024 Stevie Ray Vaughan – Couldn't Stand the Weather $19.95
00690370 Stevie Ray Vaughan and Double Trouble – The Real Deal: Greatest Hits Volume 2 $22.95
00690116 Stevie Ray Vaughan – Guitar Collection $24.95
00660136 Stevie Ray Vaughan – In Step $19.95
00694879 Stevie Ray Vaughan – In the Beginning $19.95
00660058 Stevie Ray Vaughan – Lightnin' Blues '83-'87 $24.95
00690036 Stevie Ray Vaughan – Live Alive $24.95
00690417 Stevie Ray Vaughan – Live at Carnegie Hall $19.95
00690550 Stevie Ray Vaughan and Double Trouble – Live at Montreux 1982 & 1985 $24.95
00694835 Stevie Ray Vaughan – The Sky Is Crying $22.95
00690025 Stevie Ray Vaughan – Soul to Soul $19.95
00690015 Stevie Ray Vaughan – Texas Flood $19.95
00694776 Vaughan Brothers – Family Style $19.95
00690772 Velvet Revolver – Contraband $19.95
00690132 The T-Bone Walker Collection $19.95
00694789 Muddy Waters – Deep Blues $24.95
00690071 Weezer (The Blue Album) $19.95
00690516 Weezer (The Green Album) $19.95
00690800 Weezer – Make Believe $19.95
00690286 Weezer – Pinkerton $19.95
00690447 Best of The Who $24.95
00694970 The Who – Definitive Guitar Collection: A-E $24.95
00694971 The Who – Definitive Guitar Collection: F-Li $24.95
00694972 The Who – Definitive Guitar Collection: Lo-R $24.95
00694973 The Who – Definitive Guitar Collection: S-Y $24.95
00690640 David Wilcox – Anthology 2000-2003 $19.95
00690325 David Wilcox – Collection $17.95
00690672 Best of Dar Williams $19.95
00690320 Dar Williams Songbook $17.95
00690319 Stevie Wonder – Some of the Best $17.95
00690596 Best of the Yardbirds $19.95
00690710 Yellowcard – Ocean Avenue $19.95
00690507 Frank Zappa – Apostrophe $19.95
00690443 Frank Zappa – Hot Rats $19.95
00690589 ZZ Top – Guitar Anthology $22.95

Complete descriptions
and songlists online!

HAL•LEONARD®
CORPORATION